D1203407

BUREAUCRACY AND RED TAPE

BARRY BOZEMAN
GEORGIA INSTITUTE OF TECHNOLOGY

PRENTICE HALL, UPPER SADDLE RIVER, NEW JERSEY 07458

Library of Congress Cataloging-in-Publication Data

BOZEMAN, BARRY.
  Bureaucracy and red tape/Barry Bozeman.
    p. cm.
  Includes bibliographical references and index.
  ISBN 0-13-613753-9
  1. Bureaucracy. I. Title.
JF1501.B69 2000
352.6'3—dc21

99-15766
CIP

Editorial director: Charlyce Jones Owen
Editor in chief: Nancy Roberts
Senior acquisitions editor: Beth Gillett Mejia
Editorial assistant: Brian Prybella
Marketing manager: Christopher DeJohn
Editorial/production supervision: Kari Callaghan Mazzola
Electronic page makeup: Kari Callaghan Mazzola and John P. Mazzola
Interior design: John P. Mazzola
Cover director: Jayne Conte
Cover design: Bruce Kenselaar
Buyer: Ben Smith

This book was set in 10/12 New Century Schoolbook by Big Sky Composition
and was printed and bound by Courier Companies, Inc.
The cover was printed by Phoenix Color Corp.

© 2000 by Prentice-Hall, Inc.
Upper Saddle River, New Jersey 07458

Printed in the United States of America
10 9 8 7 6 5 4 3 2 1

ISBN 0-13-613753-9

PRENTICE-HALL INTERNATIONAL (UK) LIMITED, *London*
PRENTICE-HALL OF AUSTRALIA PTY. LIMITED, *Sydney*
PRENTICE-HALL CANADA INC., *Toronto*
PRENTICE-HALL HISPANOAMERICANA, S.A., *Mexico*
PRENTICE-HALL OF INDIA PRIVATE LIMITED, *New Delhi*
PRENTICE-HALL OF JAPAN, INC., *Tokyo*
PEARSON EDUCATION ASIA PTE. LTD., *Singapore*
EDITORA PRENTICE-HALL DO BRASIL, LTDA., *Rio de Janeiro*

For my father, Glenn R. Bozeman

CONTENTS

3   BUREAUCRATIC PATHOLOGIES AND REFORM   37

4   RULES AND RED TAPE   64

5 RULES "BORN BAD": RULE-INCEPTION RED TAPE   86

6 RULES "GONE BAD": RULE-EVOLVED RED TAPE   106

PREFACE

I magine a world without bureaucracy. Would there be more or less standing in line? More or less paperwork? More or less fair and equitable treatment? More or less efficiency? The answer, of course, is a question: What does one imagine as an alternative to bureaucracy? Utopia? Feudalism? Tribal warfare? A perfectly competitive market economy?

As a form of governance, bureaucracy has had such great success in transforming the world that most citizens of industrial nations may have difficulty imagining a world without it. But just as bureaucracy has tamed the world, the world now seeks to tame bureaucracy. Bureaucracy seems to have few friends and millions of critics. Some of those critics spend a good deal of time and energy trying to reform bureaucracy. Ours is yet another era in which politicians, managers, and citizens are looking for solutions to bureaucratic problems.

Much of the dislike for government and bureaucracy is based on misinformation, no information, and information disregarded. The reasons for U.S. citizens' antipathy to government are many, complex, much studied, and still poorly understood. But only a small part of that antipathy is relevant to the purpose of identifying "normal bureaucracy," diagnosing bureaucratic pathologies, and offering up prescriptions. Putting aside prejudice, ignorance, and the blinders set in place by two hundred years of limited government traditions, why do reasonable people dislike bureaucracy?

Bureaucracy is inherently controlling. Unless all action is voluntary, coordination of activity requires control. Most of us do not like being controlled, even for the collective good. Even worse, bureaucracy strives (even if it does not always succeed) to deliver even-handed treatment and to administer policies in a disinterested manner, showing no favoritism. But, of course, most of us think of other people as "the rule" and ourselves as "the exception." Our own case is special. An institution whose business is reminding us we are not so special, that we are just one person, much like other persons, is not an institution likely to engender warm and fuzzy feelings. One of the problems with diagnosing pathologies of bureaucracy is that there are aspects of bureaucracy we find distasteful even when bureaucracy is just fulfilling its social function.

If bureaucracy is reviled even when functioning well, it is truly despised when it functions pathologically. Bureaucratic pathologies are plentiful. Nevertheless, there is one variety of bureaucratic pathology that seems more pervasive than all others: bureaucratic red tape. The term red tape has come to be associated with bureaucratic inefficiency, delays, undue paperwork, incompetence, vexing rules and regulations, overcontrol, rigidity, organizational inertia, and unresponsiveness. Red tape has become a code word for virtually every bureaucratic malady. That is exactly the problem.

Red tape, like concepts such as "politics" or "public interest," is one of those terms everyone knows, but for which there is surprisingly little shared meaning. Is red tape perceptual or objective? Is it neutral, or negative, or can red tape even be positive? Does it necessarily entail delays? Does red tape equate with bad management? Does red tape flow from rules or are rules themselves red tape? Is red tape different from "bureaucratization" or "formalism?"

THE PURPOSE OF THIS BOOK

My focus is on organizations, especially public organizations (though most of the material is relevant to private organizations), and particularly on the internal and interorganizational management of organizations. Since much of what goes on inside any bureaucracy is strongly affected by institutional actors outside, the book cannot avoid institutional politics (or economics). But there is no concern about particular politics or policies (excepting reform politics and policy), or particular problems of the marketplace.

My goal is to understand the nature of bureaucratic pathologies, why things go wrong in predictable ways. I try to develop a theory of red tape set in the context of theories of bureaucratic pathology. This is not a scientific theory, complete with axiomatic structure and formalization, but a theory in the more popular sense: ideas about how things work. After a discussion of the nature and elements of bureaucracy, I turn to the problem of distinguishing "normal" bureaucracy from bureaucratic pathology. Then I try developing a perspective on red tape, distinguishing the pathology of red tape for normal as well as other pathological characteristics of bureaucracy.

After developing a set of red tape concepts, the next concern is to explain the origins of red tape. Why is it that bureaucracies so often seem to labor under burdensome or senseless rules? Why are bad rules and regulations promulgated? How and why do useful, effective rules evolve into ineffective ones?

Once a theory of the origins of red tape has been elaborated, the focus turns to the questions of *government* red tape and why government bureaucracies often have more red tape than private ones. Chapter 8 anchors the discussion by focusing on red tape within a particular context, public policy for air quality permitting. The book concludes with some prescriptions for cutting red tape, presented within the framework of a "balance model" of reform, an approach that assumes that cutting red tape entails attention not only to efficiency, but also to accountability, performance, and fairness. Among the various prescriptions presented, a "red tape audit" is developed in some detail.

This book reinvents nothing and reengineers no one. But as we rush to reform, some discussion about the *causes* of red tape and bureaucratic pathology may prove bracing. Otherwise we may find ourselves solving the wrong problems and not making a dent in the right ones.

ACKNOWLEDGMENTS

Georgia Tech colleague Gordon Kingsley, red tape researcher brother-in-arms, read the entire manuscript and provided many helpful suggestions. He also "loaned" me one of the stories from his research. Hal Rainey, a fellow red tape researcher, read an early draft of this book and provided a great many suggestions, all of which led to considerable improvement between the first and last drafts. He is an excellent critic and it was extremely useful to have someone with his broad knowledge giving such detailed attention to my work. The book is much better because Hal is persnickety.

It was my good fortune to have Torben Beck-Jorgensen visiting (from University of Copenhagen) at nearby University of Georgia during 1996–1997. Torben read early drafts of the manuscript with great care and provided many comments and criticisms that have been incorporated throughout the book. Of the many fine critics who have shaped my thinking and work on this book, no one has helped me more than Torben.

I have benefited greatly from my red tape research collaborations, and my coauthors in these collaborations have greatly influenced my thinking about red tape. These collaborators, to whom I am grateful, include Rainey and Kingsley, Stuart Bretschneider, Sanjay Pandey,

Michael Crow, the late Steve Loveless, Leisha-DeHart Davis, Patrick Scott, and Pam Reed. I am indebted to Monica Gaughan for indulging endless discussions of my work (repaid only by interminable discussions of her work). Monica has inspired me in another way as well—as the only person who is even less tolerant of red tape than I, she provided numerous insights into its psychopathologies.

Students at three institutions, Georgia Tech, Syracuse University, and University of Michigan, helped me compile anecdotes, cases, and examples. I am particularly grateful to research assistants (all of whom are by this time professors or managers, or are engaged in some other postgraduate school existence), including Dale Jones, David Dagon, Andrew Kleine, and Stan Larmee. Kleine and Larmee helped me write the Hurricane Andrew case in Chapter 6. Leisha-DeHart Davis is coauthor of Chapter 6 and provided great expertise on the workings of environmental policy. Patrick Scott contributed to material in early versions of Chapter 4, but much of his book-related work remains on the cutting room floor (not because of quality but due to publication elsewhere [Bozeman and Scott, 1996]).

I have also discussed my ideas about red tape with a number of other organization researchers and theorists and have benefited enormously from their criticism, insight, and encouragement. In particular, I am grateful to Herbert Kaufman, who, joining me for lunch one day in Syracuse, told me amusing stories about the origins of his work on red tape and offered ideas about my work. Dwight Waldo, my long-time colleague at Syracuse University, read and commented on some of the earliest work, and his own work continues to inspire me. Larry Mohr heard many of these ideas and helped shape them into better ones, as we taught a course together at the University of Michigan.

I would also like to thank my production editor, Kari Callaghan Mazzola, as well as the following Prentice Hall reviewers who read the manuscript: Charles L. Mitchell, Grambling State University; Raymond Pomerleau, San Francisco State University; Denise Scheberle, University of Wisconsin–Green Bay; John H. Parham, Mankato State University; and Hal G. Rainey, University of Georgia.

Pat Simone was extremely helpful with early phases of the book and with keeping me going as I made a transition to middle-level university bureaucrat. Betty Joiner has provided valuable assistance, helping me with the final production of the manuscript. Most important, Betty stood guard at my office door, turning back at least some petitioners, allowing me the quiet time needed to finish the book.

With all this help, one should expect a perfect book. Unfortunately, imperfections remain. The gap between what this book is and what it should have been is due entirely to author shortcomings.

Barry Bozeman

RED TAPE
AS A BUREAUCRATIC PATHOLOGY

Bureaucracy is the cod liver oil of social institutions: It smells bad and leaves a nasty aftertaste, but sometimes it is just what you need. Even when bureaucracy is working flawlessly, it rarely draws enthusiastic praise. It is natural to feel ambivalent about bureaucracy. It is natural to rail against red tape.

As critics (e.g., Hummel, 1992; Jacoby, 1973) point out, bureaucracy is routinely controlling and insensitive to the needs of particular individuals. People are unique. Routine or disinterested treatment is not generally what we wish. If we have to stand in line for thirty minutes to obtain an automobile registration we find little consolation in the fact that others must stand in line for the same period. If disinterested application of rules results in our ineligibility for a public service, we may claim that the rules should be bent to consider our special case. We are individuals and, in most cases, we want individualized treatment. However, our interest in pressing our special, unique needs does *not* mean that the public interest is served by providing preferential treatment. It would not even be possible to tailor all government interactions to the particular needs of individuals.

Since most people feel ambivalent, at best, about bureaucracy, it is often difficult to judge whether bureaucracy is simply doing what bureaucracy does—exerting control, implementing standardized policies, functioning as a socially conservative institution—or whether it is exceeding its bounds and behaving ineffectively or pathologically. How do we separate bureaucratic pathologies, such as red tape, from socially needed rules that we may dislike because we do not personally benefit from them?

What This Book Is About

This is a book about bureaucratic pathologies, especially red tape. The purposes of this book are as follows:

1. To consider what is "normal" and what is "pathological" in bureaucratic behavior, particularly behavior related to rules and red tape
2. To develop a practical theory of the causes of red tape
3. To present ideas for changing public bureaucracies and reducing red tape

Let us consider some broad themes developed throughout the remainder of the book. One theme is the notion of bureaucratic pathology and the problem of separating dysfunction from dislike. In Chapter 2, the idea of "normal bureaucracy" is considered in contrast to pathological bureaucracy. Particular bureaucratic pathologies are identified and discussed. Chapter 3 presents and evaluates several models explaining the causes of bureaucratic pathologies.

Another theme pervading the book is bureaucratic red tape. Chapter 4 introduces the idea of a rules-based view of red tape. As we shall see later in this chapter, red tape has many meanings. Sometimes red tape is used to indicate the presence of many rules, without any consideration as to whether the rules are effective. Sometimes red tape has a neutral or even a positive connotation. Some authors speak of "good red tape," usually meaning that rules, while cumbersome, provide important benefits. In this book, the term red tape is used in a much narrower way: Red tape is rules, regulations, or procedures that do not achieve the legitimate organizational and social objectives for which they were established. Red tape is a bureaucratic pathology. A key concern in this book is the causes of this pathology. Chapter 5 suggests a number of causes for bad rules, rules that *begin* as red tape. Chapter 6 identifies several reasons why good rules *transform* into red tape. Chapter 7 gives particular attention to the question of whether public organizations have more red tape than private ones and, if so, why. Chapter 8 uses the concepts and ideas developed earlier in the book and applies them in an extended case study of environmental policy.

Much of this book is about how to change bureaucracies—how to prevent red tape and other bureaucratic pathologies, how to reform organizations from within and from the outside. Bureaucratic reform efforts often are too eager, too ambitious, and not well thought out. It is difficult to repair bureaucracies without giving full consideration to the causes of endemic problems.

Another major theme of the book is that bureaucracy is, essentially, a balancing act. Most bureaucratic reforms aim to make bureaucracy more efficient. While it is hard to argue against efficiency, efficiency cannot be the *only* goal of bureaucracy. The goals of bureaucracy (especially public bureaucracy) should include, among others, accountability, performance, and fairness. Chapter 9 presents a "balance model," considering reform in light of multiple values.

In many cases the fundamental goals of bureaucracy conflict. Accountability is costly and only rarely the most efficient path to an objective. If we mean by efficiency the ability to achieve the highest level of output for a given level of input, what about those cases where bureaucracies are efficient but, due to severe resource limits, unable to provide adequate service? Similarly, one way to achieve efficiency is to "unload" troublesome clients and concentrate services on a client pool that has fewer needs. This may be efficient, but it is not fair. Bureaucracy is a balancing act. It seeks values that may conflict and tries to find the proper balance. Unfortunately, thinking of bureaucracy as the balancing of diverse values makes reforms more difficult to design and to assess. It is much easier to say "our goal is to cut costs by 25 percent" than "our goal is to cut costs, maintain a high level of accountability, and provide high quality goods and services in a fair manner."

The red tape concept employed here is consistent with a balance model. By considering rules and regulations in light of their objectives, we focus not so much on the number of rules and regulations but on their effectiveness. In the remainder of this chapter we consider meanings of red tape and why red tape is an important topic of study.

WHY STUDY RED TAPE?

One often quoted red tape maxim is "One man's red tape is another's treasured procedural safeguard" (Kaufman, 1977). A quite different approach is taken in this book, however. If a rule, regulation, or procedure provides a "treasured procedural safeguard," then it is not red tape. It is a rule accomplishing the objective of procedural safeguard. Red tape is bad. Red tape wastes resources and fails to accomplish legitimate objectives. If the government agency has many rules because many are needed, if the rules advance the legitimate objectives of agency or clients, then there is no red tape.

Given the amount of attention this book gives to red tape, one might ask, "Is this overkill?" Most of us think of red tape as annoying but it doesn't usually rank up there with reducing world hunger or working for world peace. In fact, red tape is not even among the more popular organization theory topics. Most organization theorists have ignored the topic. Hundreds of articles and books are available on such topics as organizational conflict, leadership, and strategic planning, but red tape has

---

**BUREAUCRATIC ENCOUNTER:
RED TAPE AS AN INTER-GALACTIC PROBLEM**

On August 20, 1977, the Voyager spacecraft departed from Cape Canaveral for Jupiter, Saturn, Uranus, and parts unknown. Attached securely to the side of the spacecraft was a porcelain cartridge, a diamond stylus, and a copper phonograph record sprayed with a thin film of gold (Druyan, 1977). The package was encased in aluminum and its cover engraved with playing instructions. If all goes as planned, it should be operable for a billion years. The Voyager recording includes greetings in many languages, but most of the recording is devoted to music, not only Beethoven but the rock and roll pioneer Chuck Berry (ironically, the composer of "Roll Over Beethoven.").

One hopes that humankind's first alien encounter occurs outside earth's atmosphere, with the Voyager as medium. An earth-bound encounter would expose aliens to an aspect of human culture less exalted than Beethoven and more pervasive than Chuck Berry's widely copied *Johnny B. Goode* (the tune that made the cosmic hit parade). According to London's *Daily Telegraph*, the United Nations commissioned a group of scientists to develop a "Declaration of Principles Concerning Activities Following the Detection of Extra-Terrestrial Intelligence" (reported in *Parade Magazine*, 1991). Even the title forebodes. These guidelines, hammered out at a meeting of the International Academy of Astronautics in Buenos Aires, suggest that radio astronomers encountering aliens take the following steps. First, the observer should record the alien signal and contact other scientists and ask them to verify the signal. Then the observer should get in touch with the International Astronomical Union, which, in turn, will send out an official notification through the Central Bureau for Astronomical Telegrams. Then the Secretary General of the UN, the Institute for Space Law, and the International Telecommunications Union will be informed. The Telecommunications Union will see to it that the alien signal is cleared of human communications traffic so that the alien signal will be clear. Finally, the rest of us will be informed that we have company.

The notion of aliens being greeted by intergalactic red tape seems a wry commentary on what it means to be human. We humanoids have a prehensile thumb, language, and a talent for creating red tape.

---

not often captured scholars' attention. In light of increased public and governmental concern with red tape, perhaps the time has come to rethink and reexamine red tape.

While an easy target of humor (see box above, the first of several "bureaucratic encounters" boxes), red tape sometimes has tragic consequences. It is difficult to see the lighter side of red tape when, after having one's business wiped out by a hurricane, one must wade through a mountain of red tape before even being eligible for the loan that comes through two months late (Kilborn, 1992). Similarly, trying to rebuild one's heavily mortgaged grocery store in the wake of urban riots is hard enough, but having to deal with city hall's red tape makes the task almost insurmountable (Duignan-Cabrera, 1993).

It is not an exaggeration to say that red tape can have fatal consequences. In July, 1993, the Illinois Department of Transportation installed a traffic light at the intersection of State Highway 59 and 111th St. in the township of Wheatland—almost five years after the light was requested and authorized, and four days after two people were killed in a traffic accident at that intersection. This brought to seven the number of persons who had been killed at the intersection during the time between the authorization of the traffic light and its installation. According to the Wheatland Township highway commissioner, it took a full four years to "craft an agreement" for the traffic light. "You wouldn't believe what I had to go through to get $200,000. It took years and years…. When it comes to the process of politicking and going from one committee to another, very simple and elementary things take a long time" (Kendall and Barnum, 1993: 1).

In most instances, however, red tape is neither funny nor fatal. More often it is a frustrating barrier to achieving organizational and personal goals. Red tape makes organizations less satisfying places to work. Red tape makes clients' and customers' interactions with organizations less rewarding and more aggravating. Red tape costs organizations, citizens, and consumers.

There are many good reasons to study red tape. In the first place, knowing more about red tape gives us signals as to which aspects of bureaucracy need change. Too often, reforms are too broad and fail to identify problems except those of the most general sort. Second, red tape is something individual organizations can change. Finding sufficient resources for the organization is a daunting task, securing adequate personnel and talent, likewise, poses many problems. Often, red tape can be fixed. Third, a knowledge of red tape helps separate people problems from systems problems (more about this later). Fourth, red tape is an equal opportunity problem, as much a concern to managers as to workers, clients, and controllers. No one is exempt from the ravages of red tape. It affects the meek, the mighty, and those in between. In many respects it is remarkable that red tape has not received more attention from scholars and researchers. It goes to the heart of management and bureaucratic reform.

CONCEPTS OF RED TAPE

Most have heard the old saw about the meaning of art. When viewing an abstract picture hanging in an expensive gallery, the unpretentious Main Street critic says "I don't know much about art, but I know it when I see it." That's the way most of us define red tape—by pointing to an instance of it. But one soon finds that a bureaucratic rule that is to one viewer a Mona Lisa of bureaucratic wisdom is to another the scrawls of a dilettante. Answering the question "What is red tape?" is not so easy.

Despite the difficulty of providing a satisfactory definition of red tape, almost anyone who has worked in an organization or interacted with organizations as a customer or client would surely put red tape somewhere near the top of their list of organizational maladies. Most managers and policymakers seem to spend a good deal of time complaining about red tape, trying cut red tape, and coping with it in one manner or another. Since red tape doesn't spring up on its own, presumably some managers and policymakers spend some time creating, perhaps inadvertently, the rules, regulations, and protocols that come to be viewed as red tape. But if managers sometimes have pride of authorship for rules and regulations, understandably no one stakes a claim on red tape.

What explains this apparent avoidance of a topic so widely recognized as critical? The ivory tower syndrome cannot explain it away. While it is certainly true that scholars are sometimes captured by esoteric or arcane topics, organizational researchers are a practical lot, devoting great attention to such topics as organizational leadership, employee motivation, communication, and design of tasks and organizations. In many instances there is considerable convergence between researchers' and managers' definition of "what is important." Not so red tape. There are problems facing the red tape researcher that the leadership or motivation or communication researchers either have solved or do not face. One of these problems is that no one bothers to define red tape, on the erroneous assumption that everyone knows what it means.

While ordinary conversations about red tape usually confuse by being imprecise, scholarly deliberations about red tape often fare no better by the precision criterion. Researchers and theorists fail to distinguish among sources of red tape, perspectives of those affected by it, or, in many cases, differences between perceived and objective red tape. Scholarly treatments of red tape are often far removed from day-to-day experience with red tape. Most ordinary discussions of red tape do not include consideration of good red tape or optimal red tape. Trying to find the optimal level of red tape for an organization may intrigue organization theorists or economists, but most people think of red tape as something that needs to be fixed.

HERBERT KAUFMAN'S RED TAPE CONCEPTS

The classic book-length treatment of red tape is Herbert Kaufman's *Red Tape: Its Origins, Uses and Abuses* (1977). It is not only the best-known book on red tape, but the *only* book devoted entirely to the topic. In most

---

BUREAUCRATIC ENCOUNTER:
WHAT IS *NOT* RED TAPE—UNDERSTAFFING

The Great Flood of 1993 left many midwestern communities reeling. One of the many newspaper reports of the trials faced by flood victims was under the headline "Midwesterners Face a Flood of Red Tape" (Tyson, 1993).

On December 3, 1993, President Clinton signed a bill providing $105 million to purchase flood-plain property and help flood victims move to higher ground. In St. Charles County, Missouri, planning and zoning officials reported that the flood rendered 64 percent of the homes in the area uninhabitable. Understandably, Charles County citizens' requests for flood relief were quick in coming and frantic since their houses were "shrouded to the shingles in a uniform brown smear left by the floodwaters." But relief was not quick in coming and, the article noted, "Midwesterners who stared down a flood of biblical scale now must endure a vast backlog of paperwork."

After noting that the processing of forms and paperwork seemed to be taking an enormous amount of time and that the slow pace of relief and buy-outs had "provoked angry threats from residents of St. Charles County," the report went on to say that "... officials in St. Charles County are short of manpower and funding...." This is *not* red tape.

The problems of victims of the 1993 flood were enormous and the relief efforts did occur at a snail's pace. But if we are going to give the devil his due, let us curse the right devil. Government is widely accused of being "fat" and inefficient and it is also accused of creating red tape. Both accusations are in some instances correct. But in many instances, "red tape" is the term for things-we-do-not-like-about-government or, even more broadly, bad-things-that-happen-in-life. Quicker and more effective response to victims of natural disaster requires not only consciousness of efficiency in the processing of claims but also sufficient government personnel to support large-scale relief efforts. If we go to buy consumer electronics from a warehouse that keeps prices low by employing few people, many of whom are poorly trained, we put up with the bad service in order to get a low price. But if we get a "low price" for government service (i.e., reduced taxes) we are prone to call the bad service red tape.

The impact of personnel cutbacks on government operations is not always easy to predict, but in case studies of NASA and the Food and Drug Administration, Heimann (1995) provides evidence that personnel shortages have the sharpest impacts on agencies dealing with "nonprogrammed" decisions, ones that have to be tailored to the situation. This is a good description of most disaster relief agencies.

---

respects, it is a very good book that serves its purposes well. But despite using the term red tape on nearly every page of this 100-page book, Kaufman never actually provides a definition. This is not really surprising given Kaufman's intent to write a whimsical, widely accessible book rather than to provide a systematic, thorough-going treatment of the topic (Kaufman, 1993). He does begin the book by noting that "[w]hen people rail against red tape, they mean that they are subjected to too many constraints, that many of the constraints seem pointless, and that agencies seem to take forever to act" (Kaufman, 1977: 4–5). Thus, he includes several elements common to most discussions of red tape—vexation, constraint, and delay.

BENEFICIAL RED TAPE

Kaufman's (1977) negative concept of red tape is set side-by-side with beneficial red tape. The notion of beneficial red tape stems in part from the quite sensible point that what one person views as red tape, another may not. One line of reasoning (Kaufman, 1977: 29) might be described as an administrative "tragedy of the commons":

> Every restraint and requirement originates in somebody's demand for it. Of course, each person does not will them all; on the contrary, even the most broadly based interest groups are concerned with only a relatively small band of the full spectrum of government activities.... But there are so many of us, and such a diversity of interests among us, that modest individual demands result in great stacks of official paper and bewildering procedural mazes.

Thus, part of the reason for red tape is the sheer number of specialized demands for government action. Process protection also gives rise to red tape. Kaufman (58–59) notes, "Had we more trust in ... our public officers, we would feel less impelled to limit discretion by means of minutely detailed directions and prescriptions." Kaufman points out that much red tape could be avoided were we willing to reduce the checks and safeguards now imposed on government employees. But he does not advocate doing away with the extensive rule-based safeguards, noting that were we to do away with red tape, "we would be appalled by the resurgence of the evils and follies it currently prevents" (59).

Kaufman is certainly not the only student of bureaucracy who points to seemingly beneficial aspects of red tape. Landau (1969), who suggests an important rationale for seemingly excessive rules and procedures, makes one of the more interesting arguments. According to Landau, duplication and overlap in some cases provide important benefits. Landau (1991: 12) observes that "the deliberate removal of redundancies grinds an organization down to subsistence level, so restricting its repertoire of responses as to render it incapable of effective performance." In other words, duplication and attendant inefficiencies can sometimes provide long-run benefits.

Several writers (e.g., Benveniste, 1983, 1987; Goodsell, 1994; Thompson, 1975) argue that red tape sometimes provides benefits in the form of procedural safeguards that ensure accountability, predictability, and fairness in administrative and policy decisions. Kirlin (1996) makes the important point that government provides an institutional framework for a wide array of human activity and focusing narrowly on managerial efficiency undervalues government's role in the design of institutions and policies.

As an accountability mechanism red tape comports with—and even flows from—larger democratic and constitutional values that emphasize tolerance, diversity, and participation in the political process. Thus, according to this view, the pervasiveness of bureaucratic red tape mirrors our system of governance, a system designed to be redundant and, hence, inefficient in both structure and execution.

Consistent with Kaufman's (1977) assertion that red tape is integral to our political culture, Meyer (1979a: 230) suggests that red tape is a necessary feature of our federal system: "The quantum shift in the scope of federal activities when superimposed upon a decentralized system of state and local government created a host of intergovernmental ties where none had existed previously, and it gave rise to formal procedures governing these relationships." Meyer (1979a) also suggests that privatization—as a value ingrained within our political culture—serves as another source of red tape. As with the red tape that flows from intergovernmental relationships, this form of red tape stems from the documentation and other administrative requirements that are attached to federal funds as a means to ensure compliance with federal guidelines. But in the larger context, red tape may be viewed as a product of our political culture and the expectations that flow out of citizen demands and our constitutional system of governance. The need for adequate levels of accountability allegedly gives rise to red tape.

Several studies examining the impact of red tape point to possible benefits. Foster (1990) found that the likelihood of rule compliance is strongly mediated by factors such as client empathy and peer group pressures. In numerous instances such factors led to significant rule bending, ranging from passive noncompliance to open sabotage. While red tape is often assailed as a source of nonresponsiveness among public organizations, one study found that nonresponsiveness is related more to limited resources and to the degree of discretion workers exercise (Mladenka, 1981). Similarly, Goodsell (1981) found a favorable predisposition toward "rule bending" for clients perceived as the most needy. In this study, both physical proximity and interpersonal contact were more critical determinants of services than the extent of rules themselves. Snizek and Bullard (1983) and York and Henley (1986) report that standardization of work procedures actually enhances job satisfaction because of increasing clarification of role expectations. Baldwin (1990) was unable to detect any effects of red tape upon motivation levels among managers. But others (Blau and Scott, 1962; Sorenson and Sorenson, 1974; Ivancevich and Donnelly, 1975) have found that bureaucratization reduces job satisfaction. To sum up, some view red tape not as a pathology but as a mixed blessing—both harmful and beneficial at the same time. Usually the harm comes from its inefficiencies, costs, and the frustration it creates. The benefits arise from its protections and accountability guarantees. But the two-sided view of red tape presents confusion, perhaps an *unnecessary* confusion. We take note of studies in the "beneficial red tape" tradition, but in this book the term red tape is not associated with benefit nor is the term neutral. It is a bureaucratic pathology.

RED TAPE AS PATHOLOGY

To most people the term red tape has entirely negative connotations. Red tape is not only one of the "most enduring and universal rejection symbols in the English language," but a "classic 'condensation' symbol in that it incorporates a vast array of subjectively held feelings and expresses them succinctly" (Goodsell, 1994: 63). To put it another way, red tape has come to connote the worst of bureaucracy: gargantuan, cynically impersonal, bound up in meaningless paperwork, and beset by excessive, duplicative, and unnecessary procedures (Rai, 1983; Goodsell, 1994). Most of the bureaucracy literature treats it as a pathology rather than a positive or neutral organizational attribute. The origins of pathological red tape in theories of bureaucracy are difficult to trace but one early part of the lineage is Merton's (1940) classic study of bureaucratic personality. Merton argues that organizational demands for rule adherence lead to goal displacement among individuals working within bureaucratic organizations. Rules become ends in themselves and adherence to formalized procedures interferes with the adaptation of these rules to special circumstances. Accordingly, the rules that were designed to increase efficiency, in general, produce inefficiency in special or exceptional circumstances. Merton further suggests that sustained exposure to entrenched rules creates a tendency toward rigidity among individuals within bureaucracy. This may occur because bureaucratic organizations tend to reward rule-oriented workers more than those who display less rule orientation (Edwards, 1984).

Since Merton's path-breaking study, a number of others have followed in the same tradition of identifying red tape as a bureaucratic pathology (e.g., Argyris, 1957; Thompson, 1961; Hummel, 1982) and focusing on the role of bureaucrats and their psychological world in producing red tape (Bozeman and Rainey, 1998; Pandey, 1995).

The empirical research on red tape (reviewed in Chapter 7) has, for the most part, reflected the popular view of red tape as an organizational pathology. Buchanan (1975) describes red tape in terms of excessive structural constraints. Baldwin (1990) distinguishes between formal and informal red tape. Formal red tape pertains to burdensome personnel procedures, whereas informal red tape concerns constraints created by such external sources as the media, public opinion, and political parties. Perhaps the closest to popular usage is Rosenfeld's (1984) definition of red tape as the sum of government guidelines, procedures, and forms that are perceived as excessive, unwieldy, or pointless in relationship to official decisions and policy.

Research studies in the red tape as pathology tradition (e.g., Bozeman, Reed, and Scott, 1992) suggest that government is often the cause of red tape, whether the effect is manifested in public or private spheres. That is, red tape flows from external governmental influences and particularly governmental regulations (Baldwin, 1990), resulting in conditions of "bureaucratic inflexibility" (Rai, 1983).

The pathology tradition seems to resonate with everyday experience and is close to popular usage. The beneficial red tape tradition makes the important point that some of the rules we find frustrating, wasteful, or inefficient are nonetheless beneficial because they either ensure accountability, preserve rights of procedure, or provide protections from abuses of power.

RESOLVING THE CONFUSION OF PATHOLOGY VERSUS BENEFIT

The point made by Kaufman (1977) and others is that many of the rules and regulations and procedures viewed as red tape provide benefits in terms of control, accountability, and even public safety and security. An alternative means of making the same point is to simply distinguish between rules, regulations, and procedures that are beneficial and ones not conferring benefits, the nonbeneficial ones being red tape. This is not as easy as it sounds but is nevertheless a good strategy for sorting through bureaucratic problems.

Taking the stance that red tape is inherently a bureaucratic pathology may actually advance the normative concerns of beneficial red tape adherents. By facing head-on the need to sort good rules from bad, beneficial elements of rules from destructive ones, procedural guarantees and accountability may receive more direct attention and deliberate support. To those (such as Kaufman) who view red tape as an inevitable concomitant of government action, the crucial question is "how much red tape should you tolerate to get satisfying amounts of what you want?" (Kaufman, 1977: 60). But the counterview, advanced in this book, is zero tolerance for red tape. If rules provide accountability they are not red tape. Red tape confers no benefits and, thus, the question is not "how much do we need?" but "how do we eliminate it? If red tape were the key to preserving accountability and procedural protections then the world leaders in citizen safeguards would be the impoverished, administratively underdeveloped nations of the world that, by all accounts, greatly outpace the United States and other industrialized nations in creating red tape.

A WORKING DEFINITION OF RED TAPE

The definition provided below assumes that red tape is a pathology, not a guarantor of accountability or a facilitator of human rights. Good rules, ambivalent rules, copious rules, expensive rules—none of these is red tape.

> *Red tape*: Rules, regulations, and procedures that remain in force and entail a compliance burden but do not advance the legitimate purposes the rules were intended to serve.

We shall return to this definition in Chapter 4, but let us consider briefly just what this definition tells us about red tape. Since one of the problems with the term red tape is that it is used for multipurpose complaints about bureaucracy, it is important to separate red tape problems from the many other pathologies endemic to bureaucracy. Thus, waste is not red tape (unless caused by wasteful rules); human venality is not red tape (unless occurring under the rules); managerial incompetence is not red tape (unless aided and abetted by the rules).

This definition tells us that bad rules are not red tape unless they are *in force and entail a compliance burden*. Rules that are "on the books," but that are completely ignored, may be an offense against the tidiness of legal or organizational codes, but they are not red tape. If no one complies with the rule, there is no compliance burden (no resources expended) and, thus, no red tape.

Only those rules designed to serve a *legitimate purpose* are relevant to this definition of red tape. The key word here is "legitimate." We are using the term in the sense of "legitimate governance." Thus, official public representatives acting appropriately in their official roles must be sanctioned by the organization or, in the case of public bureaucracy, by the rule. If a manager establishes a rule that all contractors must kick back 10 percent of the cost of contracts to her personal Swiss bank account, this is a rule but not a legitimate one and, thus, has no bearing on red tape. This is bureaucratic pathology known as malfeasance.

CONCLUSION

The terms *red tape* and *bureaucracy* accompany one another so often as to imply common linguistic origin. Such is not the case. The term red tape derives from the nineteenth century British government practice of binding official government documents in red tape (Goodsell, 1994: 81). Bureaucracy is derived from the French word "bureau," a desk with many compartments.

Popular usage notwithstanding, "red tape" is not the best synonym for "bureaucracy." Nevertheless, bureaucracy and red tape are linked in so many ways that any study of red tape is necessarily a study of the nature, workings, and pathologies of bureaucracy. While some people feel that bureaucracy is an organizational form that is inherently pathological, that is not the view taken here. Fiction aside, few bureaucrats are heroes and few are villains. Bureaucracy is not so much a menace or a blight on the human spirit as a means of getting things done. Sometimes it is effective in getting things done, other times it is not so effective.

Red tape is one of the most insidious problems of bureaucracy. Indeed, it is so deeply embedded that it is difficult even to separate concerns about red tape from more general issues of bureaucratic functioning. In the next two chapters we consider the physiology of bureaucracy before we examine its pathogens. This requires focusing on some core issues. Just what is bureaucracy and how is it different from other organizational forms? Why is bureaucracy so often a target of derision? If people hate bureaucracy why is it omnipresent? If we are concerned about pathological bureaucracy we must have some notion of normal bureaucracy. But what is "normal" bureaucracy?

IN SEARCH
OF NORMAL BUREAUCRACY

Fiction provides many memorable portrayals of red tape and malevolent bureaucracy. Occasionally, fiction even celebrates heroic bureaucracy. Perhaps the most familiar bureaucratic fiction genre is futuristic science fiction—utopia gone mad in works such as Orwell's' *1984* or Koestler's *Darkness at Noon*. But there are many nineteenth century precursors warning of red tape and other more virulent bureaucratic ills. In the early nineteenth century, Charles Dickens, that most acute of social observers and an avid chronicler of red tape, wrote a scathing essay denouncing the British civil service. Later, in his novel *Little Dorrit*, he introduced the character of Sir Tite Barnacle, a British civil servant who headed the Office of Circumlocution. The responsibility of this office was to take any problem assigned to it and make it more complicated and convoluted than it already was.

Some antibureaucracy fiction contains deep philosophical renderings of bureaucracy, examining not only red tape and bureaucratic machinations, but also the alienation arising from citizens' encounters with pathological bureaucracy. Franz Kafka's *The Castle*, for example, gives more insight than any textbook into the feelings of individuals trapped in a bureaucratic maze. Other more contemporary novels, such as Ken Kesey's *One Flew Over the Cuckoo's Nest* or Heller's *Catch 22*, depict bureaucratic worlds at the same time familiar and surreal. Indeed, "catch 22" is a wonderfully evocative red tape concept: the rule that undermines all rules.

One need not go to fiction to find examples of bureaucratic malevolence. A good number of studies examine the relationship of the bureaucratic ethos of Hitler's Germany to dehumanization and depersonalization and, in turn, to the crimes committed by the regime. In addition to the fine scholarly accounts of bureaucratic totalitarianism, Albert Speer's *Inside the Third Reich* provides lasting testament to the horrors of bureaucracy gone mad as well as an understanding of the ways in which even the most sinister bureaucracies manage to recruit a nation's elite. Lest the excesses of Third Reich, or Stalinist bureaucracy, or Lon Nol's death squads be dismissed as aberrant cases that could never be repeated in democratic nations, consider the recent revelations of the U.S. government performing radiation experiments on unknowing citizens in the 1940s and 1950s. In an April 17, 1947, letter to Dr. Fidler of the U.S. Atomic Energy Commission, U.S. Army Colonel O. G. Haywood Jr. requested that "no document be released which refers to experiments with humans and might have adverse effect on public opinion or result in legal suits."

Not all government-induced hazards come from the military. One particularly infamous episode (Sanders, 1997) is the U.S. Public Health Service Tuskegee Syphilis Study, conducted between 1932 and 1972. This project charted the progress of untreated syphilis in thirty-three impoverished black men, in Macon County, Alabama. Most of these men were not informed about their case or its severity, and treatment was withheld to observe effects of the disease. According to Dr. Jackson Wright of the University Hospitals of Cleveland, the damage in public trust has been long-lasting: "We are missing critical data regarding the treatment and management of many diseases that disproportionately affect the black population" (Sanders, 1997: 9).

If irradiation and untreated syphilis are not sufficiently bracing there are many other such episodes, including the use of conscientious objectors in germ warfare experiments, the San Francisco Bay attack by the U.S. Army using serratia marcescens bacteria, and Japanese curfew (*Hirabayashi v. United States*, 1943) and internment (*Korematsu v. United States*, 323 U.S. 214, 1944; see U.S. Commission on Wartime Relocation, 1983).

Sometimes bureaucrats are intrepid. The stories of whistle-blowing bureaucrats, many of whom receive only organizational censure in return for their courage and public-spiritedness, are reminders that people in bureaucracies often behave heroically (Westman, 1991; Hunt, 1995; U.S. General Accounting Office, 1993).

In many instances, real life bureaucratic heroism comes from *not* breaking the rules. Bureaucrats sometimes work hard to ensure that even the rich and powerful are subject to the laws of government and the legitimate rules of bureaucracy. To a large extent, the story of Watergate is one of heroic bureaucrats persevering in the face of enormous political pressure (Woodward and Bernstein, 1994; Thompson, 1975). Similarly, the Iran-Contra scandal was uncovered and reported by outraged bureaucrats acting in concert with the media (Ledeen, 1988; Thelen, 1996).

BUREAUCRACY IS, BUREAUCRACY SHOULD BE

Malevolent bureaucracy, heroic bureaucracy, and normal bureaucracy exist side-by-side. Generally, bureaucracy is neither menacing nor right-eous. This does not prevent us from having strong feelings about bureau-cracy. Waiting in line for an hour when we think we should not have to wait in line at all causes us to think badly of bureaucracy. Receiving a tax refund for more than we requested, because the bureaucracy is set up to correct our arithmetic errors, causes us to think that maybe the bureau-cracy is not so bad. Our perceptions of bureaucracy, knowledge of histor-ical events in real bureaucracies, and resentments about some of the effects of bureaucracies on our daily lives, get in the way of dispassionate reflection about the nature of bureaucracy. Experience and feeling lead us directly to normative bureaucracy, not empirical bureaucracy.

Normative bureaucracy focuses on the values bureaucracy should serve and discrepancies between these values and actual bureaucratic performance. *Empirical bureaucracy* makes no judgments about the appropriateness of the values or goals of bureaucracy but, instead, seeks to identify the defining elements of bureaucracy (i.e., what separates bureaucracy from all things nonbureaucratic) and to understand "what is" rather than "what should be." Empirical bureaucracy seeks explana-tions of bureaucratic behavior without making judgments about that behavior.

Much of this book is focused on problems of bureaucracy, causes of those problems, and possible approaches to solving them. But we must begin with some notion about "what is" bureaucracy. Otherwise we may find ourselves solving problems that do not exist or ascribing faults (or virtues) to bureaucracy when, in fact the fault (or virtue) is really better ascribed to political actors to whom bureaucracy reports, to bureaucratic clients, or to particular human beings.

Before considering empirical bureaucracy, a couple of issues need to be put to rest. First, the empirical/normative distinction, while useful, is not at all clear-cut. Is a theory (e.g., Downs, 1967) providing an empirical description of bureaucracy and identifying inefficiencies a normative the-ory or an empirical one? Probably it is both. Similarly, how can a norma-tive theory of bureaucracy (e.g., Hummel, 1982) fail to provide ideas about empirical bureaucracy? Nevertheless, it is useful to distinguish between intentions to explain and intentions to criticize or change.

Generally, feelings about bureaucracy run high but empirical description and explanation get short shrift. Dispassionate analyses of bureaucracy are remarkably uncommon. But an understanding of the concept of bureaucracy and the attributes of bureaucracy is a good starting point.

WEBERIAN BUREAUCRACY

The term bureaucracy has many meanings and this ambiguity makes it more difficult to develop satisfying answers as to "what is," much less "what should be." Nevertheless, we can identify a few typical uses, each of which we shall employ here.

Bureaucracy is derived from the French word "bureau," a desk with many compartments. Often word origins tell us little about contemporary meanings (e.g., knowing "manure" is derived from a French word meaning to work with one's hands tells us little about modern usage), but the derivation of bureaucracy provides a wonderful metaphor for modern usage.

Most analyses of bureaucracy begin with the work of Max Weber, either using Weberian bureaucracy as an archetype to describe the essential elements of bureaucracy, or as a whipping boy, proclaiming Weberian bureaucracy as "closed bureaucracy," or "machine bureaucracy." Some observers (Marcuse, 1968) view Weberian bureaucracy as itself a sort of pathology. Others (Hall, 1991) take Weberian bureaucracy as a good approximation of bureaucracy and its functions and focus on ways in which bureaucracies move from Weberian characteristics to inefficient, maladapted structures. Barzelay (1992) implies that the "bureaucratic paradigm" helped improve governance by replacing the chaotic and capricious patronage-dominated administration of pre-twentieth century U.S. government, but it became too successful and entrenched, standing in the way of improved performance and accountability.

The Weberian model of bureaucracy is so familiar as to require only cursory review. Weber's analysis of nineteenth century Prussian bureaucracy sought to identify the essential elements of bureaucracy and, thus, is an archetypal model. The characteristics of Weberian bureaucracy include the following:

1. Fixed and official jurisdiction, ordered by rules and administrative law
2. Regular activities distributed in a fixed manner
3. Authority by directives according to fixed rules
4. Rights and duties of administrators prescribed by law
5. Principles of official hierarchy with levels of graded authority; firmly established superior-subordinate relations
6. Management based on written documents that are preserved in files

7. Separation of public from private lives of officials
8. Administration of bureaus that requires expertise, specialized training
9. Administration as a full-time job, a career
10. Bureau management following specific rules learned and transmitted from one official to the next

Weber described the characteristics of bureaucratic officials in the following manner:

- Office holding is a vocation, not a source of informal personal exchange or spoils.
- Official positions confer esteem.
- Officials are appointed by a superior authority.
- Positions are held for life, free from political and personal considerations, which confers independence.
- Regular compensation, fixed salary, is a function of rank.
- Hierarchical career ranks with fixed conditions of promotion, and promotion is based on exams or seniority.

As a descriptive model, Weber's archetype is widely accepted and even its critics feel that the model captures a great deal of organizational reality. For example, Carl Friedrich (1952), an early critic of Weber, took Weber to task for presenting an archetype not carefully anchored in systematic empirical observation. However, Friedrich's own examination of administrative bodies in four very different historical and national contexts uncovered many of the same characteristics identified by Weber.

Most of the controversy surrounding Weberian bureaucracy has centered on its suitability as a normative model. Despite an avowed detachment, Weber's writings strongly imply that he viewed bureaucracy as a prerequisite to economic development and as a superior way of organizing. Weber viewed modern bureaucracy as the cornerstone of organizational rationality, a value he prized highly. He noted that "the primary source of the superiority of bureaucratic administration lies in the role of technical knowledge," and contends (Merton, et al., 1952: 24) that "however much people may complain about the 'evils of bureaucracy,' ... bureaucratic administration is, other things being equal, always, from a formal, technical point of view, the most rational type." The source of rationality is technical knowledge, and technical knowledge is developed as a concomitant of bureaucratic work.

Bureaucratic administration generally entails the exercise of control on the basis of knowledge. This is the feature that makes bureaucracy rational. In addition to developing sufficient knowledge to rationalize planning and decision-making, "bureaucratic organizations ...

RESEARCH ENCOUNTER: EVIDENCE FOR WEBERIAN BUREAUCRACY IN PUBLIC AND PRIVATE ORGANIZATIONS

Most people view government agencies as "more bureaucratic" than private organizations, and there is at least some evidence (Bozeman, Reed, and Scott, 1992; Baldwin, 1990) to back up that view, depending upon what one means by "more bureaucratic." But what if what we mean by "more bureaucratic" is "more Weberian?" Are government organizations *more* likely to keep extensive written records? Are they *more* likely to be highly specialized in their tasks? Do they worry *more* about jurisdictional issues?

One way to see whether organizations have these characteristics is to use survey research and questionnaires to ask managers about their organizations. In the National Administrative Studies Project (NASP) (see Bozeman and Rainey, 1998; Rainey, Pandey, and Bozeman, 1995), hundreds of questionnaires were sent to government and private organizations in three states. In one of those questionnaires, mailed to managers in the state of New York, 365 respondents (196 government, 169 private) provided data about the Weberian characteristics of their organizations. The results are not astonishing, but there are a few surprises, including the fact that private managers view their organizations as providing greater standardization in the treatment of clients and customers. Cliché thinking tells us that in business "the customer is always right." In government, equal treatment (one form of standard) often is mandated (Aberbach, 1978).

The managers rated their organization for several Weberian characteristics on a 0–10 scale, with 5 being average. Here are the scale positions for the public and private sector respondents (G = Government, P = Private):

Hierarchy: Layers of Authority

```
                        P       G
Few       [  |   |   |   |   |   |   |   |   |   |   ]   Many
Layers       0   1   2   3   4   5   6   7   8   9  10   Layers
```

Task Specialization

```
                            P       G
Little          [  |   |   |   |   |   |   |   |   |   |   ]   Great Deal of
Specialization     0   1   2   3   4   5   6   7   8   9  10   Specialization
```

Record Keeping

```
                                P       G
Few       [  |   |   |   |   |   |   |   |   |   |   ]   Great Many
Records      0   1   2   3   4   5   6   7   8   9  10   Records
```

Formal Credentials

```
                                P   G
Little    [  |   |   |   |   |   |   |   |   |   |   ]   Great
Concern      0   1   2   3   4   5   6   7   8   9  10   Concern
```

Standardized Treatment

```
                            G   P
Much       [  |   |   |   |   |   |   |   |   |   |   ]   Highly
Discretion    0   1   2   3   4   5   6   7   8   9  10   Standard
```

have a tendency to increase their power still further by the knowledge growing out of experience in the service" (Merton, et al., 1952: 26).

Much of Weber's defense of bureaucracy rests on its alleged superiority with respect to enhancing organizations' technical efficiency. Those who do not share Weber's view that technical efficiency is the most important value of organization are less impressed with Weberian bureaucracy as a normative model.

WEBERIAN BUREAUCRACY AND NORMAL BUREAUCRACY

In light of the influence of Weberian concepts of bureaucracy on scholars' views, it is difficult to use the Weberian model as an indicator of "normal" bureaucracy. But some notion of normal bureaucracy is required if we are to know abnormal bureaucracy when we see it. As a matter of convenience, we shall take Weber's archetype as an indicator of normal bureaucracy. This is not the same as *good* or *effective* bureaucracy; rather we are taking Weberian bureaucracy as *typical* bureaucracy.

Our purpose, again, is to know bureaucratic pathologies when we see them. If we find that bureaucracies are hierarchical, or that they provide disinterested treatment to clients, then we shall not assess these behaviors as pathological. These behaviors may or may not be effective but they are not, in our terms, pathological.

"NORMAL" BUREAUCRACY

Normal bureaucracy is the nexus between straightforward descriptions of bureaucracy and views about what bureaucracy should be. If empirical bureaucracy is the actual behaviors and tangible effects bureaucracy, and normative bureaucracy is bureaucracy as we wish it, then normal bureaucracy is the bureaucracy we view as acceptable. The question, then, is this: "If we can expect a given range of bureaucratic behaviors, what behaviors within that range are acceptable?"

Normal bureaucracy depends upon society's unique political culture, qualities of political regimes, and the political-historical experiences of particular generations. What is normal (i.e., within the bounds of expectations) in one society may be pathological in another. Expectations about bureaucracy vary a good deal across nations. For example, Goodsell (1994: 71) provides data (from Rose, 1984) about citizens' responses to the question "[s]uppose there was some question you had to take to a government office ... do you think you would be treated as well as anyone else?" Whereas 83 percent of U.S. and British respondents felt they would receive equal treatment, only 53 percent of Italian citizens and 42 percent of Mexican citizens expected equal treatment. In this and many other ways, what we expect from bureaucracy varies according to political culture and nations' political histories (see Peters, 1994: 39–69).

Without some notion of normal bureaucracy there is no starting point for assessing bureaucratic pathologies. In the absence of an ability to identify normal bureaucracy, we might well find ourselves (as bureaucratic reform doctors sometimes do) killing a healthy patient.

IS WEBERIAN BUREAUCRACY NORMAL?

Scholars' continued befuddlement about the meaning of the Weberian model of bureaucracy may be explained in part by their implicit, unarticulated notions of normal bureaucracy. Those who view bureaucracy as acceptable only so long as it is humanistic, socially proactive, and self-actualizing of both bureaucrat and client are quite likely to view the Weberian model as a normative model for government gone crazy. Those who feel the role of bureaucracy is disinterestedly executing the will of the people as expressed by their elected delegates may view the Weberian model in a more positive light.

From at least one standpoint, we can safely say that the Weberian model, love it or loath it, is an accurate one. The characteristics delineated by Weber are present in virtually every bureaucratic organization; the only issue is the extent to which these characteristics dominate. Despite reformist titles such as *An End to Hierarchy! An End to Competition!* (Thayer, 1981), real life poses few, if any, instances of organizations with no hierarchy. Similarly, all bureaucracy shows some concern with jurisdiction, fixed rules, and written (including electronic) records. In short, there is a demonstrable empirical accuracy to much of the Weber model. But this does not mean that one has to either like bureaucracy or accept it as a viable organization form. Some suggest that our society is so inured to the harmful effects of bureaucracy that what we accept as normal is really pathological.

THE NORMAL AS PATHOLOGICAL

According to some critics, bureaucracy is an inherently pathological organization form. So long as executive functions rely on hierarchical, highly controlled, authority-oriented organizational schemes, pathological behavior is the only possible result. One of the best statements of the "bureaucracy as inherently pathological" school comes from Hummel (1982), who feels that pathology results from the fact that bureaucrats are expected to perform their duties disinterestedly and dispassionately. Bureaucrats' jobs also require them to address client needs partially rather than comprehensively.

According to Hummel, the basic requirements of bureaucracy—disinterestedness and restricted authority—ensure its pathology. The bureaucratic form of organization requires humans to act in ways that are not human. The human propensity is to take an interest in the client as an individual. Impersonal response to client needs undercuts the most important values of human beings, for both the client and the bureaucrat. Similarly, the natural human response is to be helpful, not to be helpful within the limits of one's jurisdiction.

Hummel has observed the following:

> Where the norms of bureaucratic detachment are carried out, the client is bound to feel himself treated with a certain coldness and without a sense of caring.... The result of this formal requirement of balance and fairness is at times the elimination of the emotional substance of everyday life, which is neither balanced nor fair (Hummel, 1982: 10).

Hummel certainly is not alone in these sentiments. A number of writers have suggested that bureaucracy is inherently pathological or inhumane because of its required impartiality and for other reasons as well. Thayer (1981), for example, ascribes a great many human ills to another feature of bureaucracy—hierarchy. According to Thayer, the imposition of hierarchy leads inevitably to alienation and, in turn, the separation of work from emotionally fulfilling parts of life.

Compounding the search for normal bureaucracy is a widespread loathing of things bureaucratic. In some instances (particularly in the United States) the antipathy toward bureaucracy is deep-seated, though often ill-founded (Goodsell, 1994: 77–101). In other instances, there are good reasons why people dislike bureaucracy, even normal bureaucracy carrying out normal functions.

BUREAUCRATIC LOATHING

Pathologies get tangled up in perceptions of bureaucracy. So, we return to the cod liver oil problem—that bureaucracy tastes bad even when it is good for you. It is important to understand bureaucracy's personally unappealing yet socially beneficial features, so as to be clear about the difference between function and dysfunction.

One problem in studying bureaucratic pathologies is that people do not like bureaucracy even when it is functioning effectively and serving the legitimate social and political purposes for which it was created. We sometimes see praise for the role of church in society, and education is seen as a secular savior, but when was the last time you saw such an elegiac account of bureaucracy?

We can distinguish three categories of bureaucracy loathing: *generalized scapegoating, big government backlash,* and *reasoned antipathy.* This book deals chiefly with the latter category, but the other two warrant some attention.

GENERALIZED SCAPEGOATING

In generalized scapegoating there is usually little thought given to exactly what it is that is objectionable about bureaucracy. Bureaucracy becomes a code word for those aspects of modern organization that we find annoying. Victor Thompson (1961: 24) uses the term "bureautics" to describe people who, because of their own failings (read "neuroses"), cannot adapt to the requirements of modern bureaucracy.

> "Bureautics" find the rationalism, orderliness, impartiality, and impersonality of the bureaucratic organization intolerable. They crave an immediate and tender response to their unique problems, whatever they may be. Bureautics are immature. They have never been weaned from habits of childhood indulgence. Bureautic behavior is not an organizational phenomenon. It is a matter of individual personality.

In his otherwise excellent book on bureaucratic pathologies, perhaps Thompson takes too hard a view of persons who consistently react negatively to bureaucracy. Bureaucracy is a convenient scapegoat. It is always there to blame when something goes wrong. It is so pervasive that we need not be too precise in our accusations.

Goodsell (1994) and Milward and Rainey (1983) argue that the public bureaucracy in the United States is more valuable and effective than generally recognized and that when public bureaucracies do perform badly, the problem is often due to external factors. Yarwood (1996) points out that unfocused bureaucracy bashing is rarely productive and can undermine the self-esteem and morale of government employees and, ultimately, the effectiveness of government. Whatever the reason for unfocused bashing, whether from "bureausis," or, more benignly, just letting off steam at the expense of a ready scapegoat, it has little directly to do with the effectiveness of bureaucracies.

BIG GOVERNMENT BACKLASH

Many people, for many reasons, do not like "big government." One of the most common reasons people don't like big government pertains to big *U.S. federal* government in general and, specifically, the federal expenditures. As of February 12, 1997, the national debt had exceeded $5 trillion (to be exact: $5,308,979,863,712.08), more than $19,900 per U.S. citizen.

As of 1999, budget forecasts were for a surplus. However, whether the federal budget is in surplus or deficit, a significant percentage of citizens seem to think the federal government is too big and too intrusive.

Anti-big government sympathies run deep. Since the beginning of the republic a fundamental principle of governance has been limited government. From the vantage point of the 1960s, the New Deal flirtation with Big Government seemed a step change auguring a new approach to governance (Walker and Vatter, 1997). From a contemporary vantage point, the period between the New Deal and the Johnson administration seems an historical aberration.

The evidence supporting the alleged growth of government is mixed. While it is true that the number of government employees continues to grow, it is not growing much faster than the general population and, in recent years, government spending has been growing at a slower rate than GDP. The federal government, which seems to be the most widely despised branch of government and is what most people mean by "big government," has been shrinking for years. The fact that much big government phobia is baseless is beside the point. For present purposes, it is beside the point that antigovernment feeling in the United States often seems puzzling to Europeans, Japanese, and the rest of the industrialized world.

Paul Light presents a more sophisticated analysis of government growth, one that focuses not just on personnel numbers, but on the "thickening of government." According to Light (1995), a number of forces, especially the perceived need for more technical and managerial help, encourage the growth of the upper- and middle-upper levels of government, with reduced accountability being one of many unfortunate results.

REASONED ANTIPATHY: WHY REASONABLE PEOPLE DISLIKE BUREAUCRACY

Much of the dislike for government and bureaucracy is based on misinformation, no information, and information disregarded. But only a small part of that antipathy is relevant to the purpose of identifying normal bureaucracy, diagnosing bureaucratic pathologies, and offering up prescriptions. Putting aside prejudice, ignorance, and the blinders set in place by two hundred years of limited government traditions, why do reasonable people dislike bureaucracy?

Inherent features of bureaucracy require individual sacrifice in order to achieve a collective good. Naturally, most of us, even the reasonable among us, do not like sacrifice. If it is for a "greater good," we may agree to sacrifice even while not being enchanted by the prospect. But there are other unsavory features of bureaucracy that are pathological, that require sacrifice but with no realization of a collective good—personal sacrifice to no good end.

In this section, we examine the reasons why reasonable people do not like the reasonable (and largely beneficial) aspects of bureaucracy. First, the structuring required by bureaucracy acts as a constraint on behavior. Second, the standardization of treatment inherent in bureaucracy thwarts our understandable desire to be treated as unique individuals. Third, bureaucracy inevitably involves delays. Before elaborating the reasons why reasonable people dislike bureaucracy, it is useful to pay some attention to the concepts of *bureaucracy* and *structure*.

STRUCTURE, FREEDOM, AND BUREAUCRACY

Modern sociologists studying bureaucracy have focused to a large extent on organizational structure. Among the many useful definitions of bureaucracy let us consider one provided by sociologist Charles Perrow (1972: 50):

> [E]very organization of any significant size is bureaucratized to some degree or, to put it differently, exhibits more or less stable patterns of behavior based upon a structure of roles and specialized tasks. *Bureaucracy, in a sense, is another word for structure.* [Emphasis added].

Bureaucratic organizations are structured organizations and, again following Perrow's usage, "more bureaucratized" organizations are more structured. While Perrow compares bureaucratic organizations to nonbureaucratic organizations, he underscores that all organizations are structured to some degree. The choice, then, is between more or less bureaucratic organizations. The key questions include the following:

1. What is achieved by structure?
2. What is lost by increased structuring?
3. What is the appropriate (to the task and goals of the organization) amount and type of structuring?

In answering these questions, we can get some insight into why reasonable people do not find bureaucracy endearing.

STRUCTURE AS CONSTRAINT:
WHAT DOES STRUCTURE ACCOMPLISH AND AT WHAT COST?

Richard Hall (1991: 48) provides a useful, unpretentious definition of organization structure: "It is the way in which the parts are arranged." Hall presents several other scholars' definitions of structure, including this not-so-simple one: "a complex medium of control which is continually produced and recreated in interaction and yet shapes that interaction: structures are constituted and constitutive" (Ranson, Hinings, and Greenwood, 1980: 3).

Hall's simple definition is useful in capturing the basic notion, but the Ranson and colleagues' definition adds some value for all its complexity. First, it makes the point that structure is patterned human interaction (a common sociologically oriented perspective on structure) and, at the same time, it is the result of that interaction. Philosophers refer to this as process-product ambiguity. The same word is used to refer to the process and to the product produced by the process. But we shall indulge that ambiguity because the term *structure* clearly means both things in the organizational literature.

According to Hall (1991), organization structure serves three fundamental functions. In the first place, it shapes organizational outputs and provides the framework for the activity intended to achieve organizational goals. Second, it regulates variations in individual behavior within the organizations; that is, it sets limits and controls certain behaviors, leaving others uncontrolled and at the discretion of members of the organization. Finally, it provides a setting for the exercise of authority within the organization, signaling who is in charge, as well as responsibilities, appropriate lines of communication, and superordinant-subordinate relationships.

If those are the functions of structure, and if bureaucracy is the structuring of organizations, then it should be clear why bureaucracy is never popular. Perrow (1972) views bureaucratization as a trade-off between efficiency and inflexibility. Too little bureaucracy, and efficiency is lost as the organization spins out of control. Too much, and bureaucracy becomes inflexible and unwieldy, stifling the very activities that the organization set up to enhance.

To this efficiency-inflexibility trade-off we can add others. Perhaps the most important of these is the trade-off between organizational coordination and individual freedom. Coordination is essential to any organization. If organizational members do not coordinate their activity, little can be achieved. While some organizational tasks rely more on interdependence than others do, few major tasks are wholly independent. Indeed, if all major organizational tasks were independent there probably would be no need for the organization. At the same time, coordination also implies control. While some control is required, the inevitable question is, how much control is necessary to ensure coordination, standardization, and efficient use of resources?

The reason bureaucracy can never be popular with persons working in the bureaucratic organization (much less those dealing with it from the outside), is that bureaucracy *inevitably* pits the interests of the organization against those of the individual. In the best of circumstances, organizational members working in a bureaucracy are called upon to limit their discretion, constrain their use of resources, and submit to hierarchical controls, in order that the organization might have the coordination and control necessary to achieve a collective purpose. To the extent that the individual organizational member's interests converge with those of the collective, the sacrifice is worth making. But in the worst of circumstances, the organizational member is called upon to submit to controls that do not promote task achievement, that do not support the goals of the collective, and that serve no legitimate social or organizational function. This is bureaucracy at its worst.

Considering the bureaucracy's need to control behavior and constrain individual discretion, we see the potential for all bureaucratic organizations to create red tape. Bureaucracy constrains, and when those constraints serve no legitimate purpose, organizations, their members, and those they serve, become ensnared in red tape.

BUREAUCRATIZATION AND STANDARDIZATION OF TREATMENT

One reason, then, that bureaucracy is unpopular is that it is inherently constraining. It constrains the individuals working within the bureaucratic organizations. It also constrains persons on the outside looking in—clients, customers, vendors, contractors. It is an unavoidable constraint, in this case the constraints flowing from standardization of treatment. In many respects, the expectation of standard treatment is a great strength of bureaucracy. Favoritism, nepotism, bribery, and other forms of corruption are inimical to modern bureaucracy; they are pathologies rather than inherent characteristics.

Standardization is often unsatisfying to individuals because most of us, in our roles as private citizens or as organizational representatives, wish to emphasize our uniqueness and the special nature of our claims. Indeed, we are unique and our claims often are special. But this is another trade-off presented by bureaucratic organization: the trade-off between *never* making an exception (itself a pathology) and the chaos of treating every case differently. The collective good requires standardization; the individual good requires some notice of special circumstances. If bureaucracy is functioning effectively, there will be times when we wish special treatment and for good reasons will not receive it. While reasonable people can recognize the value of standard treatment, that does not mean we always eagerly embrace it.

Finally, there are many instances in which unique treatment

clearly is preferable to standard treatment but simply cannot be justified on a cost basis. No one really feels that a student-teacher ratio of 35:1 leads to the most effective learning environment. But the financiers of elementary and secondary education sometimes prefer standard treatment in large group settings to the cost of tailor-made education.

BUREAUCRACY AND DELAYS

There is much truth to the stereotype of the slow-moving bureaucracy, and the delays inherent in bureaucracy rarely win it friends. Large bureaucracies rarely move fast, but sometimes the delays are for good reasons and sometimes they are pathological.

Weber was perhaps the first to emphasize the crucial role of specialization and expertise in modern bureaucracy. Specialization is both a structure and a basis for additional structure (especially vertical differentiation). In some cases specialization can speed up organizational activity—the classic example being the specialization of the assembly line. However, there are also built-in delays associated with specialization. Consider Thompson's (1961) explanation:

> Great amounts of information must be accumulated if knowledge is to be substituted for impulse, thus assuring greater effectiveness of action and greater chance of success. Since action involves many interdependent specialists, coordination time must be expended. In order that all necessary parts of the organization act in coordinated fashion, clearances must be obtained, meetings held, many copies of proposals and information memoranda prepared and properly routed. In short, if the organization could act with the speed of an individual, the organization would not be needed.

In public bureaucracies delays are compounded because of the interdependence of public organizations. Public organizations are never "free agents"; their goals are contingent on the purposes, objectives, and activities of other official actors. The need to coordinate not only within the organization but also externally leads to even further delay. In some cases the delays produced by bureaucracies are for very good reasons, such as ensuring safety, protecting organization coffers from thieves, ensuring that political officials are well-informed, and providing better or more equitable service. In those cases, bureaucracy is behaving as bureaucracy and the delays may be well-advised. In other instances, the delays may be due to bureaucratic system pathologies. An example cited in the Report of the National Performance Review was the changing of a light bulb at the U.S. Department of Energy Rock

Flats plant (Gore, 1993a: 69). Safety procedures called for a planner to meet with six others, talk with other workers who have done the job before, conduct another meeting, get signatures from five people at a work control meeting, get project plans approved by a number of officials, wait for a monthly test, direct electricians to replace the bulb, test it, and verify the repair. In all, forty-three people and more than one thousand hours are required to change a light bulb. Whether the delays are valid or a product of bureaucratic pathology, people don't like delays. The image of bureaucracy suffers as a result.

BUREAUCRACY AND AMBIVALENCE

Winston Churchill remarked famously that democracy "is the worst form of government—except for all the rest." Mark Twain said, with equally delightful irony, "the reports of my death are greatly exaggerated." We can mix aphorisms to gain some insight into bureaucracy— it is the worst form of organization, but the reports of its death are greatly exaggerated. Despite efforts to *Manage without Managers* (Martin, 1983) and attempts at *Breaking Through Bureaucracy* (Barzelay, 1992), bureaucracy persists, even flourishes. If one searches for truth in book titles, Henry Jacoby's (1973) *The Bureaucratization of the World* comes closer to the mark. As Jacoby notes, dissatisfaction with bureaucracy arises not only from red tape and bureaucratic inefficiencies but also from a deeper source—a feeling of dependence upon bureaucracy, a dependence fed by the complexities and specialization of societies. We do not love bureaucracy, but we need it, at least until we devise workable alternative organizational schemes that permit us to retain the features of bureaucracy that we embrace eagerly—predictability and stability, rationality, reliance on expertise, equitable treatment—while discarding the features we hate—rigidity, inability to deal with special needs, and a setting of barriers between officialdom and citizens.

A key to understanding bureaucracy is its costs—not the costs as reflected in big government and taxation, but its costs in terms of human desires. Even when it is functioning "normally" it is costly, requiring citizens to pay tribute to authority. When bureaucracy is functioning "pathologically," it exerts much greater costs, impairing not only efficiency (the very value it is specifically designed to achieve) but also costs in human patience, dignity, and justice.

Let us consider a fanciful question, given the near-universal dissatisfaction with bureaucracy: Is it possible that human beings are just not rational? Above all else, bureaucracy strives for rationality. When taken as a collective good, when benefits of rationality are conferred on society as a whole, humans often value rationality. But when applied to the specific case, the individual citizen has decidedly mixed feelings about rationality. If we look at the entire sweep of human existence, humans have not had much time to adjust to the values of rationality, predictability, and impersonality. Until quite recently, almost all human beings lived in traditional societies (in the anthropologists' terms), where groups were based on kinship and face-to-face interaction. Traditional societies have many limitations. Sometimes the face-to-face interaction is threatening of life and limb and there are few if any social avenues for mitigating the threat or redressing harm if the threat is carried out. Traditional societies have difficulties developing sophisticated economies, developing large-scale public works projects (despite the view in some quarters that the Great Pyramids were built by interstellar visitors, the best evidence is that they were enabled by bureaucracy), and public health systems. By the same token, traditional societies have difficulty mounting large-scale warfare and are often ineffective means of achieving genocide. The key point here is not that life is full of trade-offs, but that humankind just may not be ready for bureaucracy (or ready to give it up).

NORMAL OR PATHOLOGICAL BUREAUCRACY? A CASE STUDY

A challenge to students of bureaucracy, not to mention practitioners, is to determine from the evidence of daily life whether the seemingly crazy interactions we have with bureaucratic organizations are really just "normal craziness," or manifestations of pathology. Without some ability to diagnose, we cannot cure.

Making a diagnosis requires a case. Let us consider the bureaucratic encounter presented in the box on pages 31–33. Is this a case of bureaucratic pathology?

DIAGNOSIS: "NORMAL" BUREAUCRACY OR PATHOLOGY?

The case presented in the box on on pages 31–33 illustrates wonderfully the ambivalence of "normal" bureaucracy and the ease with which normal bureaucracy can develop pathologies. The case also illustrates that it is not so easy to sort all this out. Before considering the author's "disinterested" analysis of the case (see box on page 34), the reader may wish to provide an interpretation, focusing on sorting out the actual problems with bureaucracy from the expectations and prejudices of Stanley B.

> ### BUREAUCRATIC ENCOUNTER: NORMAL BUREAUCRACY IN THE PEACH STATE—HOW DO YOU KNOW IT WHEN YOU SEE IT?

Consider the case of Stanley P., a portrait in ambivalent response to bureaucracy. This is a petty case, no heroes, no villains, and small stakes. But this simple case describing the travails of travel reimbursement suggests (1) why actual humans (as opposed to textbook humans or "disinterested, rational observers with perfect information") feel ambivalent about bureaucracy and (2) why it is difficult to sort out the normal and the merely inefficient from the pathological.

Stanley P., a mild-mannered professor, had a research grant from the Environmental Protection Agency. The objective of the project was to evaluate the costs and benefits accruing from the implementation costs of new air quality regulations. As part of this grant, Stan traveled a great deal, flying several times to collect data in each of five states (not to mention an occasional side trip to Washington). At the time of this story, Stan was employed at a major university in the southern United States.

Though Stan wrote a proposal to the EPA the grant was, from a legal standpoint, to his university, with Stan designated as "principal investigator" (or, roughly, project manager). This is routine. Government research funds are granted not to professors but to their institutions. And since the university is a *state government* institution, it is also routine, for the budgeting and accounting for the grant to be subject to all the states' budgeting and accounting regulations, including those for travel and per diem.

Since Stan was required to travel a great deal to gather data for this project—and since he was, in general, a public-spirited person committed to minimizing taxpayer expense—he was, generally, quite careful to book airfares well in advance and achieve economies in transportation expenses. The state government had negotiated with two airlines to provide a "contract rate" to most cities, but Stan and his coworkers quickly learned that the contract rate was often above, sometimes several hundred dollars above, fares that could be obtained from any reasonably diligent travel agent. Stan routinely shopped for the best rate, rather than simply taking whatever was on the state contract. Certainly this posed no problem for anyone and, during the three-year course of the grant, Stan saved about $3,000 compared to the cost of simply booking the contract airlines in every case, even if the contract rates were more expensive. True, Stan (and his administrative assistant) had to spend more time doing it this way, but not only was Stan public-spirited, but he had a strong interest in spending the grant money as efficiently as possible. Money saved from the travel budget could be used for some other research purpose, including such noble purposes as employing graduate students and paying their tuition.

And now we come to the climax of this small bureaucratic drama. In one particularly hectic week, Stan had to travel, yes, all in the same week, to Baton Rouge, Louisiana, Washington, D.C., San Jose, California, and then back to Washington. Two of these trips were not of the sort that could be

> ### BUREAUCRATIC ENCOUNTER: NORMAL BUREAUCRACY IN THE PEACH STATE... (*CONTINUED*)
>
> easily planned, so Stan booked them at the last minute and while on the road. Haste makes waste.
>
> Now we move forward in time two months. Due to the normal workings of state bureaucracies, not all of Stan's travel expenses had as yet been reimbursed but, to his delight, the Baton Rouge expense check showed up in only two months time (well below the average time). There was a form attached to it which noted "$230 allowable air travel, state contract." But Stan requested $410 because that was the cost of the ticket he had booked. Stan was, he reports, furious with himself for not remembering either to get a contract airline or to get a fare below the state contract rate. But he was also a little vexed by the bureaucracy.
>
> #### On Being Human: Rationality and Rationalization
>
> Now for the diagnosis. In this case, the bureaucracy performed as a bureaucracy performs. In most respects it did what it was supposed to do—enforcing a rule that is in the interest of the people of (let us call it, for anonymity's sake), the Great Peach State. The general idea of a state airline contract is a good one (though in many cases it seemed to Stan that the people who negotiated it must have been involved in setting prices for Defense Department toilet seats). In many cases the state contract does provide a cheaper fare than is provided by "walk-up" no-advance-purchase approaches to buying tickets—indeed it was more than $200 cheaper than the ticket booked for our friend. Why should the people of the Great Peach State pay for the carelessness of state employees? Conclusion: The bureaucracy worked.
>
> But if the bureaucracy worked so well—preserving the values of rationality, predictability, and fairness (Stan is not the only one to have tasted the state accountants' swift justice)—how could our Stan possibly find fault? Answer: Stan is a human. Just as the bureaucracy played out its role—giving Stan no special treatment, applying legitimate rules—Stan played out his role—wanting but not receiving special treatment, caring less about the legitimacy and fairness of the rules than the fact that they did not, on this occasion, favor him. While he could see the theoretical value of this execution of bureaucratic will, Stan was less interested in democratic theory than in the $200 or so out of his pocket.
>
> Stan's typical, self-interested cupidity has no direct bearing on our diagnosis of the workings of bureaucracy, but his reasoning patterns are instructive. First, and this is important to note, Stan fully realized that he was being dealt with fairly and that the outcome was in the best interest of the people of the Great Peach State, even if not in his narrow self-interest. Nevertheless, Stan asked several questions that, taken together, expose him as a creature not well suited to obedience to the norms of bureaucratic rationality; that is, a human being.

Question one: "Why does the efficiency seem to go only in one direction? Why do we employ rules to punish undue costs but not reward savings?" Stan saw no evidence that the thousands of dollars he had saved by *not* following the routines of the state contract were banked as an offset for that day in which he mistakenly booked a flight that cost too much. If he were not public-spirited, he might even have been tempted to save himself the trouble of routinely searching for a fare better than the quite modest savings (compared to full-fare) offered in the state contract.

Question two: "In the enforcement of rules, is there no capacity to see the big picture?" The grant that Stan brought into the people of the Great Peach State entailed more than $400,000 in federal funds. From this money, a substantial portion went into travel and other research expenses, four graduate students received salary and tuition, two faculty members (not Stan) received summer salaries, and the university received "indirect costs" (i.e., extra money to pay bills and to do good things) of about $130,000. Presumably, the EPA was receiving something of interest to them (they did, after all, decide to award the grant) and, parenthetically, the results of the study were being used by the environmental agency of the Great Peach State. Stan benefited enormously in terms of the ability to perform research of interest, but his own financial balance sheet for the project was minus-$200.

Question three: "While it is generally better to give than to receive, should this nostrum apply to interest paid?" During the life of the grant, Stan paid for travel expenses (airfare, rental cars, lodging, and meals) and was later reimbursed by the Great Peach State. This is routine. It is also routine for anyone who is not fabulously wealthy to pay such expenses by credit card rather than by cash. Unfortunately, most credit cards charge interest. This is no problem if the bills are paid in full each month with no balance carried. Stanley B. carried a balance. The least amount of time required for reimbursement was six weeks, the most three and one-half months. Given prevailing credit card interest rates, the balances carried for travel expenses pertaining to the grant added up to $137. In Stan's self-interested view, he could not help but reflect upon the fact that the Great Peach State had a much larger bank balance than his and should not require loans from his comparatively meager resources.

Question four: "Why a form without a name?" Stan mused as follows: If I am going to make an unplanned contribution of $200 to the Great Peach State, would it not have been preferable for the person who provided the form to have either called me on the phone, written a letter, or at least put his or her name on the form? Would this not have been a more human and more satisfying means of communicating bad news?

> ### BUREAUCRATIC ENCOUNTER: AN INTERPRETATION
> ### OF STANLEY B.'S BUREAUCRATIC ENCOUNTER
>
> In assessing Stanley B.'s complaints, sorting pathetic whining from actual worrisome issues, let us begin by noting that there is no right answer. But here is one assessment. Regarding his complaint that his previous efficiencies are not rewarded but that his instance of mismanagement is punished—this seems largely in the pathetic whining category. This is not pathological bureaucracy; it is simply our friend wanting a pat on the back (and probably special treatment) for simply having done his job as a public servant—being as effective as possible with minimal cost.
>
> Likewise, Stan's argument about the value of the grant as a whole is a complete canard. In the first place, the overall value of the grant has no relationship to the nature of this managerial transgression. We did not, after all, say that Watergate should be overlooked because President Nixon had taken the valuable step of opening China. Again, pathetic whining.
>
> What about the argument that the "bad news" was delivered anonymously on a form? Our friend is actually on to something here, but he has not located a pathology, only a common and commonly vexing attribute of bureaucracy. Impersonality is a value that cuts both ways in bureaucracy. On the one hand, we like the fact that we don't necessarily have to know our mail carrier's name (or even, necessarily, provide a Christmas gift!) in order to get good, reliable service. But we do not like the fact that when we are engaged in unpleasant dealings with the bureaucracy we often seem confronted by faceless authority. So this is not pathetic whining; our friend is reacting to bureaucracy with the ambivalence that "normal bureaucracy" deserves.
>
> Finally, we have the question about delays, interest charges, and credit card balances. While there is some pathetic whining to be weeded out here, there is also, *finally*, an incipient pathology. Unless we can demonstrate that there are good reasons (e.g., enhanced accountability, need for special scrutiny) for reimbursement taking as much as three and one-half months, we should harbor suspicions of bureaucratic pathology. It is one thing to criticize bureaucracy for being itself (i.e., impersonal), and quite another to take issue with bureaucracy for not advancing the values it is supposed to serve, including rationality and efficiency. Reimbursement in less than three and one-half months should be possible even while preserving accountability, keeping records, and maintaining the requirements of hierarchy and control. Here we have the symptoms not of bureaucracy but of bureaucratic pathology.

CONCLUSION

Even if we set aside prejudices about bureaucracy, identifying the normal poses a difficulty. A major difficulty in sorting out bureaucracy and pathology flows from the fact that, ideal types notwithstanding, bureaucracy and administration almost always entail trade-offs among values. When one value is maximized (such as efficiency) it is often at the expense of others (such as fairness). As mentioned previously, bureaucracy is a balancing act and bureaucratic reform requires a balance of values. The concluding chapter of this book employs a balance model of organizational reform, arguing that analysis of red tape must take into account at least four core values: efficiency, accountability, performance, and fairness. The balance model's essential point is easily communicated—bureaucracy, especially public bureaucracy, is not about maximizing values but optimizing multiple and sometimes conflicting values (Antonsen and Jorgensen, 1997; Fredrickson, 1996). This point is easy enough to understand, but it presents considerable difficulty in its execution.

Most of the pathologies of bureaucracy are of the "too much of a good thing" sort (see Cope [1997] for an analysis of values trade-offs in budget reform). Control is useful for coordination, but overcontrol is pathological; standardization promotes equity and efficiency, but too much or ill-placed standardization can be highly destructive; rules, regulations, and procedures are part and parcel of every bureaucracy, but dysfunctional ones waste considerable energy to no one's benefits. But how is one to determine differences among control and overcontrol, standardization and rigidity, necessary and useful rules, and wasteful and nonproductive ones? What is normal?

One of the reasons so many find fault with the Weberian model of bureaucracy is that any "pure" organizational type is flawed. Pure types are, by definition, out of balance. In Weberian bureaucracy the chief imbalance is efficiency and standardization. When these are achieved at their maximal level it is necessarily at a cost of reduced empathy and personalism and, in many instances, reduced performance. As we have seen from studies (e.g., LaPorte and Consolini, 1991) of high reliability organizations such as NASA or air traffic control agencies, the highest levels of performance are neither cheap nor efficient. As we have seen from studies of welfare caseworkers (e.g., Scott, 1997; Kelly, 1994), control and fairness sometimes work at loggerheads.

Perhaps we can determine normality in the empirical sense by "organizational benchmarking." For example, given organizations of the same type and function, what is the median response time (delay), what is the median number of sign-offs required, and what is the typical level of formalization and standardization. While we must remember that "average" is not always "good," organizational benchmarking can help in our search for the normal. This benchmarking approach is examined in more detail in Chapter 8, which reviews research comparing red tape in public and private organizations. In the next chapter we turn our attention to possible causes of bureaucratic pathologies. As we shall see, many pathologies can be viewed as bureaucracy out of balance.

What, then, is normal bureaucracy? While the search for a concrete concept of normal is misguided, because "normal" depends on expectations and individuals' and groups' values, one notion of normal provides a good starting point. The statistical use of normal may serve best. Given the important values of bureaucracy, including, among others, efficiency, accountability, performance, and fairness, is any particular bureaucracy (or any particular agency) within the normal range? That is, does it hover around the central tendency for each of those values, or is it one or two standard deviations from the norm? While this perspective will not give us an objective assessment of good or bad bureaucracy, it will give us some insight into the character of particular bureaucracies, insights that permit us to compare the values bureaucracy against the values that each of us brings to assessing bureaucracy. Such an approach may disappoint both organizational philosophers and organizational scientists, but will likely have some appeal to organizational pragmatists trying to make their way in a world of trade-offs and conflicting values.

BUREAUCRATIC PATHOLOGIES AND REFORM

> Is government inherently incompetent? Absolutely not. Are federal agencies filled with incompetent people? No. The problem is much deeper....
>
> —Gore (1993: 3)

> [T]he Federal Government has significant deficiencies from managerial and operating perspectives, resulting in hundreds of billions of dollars of needless expenditures that taxpayers have to bear each year. The reports make clear that these deficiencies are not the result of a lack of competence or enthusiasm on the part of Federal employees.
>
> —President's Private Sector Survey on Cost Control
> (Grace Commission Report, 1982: 12)

The urge to fix bureaucracy runs deep. During virtually every era of U.S. history, some bureaucratic reform is touted. But despite a tendency for perpetual incremental reforms, U.S. public policy cycles are such that sweeping bureaucratic reform goes to the top of the policy agenda every once in a while.

REFORM AT THE MILLENNIUM

To use Paul Light's (1997) metaphor, the tides of reform come sweeping in, then go out again, leaving much flotsam and jetsam cast along the shore. But despite the seeming inevitability of reform tides, the timing and magnitude of their ebb and flow is not so easily explained. Sometimes there is a clear-cut incident leading clearly to reform demands. Thus, the Watergate affair and the near impeachment of a sitting president led to reforms. More broadly, the excesses of Jacksonian democracy led to reforms. In other cases, reform efforts relate to the priorities and interests of particular individuals. Herbert Hoover was a socio-technical engineer who believed that science and technology should be used to reform the ills of government. Jimmy Carter, the quintessential outsider, a southerner who had never held a Washington position, was psychologically well prepared to push reforms of the Washington bureaucracy from which he sought to distance himself.

Recent reform efforts, centering on the Clinton-Gore administration's National Performance Review (Gore, 1993b; Kettl, 1994; Clinton and Gore, 1995; National Performance Review, 1996) and on the U.S. Congress initiatives under the Government Performance and Results Act (USGAO, 1997), have no obvious origins in bureaucratic or executive branch corruption. No particular historical marker coincides with these reform efforts. But thousands of employees in hundreds of government agencies will have their professional lives altered by a set of related activities designed to reform bureaucracy and increase productivity.

In all likelihood, the most recent bureaucratic reform efforts will cost billions of dollars to implement. Pilot projects underway at federal agencies include decentralizing the Army Corps of Engineers, changing inspection policies of the Coast Guard, improving data availability at the Veterans Health Administration, and implementing agency-wide plans at the Federal Emergency Management Agency. These illustrate the hundreds of "reinvention" and "reengineering" projects. Under the Government Performance and Results Act, most agencies are required to develop strategic plans and performance measures as well as integrate outcome "metrics" into their budget request and planning processes. In sum, the effort now put behind reforming the U.S. bureaucracy is likely consuming more resources than used for all programs in many nations' governments. Are things really this bad? If so, why?

In this chapter we begin by examining the nature of bureaucratic pathologies, theories about what is wrong with bureaucracy, and then return to issues of bureaucratic reform. This is not to say that bureaucratic reform efforts are usually guided by underlying theories of pathology. Excepting one all-encompassing theory of bureaucratic failure—the notion that government bureaucracy does not work because of market inefficiencies—reform efforts include more "remedies" than "diagnosis."

SYSTEMIC PATHOLOGY

Most bureaucratic reforms begin with the optimistic notion that faults lie in "the system," not the individual. This is neither wishful thinking nor timidity about placing blame. Certainly no one would accuse the Grace Commission, known formally and quite accurately as the President's

Private Sector Survey on Cost Control (1982), as being "soft on government bureaucrats." Critics (e.g., Goodsell, 1984) note the harshness of the assumptions of the commission. But the Grace Commission recognized that system flaws provide reformers a better target than human frailty.

Why do so many systems fail? One obvious way that "bad" bureaucratic systems arise is that Congress, the presidency, and the judiciary place requirements on the federal bureaucracy that bureaucrats are often powerless to change. Similarly, bureaucracies at other levels of government are subject to state, local, or county legislators and courts, as well as to federal officials. To the individual bureaucrat, who may not have been consulted by any of the distant entities promulgating management systems and procedures, the source of the system constraints may matter little.

Often persons with little or no knowledge of the organization or clients affected create the rules shaping bureaucratic behavior. Sometimes people long dead created the rules. Whether rule makers passed away generations ago, or simply moved to other agencies, many of the rules under which bureaucratic officials labor were written by persons unknown and, sometimes, for purposes unknown. The fact that the rules may no longer serve any purpose of interest to the organization usually has little or no bearing on the ease with which they may be changed.

The very notion of an organization implies a disjunction between the individual and the rules under which the individual operates. This does not mean, however, that rules and procedures are created by black magic or that management systems are less immutable. It simply means that we must look to system sources of system problems.

PEOPLE PATHOLOGY

It is easy enough to understand why few informed people spend much time tracing bureaucratic pathologies directly back to the bureaucrat. While the occasional yahoo argues that "bureaucrats are just no damned good," bureaucrat bashing does not achieve much (Milward and Rainey, 1983). In the first place, excoriating 16,985,805 people, the reported number of government employees in 1995 (http://www.census.gov/ftp/pub/govs), is not a friendly act. More important, our daily experience tells us that bureaucrats differ, as do all individuals. Most of us interact directly with thousands of bureaucrats during our lives, including the surly, the dim-witted, the hard-hearted, the nitpickers, the friendly, the bright, the kindly, and the judicious. Public bureaucracy is widely vilified but, at the same time, results from Harris polls tell us that 73 percent of respondents who recently interacted with federal bureaucrats found them "helpful" and, in a Michigan poll, 76 percent indicated that bureaucrats treated them "fairly" (reported in Goodsell, 1994: 8). In short, bureaucrats may not be perfectly representative of the citizenry of the United States—for one thing they are much better educated—but they are quite a cross-section of humanity.

Another good reason for focusing more on systemic than individual sources of pathologies is that blaming the system does less to undermine the spirit and work environment of bureaucrats. It is difficult enough for professional bureaucrats to continually read in the press that they are inefficient or malevolent, but if policy-makers, especially elected officials, jump on the bashwagon then morale cannot help but suffer.

Probably the single best reason for emphasizing system pathologies is that the potential for sweeping change is at that level. If we were to find that all the problems of bureaucracies flow from the fact that (to pick a number) 30 percent of bureaucrats are "no damned good" what have we achieved? It would not be easy or effective to fire people in large bunches. It would not be easy to determine who is part of that odious 30 percent. System solutions work better, at least as remedies for sweeping problems.

Having said all that, it makes little sense to completely ignore people problems. While recognizing the validity of organizational and institutional level approaches for reform-minded policymakers and analysts, there is nevertheless much to be learned by focusing on the psychology and behaviors of individual bureaucrats. In some instances, such a focus provides fresh insight into such widely held but empirically questionable assumptions as the inferiority of the public sector work force (e.g., Crewson, 1995) or the expected but unrealized exodus from the federal bureaucracy (Lewis, 1991). Sometimes empirical research surprises us in quite different ways by questioning assumptions about public managers' higher ethical standards (Wittmer, 1992; Wittmer and Coursey, 1996) or greater social service commitment (Jurkiewicz, Massey, and Brown, 1998).

It is diplomatic to blame systems but people create systems and, in many respects, systems *are* people. Sometimes people are inept or unproductive or uninspired. If they are *randomly* inept or inefficient then the problem may still be of theoretical interest but probably has little salience to reformers. But if particular people with particular pathologies self-select into bureaucratic jobs, then the problem commands more attention, even if solutions remain in short supply.

MERTON AND THE "BUREAUCRATIC PERSONALITY"

One of the best known students of bureaucracy, sociologist Robert Merton, presents a relatively sympathetic view of bureaucracy. Merton (Merton, et al., 1952: 24). contends that "however much people may com-

---

RESEARCH ENCOUNTER:
THE BUREAUCRATIC PERSONALITY REVISITED

One recent study (Bozeman and Rainey, 1998) revisited Merton's questions about the bureaucratic personality. Working with survey data from more than 300 public and private managers, the researchers focused on bureaucrats who expressed a need for *more* rules and regulations. Surprisingly, 19 percent of the managers believed there was a need for more rules and regulations. Was this perceived need for more rules owing to problems in the organization or to peculiarities of personalities of the bureaucrats who desired more rules?

The authors examined a number of characteristics of organizations, including how long the organization takes to perform certain core tasks, how many people are required to sign off before proceeding with a task, and how many administrators versus production workers are in the organization. In addition, personality attributes of the individual bureaucrats were examined to determine whether these personality attributes or the organizational characteristics were most strongly related to the perceived need for more rules.

Table 3-1 (on page 42) shows that the need for more rules is not significantly related to the amount of time taken for core organizational tasks (such as hiring a new employee). The desire for more rules *is* related to the levels of organizational authority and the number of records kept in the organization, but perhaps not in the way some might expect. Those bureaucrats expressing the need for more rules tended to work in "flatter" organizational hierarchies and in organizations where fewer records are kept.

Bureaucrats' need for more rules had little to do with characteristics of their organizations. Instead, results showed a strong relationship between the perception of the need for more rules and the personal attributes of the bureaucrat. Bureaucrats desiring more rules tended to have lower job satisfaction, greater personal alienation, high insecurity, pessimism, and distrust. These findings reinforce Pandey's study (1995), which found no relationship between perceptions of red tape and either the number of rules and regulations in an organization or the amount of time required for the organization to accomplish core tasks.

What does one make of the alienated manager who wants more rules? It is not so clear whether alienated managers are made unhappy by their jobs or whether they bring their unhappiness to bureaucracy. Whatever the origins of these feelings, they seem to be a major culprit in creation of additional rules and, perhaps, red tape.

Finally, it is worth noting that the Bozeman and Rainey study found only 13 percent of *public* managers feel that there are not enough rules and procedures in their organizations, but twice as many (27 percent) *private* managers feel there are not enough. Research (e.g., Bozeman, Reed, and Scott, 1992; Rainey, Pandey, and Bozeman, 1995) using objective and perceptual measures of red tape consistently shows more rules and more red tape in *public* organizations. Does this mean there really are too few rules in many private organizations?

Source: B. Bozeman and H. Rainey. 1998. "Organization Rules and the Bureaucratic Personality," *American Journal of Political Science* 42, 1: 163–189.

TABLE 3-1   CORRELATIONS OF RESPONDENT'S PERCEIVED NEED
FOR MORE RULES WITH "OBJECTIVE" MEASURES OF RED TAPE

NEED MORE RULES

−.156 (p<.001)	The number of layers of organizational authority
−.219 (p<.000)	Records kept
−.079 (p<.101)	Time required to hire a full-time employee
.021 (p<.676)	Time required to buy equipment costing more than $10,000
−.022 (p<.648)	Time required to begin a major project

Note: Correlations are Kendall's Tau-b.

plain about the 'evils of bureaucracy,' ... bureaucratic administration is, other things being equal, always, from a formal, technical point of view, the most rational type"

Perhaps this more benign view of bureaucracy enabled Merton to examine the bureaucratic personality. The key to Merton's bureaucratic personality explanation can be summarized in a question Merton pondered nearly sixty years ago (Merton, 1940: 567): "Inasmuch as ascendancy and submission are held to be traits of personality ... do bureaucracies select personalities of particularly submissive or ascendant tendencies?... Does promotion through the seniority system lessen competitive anxieties and enhance administrative efficiency?"

In the more than fifty years that have elapsed since Merton's questioning of the nature of self-selection into bureaucratic careers, we still know remarkably little about the interaction among personality, structure, and bureaucratic behavior. The handful of studies conducted (e.g., Baker, Etzioni, Hansen, and Soutag, 1973) continue to underscore the importance of differences in individual response to bureaucratic environments, but research remains scarce.

SYSTEMS FAILURES IN MANAGEMENT, PEOPLE FAILURES IN WORKERS

A final note on people versus systems. Most reformers and reinventors avoid castigating individuals or groups and focus on the system. But in those cases where the individual worker, not the system, is identified as the "problem," the chances are excellent that the alleged problem worker is not a manager and is a union member. Much of the management and organization theory literature has a not-so-subtle bias against nonmanagement and union employees. Managers are given the benefit of the doubt. If we just get our political and managerial systems worked out, free up the creative manager, everything will be fine. Indeed, this is often true. The need to empower the hourly wage worker is not so widely proclaimed. Consider the following quotes from a recent reinventing manual. The first is a "top manager" diagnosis of organizational problems:

> The system is not sophisticated enough yet. We're provincial. You need well-trained technocrats who are highly professional and paid quite well.... (Osborne and Plastrik, 1997: 5)

By contrast,

> Now we go and say, "This guy is abusing sick leave, what are you going to do about it?" We've got it down from 18 days average three years ago to single digits. (Osborne and Plastrik, 1997: 4)

The second quote is from a union official. So, in this case there is no evidence of a "plot" to blame unions. It is simply the case that most reform efforts pay less attention to systemic problems, incentive "systems," and self-actualization of workers lower in the hierarchy. Is this classism rearing its ugly head? Is it an understandable result owing to the fact that most people who write management books and originate government reforms are not hourly workers? Is it a reflection of lesser organizational or job commitment of workers lower in the hierarchy?

THE PATHOLOGIES

Bureaucracy succeeds, bureaucracy fails. Not all failures stem from pathologies. In fact, probably a minority of significant failures can be traced directly to pathologies. Failure seems a chance visitor in many instances, or at least chance plays a role along with individual performance breakdowns. In many instances, failures say much more about the difficulties of the task than about the will, ability, or commitment of the performers. Thus, distilling *pathologies* from the many instances of bureaucratic failure caused by unique events presents a conceptual challenge.

Those who have given some attention to identifying and characterizing bureaucratic pathologies (e.g., Hood and Dunshire, 1981; Downs, 1967; Caiden, 1991) have come up with extensive lists, but lists that overlap to a surprisingly small degree. Caiden (1991) presents the most extensive list of bureaucratic ills. Table 3-2 (on pages 44–45) gives his alphabetic list of more 175 "bureaupathologies." It is bracing that red tape is just one of this list of 175.

Caiden's article (1991: 490) emphasizes a point central to the analysis of bureaucratic pathologies: Bureaucratic pathologies generally are not due to individual incompetence, and they cannot be cured simply by replacing less experienced managers with more experienced managers.

TABLE 3-2   LIST OF BUREAUCRATIC PATHOLOGIES

Abuse of authority/ power/position	Footdragging	Lack of performance indicators
Account padding	Framing	Lack of vision
Alienation	Fraud	Lawlessness
Anorexia	Fudging/fuzzing (issues)	Laxity
Arbitrariness	Gamesmanship	Leadership vacuums
Arrogance	Gattopardismo (superficiality)	Malfeasance
Bias	Ghost employees	Malice
Blurring issues	Gobbledygook/jargon	Malignity
Boondoggles	Highhandedness	Meaningless/make work
Bribery	Ignorance	Mediocrity
Bureaucratese (unintelligibility)	Illegality	Mellownization
Busywork	Impervious to criticism/ suggestion	Mindless job performance
Carelessness	Improper motivation	Miscommunication
Chiseling	Inability to learn	Misconduct
Coercion	Inaccessibility	Misfeasance
Complacency	Inaction	Misinformation
Compulsiveness	Inadequate rewards and incentives	Misplaced zeal
Conflicts of interest/ objectives	Inadequate working conditions	Negativism
Confusion	Inappropriateness	Negligence/neglect
Conspiracy	Incompatible tasks	Nepotism
Corruption	Incompetence	Neuroticism
Counter-productiveness	Inconvenience	Nonaccountability
Cowardice	Indecision	Noncommunication
Criminality	Indifference	Nonfeasance
Deadwood	Indiscipline	Nonproductivity
Deceit and deception	Ineffectiveness	Obscurity
Dedication to status quo	Ineptitude	Obstruction
Defective goods	Inertia	Officiousness
Delay	Inferior quality	Oppression
Deterioration	Inflexibility	Overkill
Discourtesy	Inhumanity	Oversight
Discrimination	Injustice	Overspread
Diseconomies of size	Insensitivity	Overstaffing
Displacement of goals/objectives	Insolence	Paperasserie
Dogmatism	Intimidation	Paranoia
Dramaturgy	Irregularity	Patronage
Empire-building	Irrelevance	Payoffs and kickbacks
Excessive social costs/complexity	Irresolution	Perversity
Exploitation	Irresponsibility	Phony contracts
Extortion	Kleptocracy	Pointless activity
Extravagance	Lack of commitment	Procrastination
Failure to acknowledge/ act/answer/respond	Lack of coordination	Punitive supervision
Favoritism	Lack of creativity/ experimentation	Red-tape
Fear of change, risk	Lack of credibility	Reluctance to delegate
Finagling	Lack of imagination	Reluctance to make decisions
	Lack of initiative	Reluctance to take responsibility

TABLE 3-2   LIST OF BUREAUCRATIC PATHOLOGIES (CONTINUED)

Remoteness	Soul-destroying work	Unfairness
Rigidity/brittleness	Spendthrift	Unnecessary work
Rip-offs	Spoils	Unprofessional conduct
Ritualism	Stagnation	Unreasonableness
Rudeness	Stalling	Unsafe conditions
Sabotage	Stonewalling	Unsuitable premises
Scams	Suboptimization	and equipment
Secrecy	Sycophancy	Usurpatory
Self-perpetuation	Tail-chasing	Vanity
Self-serving	Tamping	Vested
Slick bookkeeping	Territorial imperative	Vindictiveness
Sloppiness	Theft	Waste
Social astigmatism	Tokenism	Whim
(failure to see	Tunnel vision	Xenophobia
problems)	Unclear objectives	

Source: From Gerald Caiden, "What Really Is Public Maladministration?" *Public Administration Review* 51, 6 (November/December 1991): 492.

Bureaupathologies are not the individual failings of individuals who compose organizations but the systematic shortcomings of organizations that cause individuals within them to be guilty of malpractices. They cannot be corrected by separating the guilty from the organization for the malpractices will continue irrespective of the organization's composition. They are not random, isolated incidents either. Although they may not be regular, they are not so rare either.

"FIRST GENERATION" AND "SECOND GENERATION" PATHOLOGIES

Much of the work dealing with bureaucratic pathologies comes from the bureaucratic politics literature and focuses on pathologies of public bureaucracies. William Gormley (1989) has developed a particularly useful framework. He begins by presenting a set of "first generation" pathologies discussed in many of the best-known works in the bureaucratic politics literature (e.g., Rourke, 1984; Tullock, 1965; Seidman, 1970). These pathologies include the following:

1. *Clientelism*—Agencies defer to clientele groups, demonstrating favoritism that runs contrary to the public interest.
2. *Incrementalism*—Agencies resist change and tolerate only modest departures from the status quo.
3. *Arbitrariness*—Agencies demonstrate arbitrary and capricious behavior in their handling of individual cases.
4. *Imperialism*—Agencies seek to expand their resources without regard to cost constraints.
5. *Parochialism*—Agencies miss the "big picture" by focusing narrowly on a limited set of purposes and goals.

According to Gormley, attempts to reform these first generation pathologies have, perversely, given rise to a second generation of pathologies as overcontrolled, distrusted bureaucrats have adjusted their management strategies to be more and more cautious and "by the book." These second generation pathologies include the following:

1. *Beancounting*—Agencies that focus on outputs, not outcomes, in order to generate statistics that create the illusion of progress.
2. *Proceduralism*—Agencies that adopt uniform procedures in order to rebut charges of arbitrariness and unfairness.
3. *Avoidance*—Agencies that escape restrictions by avoiding actions that raise suspicions, even when those actions seem appropriate.
4. *Defeatism*—Agencies that abandon public interest goals in the face of tight controls and painful insults.

Second generation pathologies, Gormley tells us (1989: 112) are in large measure a product of "bureau-bashing," whereby "... politicians, judges and scholars have unleashed a withering barrage of antibureaucratic rhetoric." The notion of bureau-bashing as a generator of pathological response is convincing. Persons and organizations under a constant state of psychological siege might well be expected to react with defeatism, avoidance, proceduralism, and beancounting.

While Gormley's framework does a good job of summarizing widely cited bureaucratic pathologies, his "causality" may be indirect. While it certainly seems to make sense that bureau-bashing might give rise to a number of unfortunate responses, many of these "second generation" pathologies are as old as bureaucracy itself and, thus, can hardly be attributed chiefly to recent control-oriented reform efforts. However, it may well be the case that bureau-bashing and attendant controls have exacerbated tendencies toward proceduralism and beancounting.

Theories of Bureaucratic Pathology

THE GOAL AMBIGUITY MODEL

Having identified particular bureaucratic pathologies, we turn to theories about the *causes* of pathologies. The literature criticizing bureaucracy is vast. Many studies document bureaucratic failure. While there are a great many studies providing explanations of particular bureaucratic failures, less common are explanations of generalized failure.

One general explanation of bureaucratic pathology is the *goal ambiguity model*. The goal ambiguity model tells us bureaucracy fails because bureaucrats have ambiguous goals. This ambiguity brings out the worst in bureaucrats, including a concern with minutiae, attempts to control matters that cannot be controlled, and an emphasis on process to the detriment of outcome. Some treatments (Thompson, 1961) of goal ambiguity focus on its psychological impact on mangers, suggesting that goal ambiguity leads to personal insecurity and, in turn, psychological problems lead to pathological behaviors. Others (e.g., Nutt and Backoff, 1992) discuss the harmful effects of goal ambiguity without reference to any underlying psychological dispositions. The goal ambiguity model reflects one of the best-known maxims in the literature on public organizations and public management—that public organizations have ambiguous goals and bureaucratic failures result from unclear goals.

The fullest treatment of the goal ambiguity model is presented in Victor Thompson's (1961) *Modern Organization*, a work by a political scientist, steeped in the assumptions of organizational sociology, offering an explanation rooted in psychology. "Bureaupathology," according to Thompson, flows from personal insecurity. Bureaupathology involves "the appropriation of major aspects of bureaucratic organization as means for satisfaction of personal needs" (1961: 153). This occurs because of individuals' personal insecurity. In Thompson's view, personal insecurity gives rise to managerial efforts to exert control, where control is defined as requiring that "subordinate behavior correspond as closely as possible with one set of preconceived standards" (1961: 154).

In Thompson's view, the insecurity of top level bureaucrats is pandemic. The farther one goes up the bureaucratic hierarchy, the greater the distance between the performance of task and responsibility for the task. In the upper echelons goals are broader, responsibilities broader, tasks broader, and performance monitoring is necessarily less precise. Thus, it is harder to know whether one is "doing a good job," and effectiveness is increasingly subjective as one moves up the hierarchy.

Compounding the insecurity of senior line bureaucrats is the fact that the work of bureaucracies is increasingly technical and performance is under the control of technicians. Senior managers, nontechnicians by the very nature of their job, have responsibilities for tasks they do not perform and sometimes do not fully understand.

Thompson delineates a number of bureaupathological behaviors, each of which can be thought of as Weberian bureaucracy run amuck. In each instance, a component of Weberian bureaucracy is taken to an extreme with the result that an organizational attribute normally beneficial or benign becomes pathological. These pathological behaviors include the following:

    1. *Drift toward quantitative compliance*: This entails an exaggerated dependence on system controls, especially numbers, to manage and make decisions. Standard operating procedures, rules, and regulations allow the manager to shift the burden of decision-making to "the system," thereby depersonalizing decision-

making and minimizing the likelihood of confrontations with subordinates.

2. *Exaggerated aloofness*: While some degree of disinterestedness is required in formal organizations, exaggerated aloofness occurs when the bureaucrat fails to recognize the rights of the individual client or deals with the client in a manner that is purposefully cold and distant. The reason for this approach, according to Thompson, is that bureaucrats "tend to seek satisfactions from the abstract values of the enterprise rather than from the concrete values of personal service to a client" (162).

3. *Resistance to change*: Most bureaucracies are inherently conservative because they rely on routines. Resistance to change is pathological if bureaucrats' insecurities lead them to view any change as threatening and if those insecurities lead them to undermine positive change.

4. *Insistence on the rights of office*: Sometimes the bureaucrat "exaggerates the official, nontechnical aspects of relationships and suppresses the technical and the informal. He stresses rights, not abilities" (164). The focus on rights rather than abilities, on channels rather than task, may reduce personal insecurity but often undermines the viability of the organization.

The following is a summary of Thompson's goal ambiguity logic:

1. Managers' responsibility and task domain expands as they move up the organizational hierarchy.
2. Managers become more removed from specific tasks.
3. Managers face more uncertainty about the effectiveness of task performance.
4. Because of uncertainty managers seek inappropriate control (such as focusing only on the measurable or giving too much emphasis to procedures).
5. Finally, managers pass this control orientation down the organizational hierarchy.

The goal ambiguity model is a popular one. As Rainey (1989: 238) notes, the goal ambiguity hypothesis is "the most frequent observation in all the relevant literature [comparing public and private organizations]." Many well-known studies in the public management literature include the assertion about lack of goal clarity leading to poor performance in public organizations (e.g., Allison, 1979; Lynn, 1981; Blumenthal, 1983). Nutt and Backoff (1992: 44) present a succinct summary of the goal ambiguity model as represented in the public management literature:

Public organizations often have multiple goals that are both vague and conflicting. There is no 'bottom line' that can be used as a proxy measure of success in most public organizations. Instead, the demand of interest groups, flux in missions, and manipulation by important stakeholders and third parties cast a complex and confusing set of expectations that are frequently in conflict.

Despite the great popularity of the goal ambiguity model, research findings provide limited justification. On the one hand, empirical research supports Thompson's contentions about the *effects* of goal ambiguity. On the other hand, it is not clear that public managers feel they have more ambiguous and uncertain goals. In separate studies using diverse organization data, Rainey (1983), Lan and Rainey (1992), Baldwin (1987), Coursey and Bozeman (1990), and Bozeman and Kingsley (1998) all report no significant difference between public and private managers' goal ambiguity. One particularly relevant study (Rainey, Pandey, and Bozeman, 1995) examined data collected from a sample of 150 business managers and public managers in state and city government. The study found that goal ambiguity is related to red tape and rule formalization but not to sector. That is, public sector managers are no more prone to goal ambiguity, but managers, in *both* sectors, who perceive more goal ambiguity are more apt to experience red tape and formalization. While it is difficult to ignore these accumulated findings, it is possible that the results are very much dependent on the managerial level studied (Brower and Abolafia, 1997).

THE UTILITY MAXIMIZATION MODEL

In his sweeping analysis of bureaucracy, Anthony Downs (1967: 2) begins with the assumption that "bureaucratic officials, like all other agents in society, are significantly—though not solely—motivated by their own self-interests." Bureaucratic failures result when there is a clash between the self-interests of bureaucrats and the legitimate interests of the organization as a whole.

Utility maximization approaches are an outgrowth of positive economics (Friedman, 1953). Beginning in the 1960s, a number of economists and political scientists began to apply the methods and techniques of positive economics to the study of public policy and government. The result was the literature, now vast, that is now called "public choice." While the public choice approach focuses more on policies than organizations, some have developed applications to understanding bureaucracy (e.g., Hammond and Miller, 1985; Maser, 1986).

Downs's *Inside Bureaucracy* was an early and particularly accessible attempt to apply concepts and theories of utility maximization to bureaucratic organizations, especially public bureaucracies. Downs's theory revolves around the nature of individuals' incentives to participate in organizations. He even develops a typology of bureaucrats (e.g., "zealots," "climbers," "conservers") as a sort of shorthand for the incentives each represents.

The basic notion of the utility maximization model is that bureaucrats should be viewed as simply maximizing their self-interest and the key to performance is to align the self-interests of bureaucrats with goals of the organization. While there are a number of ways in which this can be brought about, it is particularly difficult to do so in public organizations because there are "distortions" in incentive systems and there are no market signals by which to judge performance. Downs's work in many ways anticipates the influential and, in most respects, more sophisticated work of Oliver Williamson (1975). Williamson views market and hierarchy more as a choice process influenced by perceived transactions costs and problems of coordination across markets.

Among Downs's many varieties of conflicting interest, the type most relevant for present purposes relates to control. Downs propounds three "laws" relating control problems to organizational size. These include the following:

1. No one can fully control the behavior of a large organization ("Law of Imperfect Control").
2. The larger any organization becomes, the weaker is the control over its actions exercised by those at the top ("Law of Diminishing Control").
3. The larger any organization becomes, the poorer is the coordination among its actions ("Law of Decreasing Coordination").

There is one "law" particularly relevant in that it explains a behavior dynamic that accounts for a number of seemingly pathological outcomes. The "Law of Counter Control" states that "the greater the effort made by a sovereign or top-level official to control the behavior of subordinate officials, the greater the efforts made by those subordinates to evade or counteract such control" (Downs, 1967: 147). Downs points out that subordinates have their own weapons to combat the control efforts of supervisors. Among others, subordinates develop extensive communications networks, part of the informal organization, as an alternative to the legitimate communications networks dominated by top officials.

Consistent with many economic interpretations of organizations, many of the problems flowing from organizations are traced to the substitution of hierarchical control for market control. Taking together various Downsian laws, we can reconstruct his logic as follows:

1. In the absence of the market as an allocator of organizational resources and pursuits, hierarchy takes its place.
2. Hierarchy cannot fully control an organization.

3. The larger the organization, the poorer the coordination among its activities.

Particularly relevant to present purposes, Downs presents an unusual view of red tape. He considers red tape as a "quasi-price," a non-monetary cost levied by nonmarket organizations on persons or other organizations seeking information. These quasi-prices, which include red tape and delays, are designed to discourage requests for information flow and activity and to "ration limited resources so they will be available to those truly anxious to use them" (188). In other words, agencies set up red tape as a hurdle that serves as an indictor of need. Those willing to jump the hurdle have given evidence of their need and, in most cases, are served. Those unwilling to jump the hurdle are not served, thereby reserving the scarce resources of the agency.

At least as represented by Downs, the utility maximization model has many flaws as a theory of bureaucratic pathology. Most important, there is little to distinguish pathological behavior from effective or even normal behavior. Perhaps the chief value of a utility maximization framework is that it provides some hope of relating organizational dysfunctions to the behavior of individuals. The approach requires a focus on the motives, interests, and behaviors of individuals as they react against the requirements of the organization.

PROPERTY RIGHTS AND PRINCIPAL-AGENT MODELS

The utility maximization model is not the only economics-influenced approach to understanding bureaucratic pathology. The property rights model (see De Alessi, 1969, for an overview) provides one of the more comprehensive explanations of the failures of bureaucracy, particularly failures in public bureaucracy. The principal-agent model is, in some respects, more general (Ross, 1973) and has recently been more popular among students of bureaucracy (Mitnick, 1980; Moe, 1984; Bendor, Taylor, and Van Gaalen, 1987).

The property rights model traces its lineage back at least as far as the pioneering work of Berle and Means (1932). Berle and Means were concerned about the rise of a managerial class and the separation of ownership and control of the organization. The property rights model (e.g., De Alessi, 1969; Demsetz, 1967) assumes that many bureaucratic dysfunctions arise from the absence of oversight from wealth-seeking entrepreneurs. In the private firm the wealth-seeking entrepreneur works to combine the optimal production inputs to produce goods and services as efficiently as possible, the rationale being that the margin between input and price should be as large as possible because the entrepreneur's economic well-being hinges on that (profit) margin. Not surprisingly, public sector organizations are inevitably viewed as less efficient because there is such extreme separation of ownership (the public at large) from operation (by bureaucrats without a pecuniary interest in the organization).

A related source of inefficiency derives from the fact that there are no rights of property transfer in public agencies. Since public programs (most of them, at least) are financed indirectly through tax dollars and since the "investor" (i.e., taxpayer) is unable to make "portfolio adjustments" (i.e., choose to invest in some public programs and not others), there are natural tendencies toward inefficiency. This ability to transfer property rights is, allegedly, a force for efficiency in the private sector even in those circumstances where there is a sharp distinction between ownership and control of operations.

Since public organizations are viewed as inherently flawed, at least from a technical efficiency standpoint, the property rights prescription is straightforward—put economic activity in the private sector if at all possible, either through direct control, contract, or privatization of public operations.

A good introduction to the prescriptions that flow from privatization assumptions is E. S. Savas's *Privatizing the Public Sector* (1982). The book is significant not only because it provides good, forceful arguments for the alleged benefits of privatizing, but its premises influenced Reagan administration policy.

Privatization is no less popular today than during the heyday of the Reagan administration. If anything, it has become even more popular as state and local governments search for more economical ways of delivering goods and services. Privatization has numerous advocates and some clear advantages. In many instances, privatization introduces competition and saves money, often with no decrement in the quality of service. Three-quarters of the city and county executives responding to a 1987 survey reported savings of 10 percent or more from a wide variety of privatization efforts (U.S. Bureau of Census, 1987). When the profit motive is clear, privatization provides efficiency motivations and strong profit-motivated management oversight (Vickers and Yarrow, 1991).

But privatization also has its critics. Privatization can promote contempt for public service and the role of the public sector and can reinforce stereotypes and expectations of government inefficiency (Starr, 1989; Beck Jorgensen, 1993). Private contractors are not always more efficient. The relative efficiency of private contractors seems to depend on the presence of competition. For example, studies of privatization of utilities have shown few efficiency or productivity gains (Donahue, 1989).

The evidence for the property rights model of bureaucratic pathology is difficult to assess. Most of the work is in the positive economics tradition and there have not been a great many efforts to verify empirically the claims of property rights theorists. Comparisons of public and private organizations and services have been made in a few organizational

---

RESEARCH ENCOUNTER:
"THE THEORY OF THE SECOND BEST"

One of the most interesting recent assessments of privatization is Kuttner's (1997) *Everything for Sale*. Unlike some boosters of generalized solutions, Kuttner gives thought to particular circumstances under which market-based delivery of goods and services is most effective. According to Kuttner, market solutions are most likely to succeed when the classical assumptions of the free market are most closely approximated. These include the following: (1) Consumers have "perfect information." (2) There is "perfect competition"; barriers to market entry are low, and hence many suppliers of a service are present. This assumption makes sure that there are no monopolies and prices are hence set by theory of supply and demand. (3) There is mobility of the factors of production, including capital and labor. (4) There is an absence of externalities (spill-over effects), especially negative externalities.

Free market assumptions are never met entirely, in part because some, such as perfect information, are ideal. This leads to Kuttner to cite the "Theory of the Second Best." According to this theory, first proposed more than three decades ago by Lancaster and Lipsey (1956), when markets depart significantly from the ideal and yield nonoptimal outcomes, attempts to make allocation systems more market-like yield worse outcomes than if left alone. Kuttner provides examples from the health-care industry and banking industry, which serve as models for second-best markets.

---

realms including hospitals (Lindsay, 1976; Clarkson, 1972); utilities (Neuberg, 1977; Di Lorenzo and Robinson, 1982) and, perhaps most familiar, Davies' (1971, 1977) studies of airlines. However, almost all of these studies have been focused on differences between public and private sector organizations' technical efficiency. While the findings are not perfectly consistent with the key assumptions of property rights theory, it would seem implausible that public sector organization, often providing a good or service *because* of market failure, would be as efficient as private sector ones. The dice are loaded.

One of the most relevant empirical tests of property rights theory is Clarkson's (1972) comparison of public and private hospitals. Interestingly, he hypothesized that because of owner oversight, owners (and their managerial representatives) in private hospitals would exert direct control of activities, but managers of nonproprietary hospitals would seek control indirectly through more meetings, more specific bylaws, increased rules and procedures, and more formal budgeting and accounting practice. In brief, such organizations will be more formalized and have more red tape. The empirical results supported Clarkson's expectations.

A major advantage of the property rights model is that it provides a simple but plausible explanation for organization failure—the clouding of incentives due to the absence of a profit motive. But it is perhaps a better explanation of efficiency differences between public and private sector than a theory of bureaucratic pathology. For all their alleged owner-induced efficiency, most business enterprises fail. Property rights theory tells us much about public organization failure but it has little to say about private sector failure or public sector successes.

The principal-agent model has much in common with property rights assumptions but a different developmental lineage. The key issue in principal-agent models is the view of human relations as contractual between a buyer of goods and services, the "principal," and a provider of good and services, the "agent." Viewed from the standpoint of economic rationality, it is the agent's interest to provide minimally acceptable goods and services at the greatest acceptable price and the principal's to seek the lowest possible price for an acceptable quality of goods and services. Often the analysis centers on information disparities between the principal and the agent. In most cases, such as a physician-patient or lawyer-client relationship, the agent will have specialized knowledge not easily obtained by the principal. This "information asymmetry" leads to many key issues of principal-agent theory, such as the amount of time and resources the principal should devote to monitoring and information acquisition.

Most applications of principal-agent theory to bureaucracy have focused on relations between public officials, especially legislators, as the principal and bureaucrats as agents (Wood and Waterman, 1991; Waterman, Rouse, and Wright, 1998). The theory is appealing because it addresses a classic problem in bureaucratic politics: the ability of elected officials to acquire the knowledge to exercise oversight (Wilson, 1887; Goodnow, 1900).

Similar to the property rights model, the principal-agent models focuses on "shirking." Given the incentive for the agent (the bureaucrat) to provide services at a relatively low level and the principal's (legislator, governor, OMB official) limited ability to obtain information required for oversight, how is shirking minimized? Principals must pay a "specification cost" (Mitnick, 1980) to set the minimal level of acceptable quality and a "policing cost" to monitor and enforce compliance. But what is the appropriate level of cost? Obviously, there is some level of information acquisition and monitoring that becomes impractical as well as too costly. Moreover, this is in some ways the key question of bureaucratic reform: What price should we pay for control of the bureaucracy?

As Waterman and Meier (1998) have pointed out in a recent paper evaluating and extending principal-agent theory, there are many ways in which the assumptions of the theory are unrealistic. For example, applications usually assume a two-party relationship. But not only are there more parties to most policy and public management issues than just legislative principals and bureaucratic agents, even these principals and agents are not monolithic in their goals and interests. Political institutions are composed of coalitions and most principal-agent models cannot accommodate the complexities of coalition relationships and "multiple contracts." But as a starting point to focus on the problems of information asymmetry, information costs, and the need for control, the principal-agent model provides helpful insights.

THE MALADAPTION MODEL

The ultimate systems pathology model, the maladaption model deemphasizes the role of the individual and looks instead at the fit of the organization and its structure to the demands of its environment. There are two distinct strains to this model, one flowing from the 1960s–1970s work on "contingency theory," relating structure to environment, the other flowing from the more formalized explanations of "population ecology theory," which, roughly, can be viewed as the application of evolutionary theory to the study of organizations. In either case, the answer to the "why is the organization dysfunctional?" question is "because its structure is not suited to its environment."

With the conspicuous exception of Kaufman's (1986) work on time and changes in bureaucracy, the maladaption model has not had much impact on *public* organization theory. Indeed, most people working in the adaptation-maladaption tradition tend to recognize public ownership as just one of many taxonomic attributes, no more important than most.

Early contingency theorists were strongly motivated by applied questions, particularly seeking to determine the appropriate organizational structure or design for a set of environmental contingencies. Thus, Burns and Stalker (1961), in their early contingency theory study *The Management of Innovation*, were driven by their concerns about the impact of environmental change on the Scottish electronics industry and just what structural response seemed an effective adaptation. Similarly, Joan Woodward (1965) sought to understand the elements of technological processes and production systems and their implications for the structuring of organizations. During the late 1960s and much of the 1970s, contingency theorists focused on uncovering empirical evidence about the reciprocal effects of organizational function and technology, environment, and structure.

These efforts reported such factors as the relationship between size and formalization (e.g., Blau and Schoenherr, 1971) and structure and task routine (e.g., Hage and Aiken, 1969). Later, in the same applied research tradition that gave rise to contingency theory, a number of scholars turned their attention to developing prescriptions for organization design (e.g., Nystrom and Starbuck, 1981).

Population ecology theory, which seeks to understand the ways in which populations and sets of organizations are born, evolve, and die, built on a different strand of contingency theory. Whereas the organization designers embraced the empirical findings about the fit of structure to environment (e.g., Child, 1972), the population ecology theorists were more taken with the efforts of the contingency theorists to develop sophisticated empirical taxonomies of organizations (e.g., Pugh, Hickson, Hinings, and Turner, 1969).

Population ecology theory has a number of benefits for those interested in understanding bureaucratic pathology. The basic assumptions of the population ecology model can be stated simply:

> Environmental pressures make competition for resources the central force in organizational activities, and the resource dependence perspective focuses on tactics and strategies used by authorities in seeking to manage their environments as well as their organizations. The three stages of variation, selection, and retention constitute a general model of organizational change, which explains how organizational forms are created survive or fail, and are diffused throughout a population. (Aldrich, 1979: 28)

In population ecology terms, organization structures and organizations survive because they are adapted to the demands of their environment. If they are maladapted they usually do not survive. An interesting implication is the role of government status (or government subsidy) in the population mix. If organizations evolve due to a selection of environmentally adapted attributes, what about when the organization is "artificially" sheltered by its government status? Does this qualify as an undesirable disruption of "natural" selection, one that permits pathologies (as well as maladapted structures) to thrive? Or is government support itself a resource to be managed (Bozeman and Straussman, 1990)?

The maladaption model's chief utility is recognizing that bureaucratic structures should not be evaluated out of context. A set of structures that may appear inherently dysfunctional may well conform to the needs of some environments and particular environmental dictates. Similarly, the maladaption model cautions against static organizational assessment. If environments change, the organization's suitability to the environment must change.

The maladaption model has many of the same theoretical limitations as population ecology theory in general. In the first place, there is always some danger of circular reasoning (e.g., "the environment conduces structure, the structure meets the demand of the environment, the structure must be adaptive"). Second, environmental adaptation is a broad and often not terribly meaningful standard. Other than survival, what is meant by adaptation? Because of these limitations, the maladaption model is not terribly useful for assessing particular organizations. The focus on sets of organizations and their environmental fitness renders the analysis of any particular organization problematic.

PATHOLOGY MODELS AND REFORM

The explanations of bureaucratic pathology presented here certainly are not exhaustive. To the models presented, we could add others based on culture (Crozier, 1964; Schein, 1985), organizational change and development (Golembiewski, 1985), and participation (Bryson, 1988), to name just a few. But the four models highlighted here seem particularly relevant to contemporary reform efforts, as shown in Table 3-3.

Most systems-oriented reforms contain one or more theories about pathology. As we see from Table 3-3, some of the most popular prescriptions among today's reformers line up well against the four pathology models presented. Let us focus briefly on the reform prescriptions now sweeping across the federal bureaucracy and consider implications for understanding and addressing bureaucratic pathologies.

TABLE 3-3   REFORM IMPLICATIONS OF PATHOLOGY MODELS

	GOAL AMBIGUITY	UTILITY MAXIMIZING	PROPERTY RIGHTS AND PRINCIPAL-AGENT	MALADAPTION
PROBLEM	Personal insecurity and unclear goals	Immutable self-interest	Lack of owner oversight, limited portability of wealth; asymmetry of information between principal and agent	Organization and structures not suited to environment
CURE	Clear goals, psychological counseling	Mesh personal and organizational goals	Privatize; monitoring, regulation	Align organization with environment
REFORM PRESCRIPTION	Performance-based management	Incentive structuring	Market-based alternatives; goal alignment	Strategic planning and management

A PHILOSOPHY OF BUREAUCRATIC REFORM:
THE CASE OF THE GOVERNMENT PERFORMANCE
AND RESULTS ACT OF 1993

The Clinton administration's National Performance Review (Gore, 1993a) has, deservedly, received a great deal of attention. After establishing advisory and working groups throughout the federal government, more than 250 "reinvention laboratories" have been established at sites ranging from the Miami International Airport to an Alaska-based Department of Interior library on natural resources (Gore, 1996). While the level and diversity of reform activity under the National Performance Review is impressive, the government reform that may well have the broadest impact is the set of activities required under the Government Performance and Results Act (1993). The act, now known to most federal bureaucrats as GPRA (usually pronounced "GEPRA"), will engage literally millions of government workers at a cost of billions of dollars. To use bureaucratic parlance, it puts government reform on the radar screen. In many ways, GPRA is an excellent case study of the philosophy of reform (Radin, 1998). After reviewing some requirements of GPRA, we consider here just what it implies about assumptions and perceptions of bureaucracy.

GPRA requires the adoption of strategic planning and performance measurements throughout the federal government. Its requirements are quite specific and considerable, including a strategic plan, a related performance plan, input measures, output measures, outcome measures, impact measures, and criteria for goal development. It is economically rational management taken to its zenith: explicit and measurable goals, explicit measures of performance, ties of measures to budgets.

While it is not easy to pick an exact date for the origins of GPRA, the introduction by Senator William Roth (R-Del.) of S. 3154, the "Federal Program Performance Standards and Goals Act of 1990," introduced in October, 1990, is the formal beginning of legislative ideas that evolved into GPRA. On January 14, 1991, Senator Roth introduced a version, S. 20, that was quite similar but with a "Findings and Purposes" section that included information from the Office of Management and Budget on government management failures. It took two years to hammer out the details about the specific requirements of the act and to reconcile a House of Representatives version. Finally, in 1993 the act was signed into law and hundreds of thousands of federal managers (and almost as many consultants) began in earnest to reflect on the meaning and likely impacts of GPRA.

The goals of GPRA are to improve the efficiency and effectiveness of federal programs by establishing a system to set goals for program performance and to measure results (GAO, 1997: 3). The act is to be phased in over several years and will ultimately require agencies to prepare multiyear strategic plans, annual performance plans, and annual performance reports.

It starts with strategic planning. In 1997 and 1998 agencies of the federal government were actively preparing, revising, submitting, and resubmitting strategic plans. The strategic plans include the agency's mission statement, general goals and objectives, and the strategies the agency will use in pursuit of those objectives. In forming plans, an agency must consult directly with Congress and agency "stakeholders," groups and individuals who have a strong link to the agency's activities. The first round of strategic plans was submitted in September, 1997, and Congress provided an informal "grade" for the plans. None of the plans received a "passing" grade of 70. The agencies then revised plans in consultation with Congress.

The next step was submission of annual performance plans, starting fiscal year 1999. The annual performance plans must contain an agency's annual goals, performance measures reflecting the extent of accomplishment of those goals, and resources the agency needs to meet its goals. Starting March 31, 2000, agencies are required to submit yearly performance reports, relating performance to goals and summarizing results of performance evaluations. Agencies gained experience with these new procedures in pilot projects underway between 1994 and 1997.

The GAO (1997: 6) judged early GPRA implementation as mixed, noting several problems:

- Overlapping and fragmented program efforts
- Limited control of federal agencies to accomplish objectives when there are many relevant nonfederal actors
- Lack of results-oriented performance information
- Difficulty of instilling an organizational culture focusing on results.
- Problems linking performance to the budget process

While it is certainly too early for a definitive assessment of the impacts or results of GPRA, most of which has not even been implemented at this time, the entire thrust of GPRA says much about the nature of reform and assumptions of what is wrong with bureaucracy.

The Senate Committee on Government Affairs issued a report (U.S. Congress, 1992) on GPRA and this is perhaps the best source of knowledge about the assumptions and motives underlying the act. Table 3-4 (on page 60) presents excerpts from the report in which each of the primary instruments of GPRA is discussed, along with a rationale.

The rationales and instruments described in Table 3-4 seem to have an underlying reform philosophy that says "the *problem* is ambiguity and lack of specificity," and "the *solution* is to measure and act upon the measures." This is an approach that would have warmed the heart of Luther Gulick and Frederick Taylor, two pioneers of scientific management. That is not a criticism: Gulick, Taylor, and others from the classical school of management theory presented many valid points. In all likelihood, much can be accomplished by having more precise goals and better measures.

TABLE 3-4   GPRA AND ITS RATIONALE

GPRA REQUIREMENT	DESCRIPTION	RATIONALE
Strategic plans	"Strategic plans are the starting point and basic underpinning for a system of program goal-setting and performance measurement. A multiyear strategic plan articulates the fundamental missions of an organization and lays out its long-term general goals."	"The clearer and more precise these goals are, the better able the organization will be to maintain a consistent sense of direction, regardless of leadership changes at the top.... Even when a change in administration brings about a shift in political philosophy, the program's mission and long-term general goals remain intact."
Performance plans	"[P]rogram performance plans are what provide the direct linkage between an agency's longer-term goals and what its managers and staff are doing on a day-to-day basis. These plans are often hierarchical in form, showing what annual performance goals need to be accomplished at each level in order for the next higher level to meet its own goals."	"Performance goals may relate to either 'outputs' or 'outcomes.'... A common weakness in program performance plans is an overreliance on output measures, to the neglect of outcomes."
Performance reports	"[P]rogram performance reports are the feedback to managers, policy-makers, and the public as to what was actually accomplished for the resources expended."	"While the nature of some of what is measured may change periodically, that should not be a frequent, widespread occurrence."
Performance budgeting	A performance budget shows "a direct relationship between proposed spending and expected results, along with the anticipated effects of higher or lower amounts."	"During this time of very tight budget constraints, it is important that Congress have a clear understanding of what it is getting in the way of results from each dollar spent and how those results would change with an increase or decrease in funding."

Source: Compiled from U.S. Congress, 1992: 14–17.

As the embodiment of a rationalist approach to fixing bureaucracy, GPRA presents both advantages and disadvantages. One advantage is that its proponents have an empirical orientation. They did not simply make blind assumptions about the level of planning and information currently extant in government. Studies were commissioned to learn about existing practices. Indeed, since 1973 the GAO has provided Congress with more than seventy-five studies assessing federal agencies' evaluation and performance measurement activities. Nor can they be faulted for assuming that bureaucratic reforms are costless. While one may disagree with estimates that GPRA will cost no more than 1 percent of program expenses (U.S. Congress, 1992: 13), at least some consideration is being given to implementation costs.

Another advantage of GPRA is the insistence on focusing on ends ("outcomes"). As Lindblom (1959, 1977), among others, has demonstrated, it is all too easy for managers and policymakers to develop consensus around means and resources while never agreeing upon, much less measuring, ends.

Finally, though it is not often discussed (and sometimes not viewed as an advantage), GPRA has the effect of having Congress more closely involved in directing bureaucracy. Congressional oversight can be a thorny problem for bureaucrats but it is difficult to mount an argument that the elected representatives of the people should simply defer to bureaucrats.

A major disadvantage of GPRA is that, disclaimers notwithstanding, it is very much a paper-driven process. It is subject to the same loss of energy and bogging down as such earlier paper-driven, formalistic reform efforts as Planning, Programming Budgeting Systems (PPBS) and management by objectives (Wildavsky, 1969), each of which had many similarities to GPRA procedures. If it is fully implemented, it may collapse under its own weight. The paperwork and planning required is considerable.

One might heed President Eisenhower's admonition and assume that it is not the plan that is important but planning itself. That is, there is much to be gained by requiring systematic and thoughtful planning. Certainly GPRA can present such advantages, so long as the federal managers actually develop the strategic plans for themselves rather than (as has already begun to happen) contracting them out for consultants to develop.

There are many other hazards to effective implementation of GPRA. These include not only those listed in the GAO (1997) report, but also possibilities such as overreliance on precision, failure to adequately identify relations of means to ends, and problems of translating outcomes at one level to outcomes at the next. But more interesting than the pitfalls or possible accomplishments of GPRA is what it says as a congressionally sanctioned remedy for the ills of bureaucracy. As a philosophy of reform, the *motives* of GPRA are particularly interesting. GPRA tries to do much the same thing that many federal managers already do in so many different ways—control the uncontrollable. Consider the language in Table 3-4 about the need to keep on course even with changes in administration. Though a continuing problem, managerial and policy instability may not be amenable to a legislative solution.

Conclusion

The Government Performance and Results Act conveys a message about bureaucratic pathology and bureaucratic reform. The GPRA message is to beware of goal ambiguity. Other reforms have other implicit messages, messages about market failure, or bureaucrats' alienation and the need for "empowerment" (a major theme of the National Performance Review). The principal-agent model sets the question for GPRA: "How does one ensure sufficient investment in "specification" and "policing" between the principal and the agent?

The optimistic theme of this chapter is that there is no lack of interest or lack of prescriptions for curing the alleged ills of bureaucracy. If persistent doctoring can cure bureaucratic pathologies we are surely on the right track. The pessimistic theme is that the reform efforts, while as sure as the tides (Light, 1997), do not seem to provide much cumulative knowledge. One study of budget reforms (Downs and Larkey, 1986) showed that the introduction of planning-programming-budgeting systems (PPBS) reforms in the late 1960s had much in common with the 1970s zero-based budgeting (ZBB) reforms (Pyhrr, 1973), but the later reform made almost all the same mistakes as the earlier one. Now the adherents of GPRA seem to pay little attention to reform history.

How does one avoid the disappointments so often experienced in reform efforts? One possibility, suggested by Downs and Larkey and by Light (1997), is to just be less ambitious, to cultivate experiments rather than sweeping changes. Perhaps this advice will be tested in the implementation of the various reinvention laboratories of the National Performance Review. Another possibility, suggested in this chapter, is to give more systematic attention to the underlying theories of reform. Sober reflection on the assumptions of reform and the mechanics by which change is expected to occur at least reduces the possibilities for self-deception.

As we have seen here, the pathologies of bureaucracy are many and the prescriptions, though plentiful, are weak. Often these prescriptions pay little heed to evidence about the workings of bureaucracy and politics and, instead, embrace popular bromides. Patrick Wolf (1997) shows that throughout U.S. history the difficulties of reform have been under-estimated, with most reforms coming undone by a failure to cope adequately with political values. One especially popular and often harmful prescription is to make government more like business. Many of our theories and our cultural predisposition lead us to embrace this simple prescription. But few careful studies of pathology or bureaucratic reform attest to the prescription's power.

In this chapter our focus has been on the range of bureaucratic pathologies, theoretical interpretations, and recent reform efforts. In the next chapter we examine in depth one peculiar form of bureaucratic pathology: bureaucratic red tape. Both the pathology and prescriptions for its cure are very much wound up in perceptions, myth, and ideology. It is all too easy to simply think of red tape as a problem of efficiency. But, as we shall see, a simple efficiency concept of the problem of red tape fails to do justice to the complexity of its causes and effects. Reforming red tape requires a different reform philosophy, one that balances the needs for efficiency, accountability, performance, and fairness.

RULES AND RED TAPE
4

As a bureaucratic pathology, red tape lacks the "glamour" of such headline-grabbing pathologies as corruption. Stories of bureaucratic or political corruption make it to the front page, but red tape stories usually get inserted somewhere between the want ads and political news of nations we cannot identify on a map. However, if red tape lacks the glitz of big time pathologies, it compensates with stubborn intractability. Many corruption stories are for the ages and lead to epochal changes in policy and governance (Anechiarico and Jacobs, 1996), but red tape is for every day. Why is red tape everywhere and why is it so difficult to prevent?

In this chapter we examine the relationships between rules and red tape. If we consider the number of formal rules affecting any bureaucracy and think of every rule as a red tape "opportunity," then it becomes easy to see why red tape is so plentiful—there are so many opportunities. More interesting than the amount of red tape is its causes. How do good, well-functioning rules turn into red tape? Corruption is a bureaucratic pathology whose motives, usually centered on greed or lust for power, are often easy to understand. However, red tape turns out to be quite a bit more complicated in its motivation. Corrupt people set out to steal but bureaucrats rarely set out to create red tape. So how does it happen? In much of the remainder of this book we consider in some detail the causes of red tape. In this chapter, we take some care to define red tape and show its relationships to rules, formalization and other nonpathological aspects of bureaucracy. Much of this chapter is about developing a language for thinking about red tape and its causes and effects.

A major flaw in some concepts of red tape is lack of specificity. In particular, many fail to distinguish between rules (all rules, good and bad) and red tape (bad rules). The IRS example in the box on page 66 shows the difficulties of determining what is and is not red tape.

FORMALIZATION AS PHYSIOLOGY, RED TAPE AS PATHOLOGY

Metaphorically, red tape is a pathology affecting a bureaucratic organization's physiology. A significant part of an organization's physiology is the set of officially sanctioned behaviors embodied in the codified rules to which the organization is subject. Neither the number of an organization's rules nor the extent to which procedures are formally codified tell us anything about whether the rules work. Neither a high nor a low level of formalization is inherently "bad." The IRS case on page 66 shows that some organizations require more rules than others do and some circumstances require rules whereas others do not. In some instances, high levels of formalization enhance needed controls, accountability, or safeguards. There may be a large body of rules, but no accompanying "sickness." We reserve the term red tape for those instances in which the rules and procedures, whatever the level of formalization, high or low, serve no significant organizational or social purpose.

WHY FORMALIZATION IS IMPORTANT

Organization theorists have been quite inventive in their development of concepts and measures of formalization, but the definition provided below is simple and relevant:

> *Formalization*: "the extent to which rules, procedures, instructions and communications are written" (Pugh, et al., 1968: 75)

From this most fundamental of organizational characteristics spring much of the organization's behavior and its meaning in society. Scott (1987) provides a good account of the importance of formalization, beginning with the idea that formalization actually *defines* organization. Scott's definition of formalization is a bit broader than some in that it examines all organization structure, not just rules. According to Scott (1987: 33), "a structure is formalized to the extent that the rules governing behavior are precisely and explicitly formulated and to the extent that roles and role relations are prescribed independently of the personal attributes of individuals occupying positions in the structure." Without prescribed roles and behaviors, established through sets of formal rules, formal organizations cannot exist (Simon, 1957). If a group's behavior is entirely based on unpredictable, unlegitimated, and informal behaviors

BUREAUCRATIC ENCOUNTER:
THE IRS AND ELECTRONIC FILING

Many think of the Internal Revenue Service as one of the world's leading producers of red tape. But one recent episode shows that the IRS is as likely to be excoriated for having too few rules and regulations as it is for having too many.

The IRS, like many organizations, views computers and electronic media as a means of doing its job more efficiently and with less bureaucracy. One of the cornerstones of the IRS strategic plan is to increase electronic filing. With more than 12 million of the 115 million individual federal tax returns filed electronically in 1993, the IRS is well on its way to its objective of having 80 million returns filed electronically by 2001.

As pointed out in a newspaper article, "electronic filing has been a point of pride with the IRS, welcomed as a big stride forward along the government's vaunted information highway." The problem seems to be that "electronic filing could become a highway rest stop that beckons crooks and thieves (Rosenblatt, 1994: 1). False filing of returns by computer jumped 105 percent during 1993, according to a report of the General Accounting Office. The report estimated that more than 25,000 false returns were filed during the first ten months of the filing season, claiming bogus refunds of more than $53 million. The IRS was able to stop only about $29 million before issuance of a check.

The IRS has become "too efficient." It provides refunds so quickly to those filing electronically, and provides them with so little fuss and bother, that it has become much easier for thieves to bilk the U.S. treasury. Of course, it is the promise of fast refunds that is the very incentive that appeals to electronic filers. Thus, the imposition of additional controls will provide a disincentive for electronic filing and could prove a major obstacle to the IRS plans for a new, more efficient way of doing business. What is the moral of this story for students of bureaucracy and bureaucratic pathology? There are at least two. First, it is not sensible to equate a high level of bureaucratic structure and control with red tape. Some bureaucratic organizations, of which the IRS is a prime example, can easily justify a high level of bureaucratic control. A second point, the question of "how much structure and bureaucratic control is appropriate?" is complex and has strategic implications. Bureaucracy and formalization often pose a trade-off for the public manager since different values are often enhanced by more or less bureaucratic formalization. Thus, should the IRS increase the amount of structure and control involved in electronic filing? If so, it can expect to make life more difficult for thieves and it will almost certainly save a part of that $24 million of revenue going to thieves. Alternatively, should it maintain the current level of structure and control that enables fast returns and encourages electronic filing? If so, it is likely to get by with many fewer employees engaged in processing returns, it is likely to enhance its computerized record-keeping abilities, and, ironically, it can probably prevent or detect cer-

---

BUREAUCRATIC ENCOUNTER:
THE IRS AND ELECTRONIC FILING (CONTINUED)

tain types of fraud and abuse by having better electronic records. The answer? It all depends. It depends not only on the comparison of the amount of revenue lost to thieves as compared to the amount of money saved through greater efficiency of electronic filing. The answer depends also on such external factors as the loss of political support in Congress (and possibly the loss of appropriations dollars for computerization initiatives) as members of Congress read about electronic theft. So, the trade-offs are complicated and the stakes considerable.

---

the group is not by any conventional definition an organization. The formalization issue, then, is not "whether" but "how much."

According to Scott (1987), the organization's formal structure not only mediates performance but is also the manager's instrument of performance. The manager has little or no control over the informal, personalized, and ad hoc behaviors of employees; it is the formalized structures, as represented by rules, procedures, organizational charts, and formal plans that give direction to sanctioned behavior. Thus, the degree of formalization relates closely to the potential for managerial control of organization members' behaviors (Clegg, 1981). One of the enduring questions in organization and management is which aspects of behavior to require formally and to codify, and which aspects to keep informal and leave to the discretion of employees. The answer to that question often tells us much about the effectiveness of particular organizations.

While organizational members do not always find formal relations as satisfying as those based on informal, personalized relations, the tasks, duties, and behaviors formally prescribed in organizations' structures nonetheless offer many advantages. In the first place, it helps separate the person from the behavior. This is an advantage in that role performance does not depend on any particular individual. Thus, job mobility, promotion, and even the death of organizational members present fewer barriers to organizational stability and functioning (Gouldner, 1950; Pffefer and Salancik, 1977; Lieberson and O'Connor, 1972). The formalization of roles also has the advantage, in some cases, of easing work relationships among people who do not like one another or who do not know one another.

In sum, formalization is inherent, even defining, in modern organizations. However, each organization is unique with respect to its particular degrees and patterns of formalization. Formalization has consequences well beyond the issue of red tape. Nevertheless, an understanding of red tape presupposes knowledge of the nature and significance of formalization.

Knowing how systems of rules evolve or become more formal is relevant to knowing how rules "devolve," or become less effective. Fortunately, there is a good deal of research on the question of the origins and growth of formalization; unfortunately, almost all of it is based on analyses of private sector organizations. While studies of private sector organizations are often germane to government agencies, aspects of bureaucratic behavior affected by external political authority (Bozeman, 1987) or by structural characteristics of government, such as government personnel or procurement systems, are not well understood by looking exclusively at private organizations (Rainey, 1997).

Chapter 3 gave a brief discussion of a maladaption model for explaining bureaucratic pathologies. The maladaption model is the "dark side" of more general study of organizational ecologies and life cycles. Formalization studies rooted in ecology and life cycle perspectives are particularly useful. Langton (1984) seeks to explain formalization and rule elaboration in terms of population ecology theory, using historical examples to show that rules and other aspects of bureaucratic structure are selectively retained within an organization because they enhance its efficiency and contribute toward its success in managing environmental complexities. The more complex or uncertain the environment, the more elaborate an organization's internal administrative structure (Van de Ven, 1986).

Several factors seem to drive the elaboration of formal procedures and systems of rules. As the resource environment changes, formal rules sometimes emerge as a means to "buffer" the environment, protecting the organization from changes in the supply and plenitude of resources (Meyer, et al., 1987). In some cases, an organization creates rules in an effort to increase external perceptions of its legitimacy or professionalization. If there are external standards and those standards are adopted by the organization, then the organization may be perceived as legitimate, in conformance with others' expectations, and, for those reasons, deserving of resources (Meyer and Rowan, 1977).

Another factor giving rise to formalization is political or constituent demands (Warwick, 1975; Rosenfeld, 1984; Stevenson, 1986). Just as organizations seek legitimacy, organizations' clients likewise seek legitimacy for their political demands and look to organizations, particularly government organizations, to create value (Kirlin, 1996). One sign that political demands have been addressed is the adoption of new formal rules and structures (Seidman, 1970). In some instances, political pressures for government to create or reallocate value lead to increased formalization, in others to new programs and new agencies (Kaufman, 1986).

A RULES-BASED THEORY OF RED TAPE

Why should one embrace a rules-based concept of red tape? There are other ways to think about red tape. For example, red tape may be viewed as a matter of perception, focusing on individuals' vexation or fears about bureaucracy. Alternatively, one may view red tape purely as a synonym for inefficiency—if work is performed inefficiently red tape is presumed. But let us consider some of the arguments for red tape as "bad rules." First, it provides a focus, some ability to exclude. One of the greatest problems with analysis of red tape, as mentioned several times already, is that it has come to mean almost any problem one finds with an organization. Second, a rules-based focus is substantial and concrete. All organizations have formal rules and, thus, it is at least possible to conduct research on organizational rules. Third, a rules approach has some face validity. Many complaints about red tape refer directly to rules, regulations, and procedures that are burdensome or ineffective. [A note on usage: The term *rules* is used throughout the remainder of this book as shorthand for *formal rules*, *regulations*, and *procedures*.]

The study of organizational rules has a long history in organization theory (Gouldner, 1954; Crozier, 1964), but has for some time been neglected, only to have been rediscovered during the past decade or so. During the 1950s and 1960s, sociologists' studies of rules focused chiefly on their effects on the psychological states of individual bureaucrats or on the impacts on power relations. Merton (1940) emphasized the importance of rules in facilitating harmony and predictability among employees with different types or degrees of authority. Crozier (1964) focused on rules as a protection against one's superior and the possibility of arbitrary action.

Many recent studies of bureaucratic rules have focused on the politics and law of rule-making, examining processes more than impacts. Some studies focus on rules of one particular sort or rules pertaining to a particular policy domain, such as environmental policy (e.g., Magat, Krupnick, and Harrington, 1986; McGarrity, 1991). Others examine the relationship of rules and rules processes to governance structures (e.g., Frant, 1993) or interest groups (e.g., Furlong, 1997). Kerwin (1994) provides one of the best and most comprehensive overviews of rule-making processes, including useful information about the formulation, management, and oversight of rules. But most studies of rule-making give limited attention to the impacts of rules and the ways in which they change.

ANATOMY OF A RULE

Webster's Unabridged Dictionary provides the following as a first definition of the noun rule: an established guide or regulation for action. This is a good starting point but it needs some elaboration. First, our focus is

BUREAUCRATIC ENCOUNTER: PEPPY AUTO SUPPLY, A NONBUREAUCRATIC ORGANIZATION

Carl R. bought a boat. The used 16-foot bass boat had a motor, a trailer, and even a radar fish finder gizmo. Carl had a four-wheel drive 1997 Jeep Cherokee to pull the boat. Carl had a fishing license and a will to land the big one. Carl had a lake within fifteen minutes drive. The only thing Carl did not have was a trailer hitch. Not having any particular reason to choose one auto supply house over another, Carl picked the one closest to his home, Peppy Auto Supply, a national chain store, large and well-equipped, that had opened just a month ago. Here begins Carl's organizational encounter.

Wednesday, 2 P.M.   Carl walked into the store and was immediately greeted by not one but two employees (let us call them Mr. One and Mr. Two). *[Note: no standard approach to dealing with newly arriving customers].* Even though the store was fairly busy, especially for a weekday, the employees were obviously anxious to help. The problem was that One and Two did not know about the trailer hitches and so referred Carl to Mr. Three (all the employees in this story are Mr.s; maybe that is part of the problem), who happened to be at the back of the store at that time. After Carl had waited for about fifteen minutes, Mr. Three, also cordial and eager to please, was informed by Carl of his interest in purchasing a trailer hitch kit, an electrical kit, a two-inch trailer hitch ball, and having Peppy Auto install it on his Jeep Cherokee. Mr. Three directed Carl to the aisle Carl had found fifteen minutes ago. After looking a good deal in the catalog to match the trailer hitch style to the vehicle, Mr. Three was about ready to give up when Carl pointed out that the list was alphabetized by car manufacturer.

"Ah, yes, here it is," said Mr. Three, "Jeep Wrangler."

"No," Carl said, "it's right below that one, it's a Jeep Cherokee."

"Right," Mr. Three said, and went back to get the hitch. When he came back, Mr. Three and Carl loaded the boxed trailer hitch kit, electrical wiring for a Jeep Cherokee, and a two-inch trailer ball in the shopping cart. Mr. Three then directed Carl to Mr. Four who rang up the sale. "Can I make an appointment here for the installation?" Carl asked. "Please see Mr. Five in our Service Department," Carl was told.

Carl waited in line to speak with Mr. Five who said they don't really take appointments but urged him to bring it in on Saturday, 8 A.M., when Peppy Auto opened. *[Note: no standard for service appointments].* Carl took the shopping cart, loaded the trailer hitch kit, two-inch ball, and electrical wiring in the back of his Jeep Cherokee and took off, looking forward to having his hitch installed on Saturday morning and being on the lake by noon.

Saturday, 8 A.M.   Not wanting to be late, Carl arrived at 7:50 A.M. Walking into the store when it opened, Carl went to the service desk, met Mr. Six, the service manager, presented him with a key, and was told to come back at noon. Four hours seemed a bit long for installation of a trailer hitch. When questioned, Mr. Six confessed that he really had no idea how long it would take to install the hitch or when the mechanics would begin *[Note: no standard to queuing or for service time estimates]*.

Saturday, noon   Not ready.

Saturday, 5 P.M.   Carl finds his Jeep sitting in the Peppy Auto Supply parking lot and goes over to inspect. The trailer hitch is on but has no wiring and no ball. Carl goes in to talk to Mr. Six who says he will find out from Mr. Seven what happened. Mr. Seven tells Carl that the trailer hitch he had purchased was for a Jeep Wrangler, not a Cherokee, but they had taken the liberty of substituting the right one, so things should be okay. "Let's check," says Carl, and Mr. Seven accompanies Carl to the Jeep Cherokee. "There's no ball or electrical kit," Carl says. "I don't know why," Mr. Seven says. "Let me check with Mr. Eight who actually did the installation." Carl is told that Mr. Eight knew nothing about the need to install an electrical kit and a ball. Carl points to the service contract, which includes the installation requirements and Mr. Eight says, "Well, Mr. Six never mentioned that to me, he just said that Mr. Nine had earlier installed the wrong hitch and be sure to install the right one this time." Mr. Seven jokes, "I know how you feel, I brought my own car in today for a brake job. They did a good job of changing my oil, which I just changed a week ago, but didn't touch the brakes." *[Note: no formal requirement for checking the work order before proceeding.]*

Mr. Seven, still good-natured, says, "I'll take care of it myself." Mr. Seven puts on the right two-inch ball, but when he begins on the electrical attachment says, "This isn't the right one and we don't have the one you need in stock. I'll have Mr. Ten special order it and write up the bill." Mr. Seven says to Mr. Ten, "This gentleman had the wrong hitch installed and then we put on the right one, so he needs to be billed for the installation, credited for the hitch he's already paid for, then credit him for the electrical kit, which was the wrong one, and he's already paid for the ball." Mr. Seven then leaves to wait on another customer. Mr. Ten, understandably, seems puzzled. *[Note: no standard for connecting billing changes to billing problem]*. Mr. Ten says, "I'll bill you for the equipment, but you have to go to service to pay for the installation." After about twenty minutes work at the cash register, Mr. Ten gives Carl seven dollars and loose change and apologizes for the inconvenience.

Carl goes to the service desk and looks for the service manager (Mr. Six). Mr. Eleven is at the service desk, but Carl, beginning to catch on, doesn't really want to explain this to him. When the service manager, Mr. Six, returns, he says that installation need not be paid at the service desk and, anyway, the bill has been written up wrong. He takes Carl to talk with Mr. Ten and, after some argument, Mr. Ten rewrites the bill, spending another twenty minutes at the cash register. *[Note: no fixed procedure for handling returned inventory]*. Mr. Ten says, "Now you can pay the clerk on your way out." (Seems Mr. Ten is preoccupied dealing with a very patient lady who earlier in the day brought in

> ### BUREAUCRATIC ENCOUNTER: PEPPY AUTO SUPPLY, A NONBUREAUCRATIC ORGANIZATION (CONTINUED)
>
> her car for an oil change. She returned to find that one of the Peppy Auto mechanics had wrecked her car while driving it in from the parking lot to the garage.)
>
> Carl, thinking he is almost free, goes to the clerk (Mr. Twelve) who finds it almost impossible to make any sense out of the bill. Carl explains three times, once with the help of another customer waiting in line. Finally, the clerk gives Carl a credit for $70. Carl explains, "If you give me a credit for $70, the hitch will be free." "But you returned the hitch," says the clerk, "so I have to give you a credit." "Yes," says Carl, "but one of equal value was installed." "Well, I don't understand," says the clerk, "but if you don't want your $70 then I can't make you take it." It is now 8:00 P.M. Carl leaves, a little wiser, hoping to find some other store that has a light kit for his trailer hitch. Thanks to Peppy Auto Supply, no fish will die today, at least not by Carl's hand.
>
> There are several lessons to be learned from Carl's misfortunes. Lesson one: New organizations present risk for the consumer. Lesson two: The market works perfectly only when the consumer has perfect information about, for example, the quality of management and the inventory of auto suppliers. Lesson three (most important): Personalized attention is not always a good thing, especially when the personalized attention comes from twelve different people. *Formal bureaucratic structures and routines sometimes help!* A lack of routines for dealing with inventory, invoicing, and payment is not the beginning of Carl's trouble (Mr. One started this downward spiral) but could have saved Peppy Auto Supply and Carl a good deal of grief. Empathetic, personalized service does not solve all problems. Sometimes bureaucratic formalization is a good thing!

a bit narrower—formal, organizationally sanctioned rules, not normatively established guidelines. The focus is on three dimensions common to all rules, regulations, and procedures:

1. Behavior requirements
2. Implementation mechanisms
3. Enforcement provisions

Each formal, organizationally sanctioned rule specifies some behavior that is either required or prohibited (prohibition is just another requirement—the requirement to refrain). Requirements may be straightforward, such as "no smoking," or they may be inordinately complex, such as requirements for actions during a nuclear plant accident. In addition to setting behavior requirements, rules tell us when and how and who should implement a behavior. Implementation components of rules tell us, for example, that the no smoking provision applies to all employees at all times when they are in the office building, but that behavior is not regulated when they are on official business but outside the building. Similarly, the rules for nuclear plant accidents will set boundary conditions defining an accident and specify not only the actions to be taken but also the parties responsible for acting.

Since our concern is with formal, organizationally sanctioned rules, an enforcement provision is vital because it distinguishes between formal rules and informal, norm-based guidelines. This is *not* to suggest that informal rules are less important. Many studies (e.g., Roethlisberger and Dickson, 1939; Dubin, 1951) have documented the strength of informal norms and group-based dicta. But one does not associate red tape with informal, norm-based rules.

For purposes of a rule-based theory of red tape, a most important assumption is that a rule (regulation, procedure) is a *social* concept and has no existence without social meaning. This is because rules are all about behavioral requirements. Since a behavioral requirement of a rule is a defining characteristic, and since behavioral requirements are inherently social, it follows that rules themselves are best viewed as social artifacts.

A LANGUAGE OF RULES

Any rule can be viewed as having not only behavioral requirements, implementation mechanisms, and enforcement provisions, but, in addition, *a functional object, persons subject to the rule, a compliance resource requirement, and a rule ecology.*

> *Functional object of a rule:* the officially sanctioned objective of the rule

The functional object of the rule implies nothing about the desirability of the rule. The functional object is simply the behavior the rule seeks to induce or shape. Thus it is possible to achieve the functional object of a bad rule or to achieve the functional object in a highly undesirable way. For example, let us say that the city officials of Metropolis think that the population is growing too fast. They establish single occupancy vehicle (SOV) lanes on all major feeder highways, encouraging more people to drive by themselves and discouraging car pools. This, in turn, increases automobile exhaust pollution to an intolerable level, lowering the quality of life and stemming the growth of the city. This is a case of a (possibly) desirable functional object, controlling growth, but a very bad rule. The question of whether a rule is effective in achieving its functional object says nothing about the desirability of the functional object. Similarly, the desirability of the functional object tells us nothing about the effectiveness of the rules developed to attain it. Bad ends can be obtained efficiently; good ends can be thwarted.

While there is no logical connection between rules' functional objective and the effectiveness of the rules, compliance with rules nonetheless requires some minimal level of shared or symmetrical values. For those interested in ensuring compliance, one of the keys is the strength of the value served by the rule. Compliance may be based on fear of sanctions or others perceptions, a desire to "get ahead," or to receive positive evaluations. But in many cases, one's compliance is based on an interest identical to the functional object of the rule. Thus, even if one is a smoker, one may readily agree not to smoke indoors because one is sympathetic to the functional object of the rule—better air quality in the workplace. Similarly, owners of polluting industrial firms may actually support strong pollution controls, so long as there is a perception that their competitors are subject to the same rules and same levels of enforcement.

A rule is intended to affect the behavior of some specific set of individuals, groups, or organizations. Thus,

> *Subjects to a rule:* those people (individuals, groups, interests, organizations, or other social collectivities) whose behavior the rule seeks to remedy or reinforce

In the example of the no smoking rule, the subjects to the rule are smokers. But usually one can be more precise. If the no smoking rule is enforced at Atlanta-Hartsfield airport, the subjects to the rule are probably smokers working, traveling, or visiting in the airport. In many instances, however, the subjects are not nearly so easy to identify. Thus, for an environmental rule requiring print shops effectively to dispose of non-water soluble inks, the enforcing agency may have limited knowledge about which printers use which type of ink. In many cases, the definition of the subjects to the rule is even more complicated. States wishing to reduce auto emissions soon found out that drivers had no more idea than state officials do as to the performance level of their catalytic converters. Generally, the more specific and unique the rule is in its effects, the more difficult it is to identify precisely the subjects to the rules.

> *Compliance resource requirement:* total resources (time, people, and money) required to comply with a rule

In addition to having a behavioral requirement, all rules entail a compliance resource requirement, even if that requirement is not specified. The compliance resource requirement is the answer to the question:

"What level of resources would be needed to comply with the requirements set by the rule?" This is *not* to say, of course, that the compliance resource requirement is a good approximation of the resources that will, in fact, be marshaled to comply with the rule. From a practical standpoint, making good estimates of the compliance resource requirement is a vital part of making good rules and avoiding red tape. But in many instances, determining compliance resource requirements is a tricky proposition. Thus, when EPA requires all the companies within a given geographic attainment area meet a given standard for Nox emissions, it is almost impossible to get a good estimate of the compliance resource requirement of such a regulation.

As is the case with most social and behavioral concepts, rules-related behaviors can be thought of as having an "ecology." Thus,

> *Rule ecology:* that part of the social and physical environment that impinges upon compliance and upon the rule's effects

Rules do not exist in a vacuum. They are affected not only by external social events but also by changes in the physical world. The relevant examples are endless. Let us revisit some examples given earlier. If a literally smokeless cigarette were developed and adopted universally, the smoking rules at Atlanta-Hartsfield airport would likely be affected. This is an example of a *technological change* within the rule ecology. Similarly, the rule might change if a strong smokers union emerged and effective boycotts were implemented against organizations with nonsmoking rules. This is an example of a *socio-political change* affecting a rule.

In the case of emission standards for catalytic converters, the rule ecology might change in a great many ways. Some possibilities include the following: (1) new information emerging about the costs of bringing converters up to standard; (2) further development of solar or electrical vehicles; (3) rising (or declining) use of mass transit; (4) motorists rising up in protest, writing elective representatives about the annoyance of complying with auto inspection rules; (5) lack of service stations and garages willing to undertake inspections; (6) new scientific evidence about the effectiveness of converters; (7) the outbreak of World War III. These illustrations give some indication of the complexity of rule ecologies. The effectiveness of rules depends on a great many factors outside the sometimes simple behavior modification sphere of the rule. Technology, political action, available resources, knowledge, social change, and even world events can affect the outcomes of rules. Even the World War III example is not facetious, but rather a reminder that some changes are so dramatic as to affect most of a society's ways of doing business. During wars, depressions, and natural disasters, people are wont to say "all the rules have changed." This has both symbolic and literal meaning.

ASSESSING THE EFFECTS OF RULES: RED TAPE AND COMPLIANCE

If we view formalization as "the extent to which rules, procedures, instructions and communications are written" (Pugh, et al., 1968: 75), then an organization with twenty rules, eighteen of which are formal and two of which are informal, is highly formalized. By the same token, an organization with 200,000 rules, half formal, half informal, is not highly formalized. Obviously, it is not just the balance of formal to informal rules that affects behavior; the sheer number of rules can have independent effects on the organization's culture and members' and stakeholders' behaviors. This simple distinction is captured in the concept *rule sum.*

> *Rule sum:* the total number of written rules, regulations, and procedures in force for an organization

Note that the definition is for rules "in force." Often there are rules and procedures within an organization that no one obeys because no one is aware of them. Perhaps they have been lost in antiquity or, in some instances, there are simply so many rules that the sheer number defies human efforts to ingest information.

It is also important to note that rule sum does not make a distinction as to the source of the rules. In some cases external actors may impose the rules affecting an organization. Thus, when the U.S. Office of Management and Budget develops a new rule about how federal contractors must account for indirect costs (overhead) on federal contracts, the *rule source* is external. Other rules originate entirely within the organization. Thus, if an organization decides on its own to adopt flexible working hours and to change its work-time accounting rules accordingly, the rule source is internal. In many cases, though, it is not so clear-cut. Returning to the first example, a federal contractor may decide to change to more stringent accounting rules because it suspects that the new OMB guidelines will make it more likely that the organization will be audited. In that case the rules are not directly responsive to an external federal mandate but are internally imposed rules anticipating (perhaps accurately, perhaps not) possible external changes.

Rule sum captures the number of rules, regulations, and procedures affecting an organization; formalization tells us, regardless of the *number* of rules, the percentage of expected behaviors actually codified. However, it is rarely just the number of rules or the level of formalization that causes problems for the organization. The full impact of rules cannot be adequately determined without knowing something about the resources and energy required to comply with the rule (Foster and Jones, 1978; Foster, 1990). A new set of federal guidelines on sponsored research accounting might well have a quite different impact on, say, a small consulting firm with a single accountant than on a major university employing thirty accountants and financial managers. Thus, it is useful to distinguish between the amount of rules (rules sum) and the resources required to comply with them.

Compliance burden: total resources actually expended in complying with a rule

Compliance burden is, roughly speaking, a direct "cost" of a rule. Compliance burden is *not* the full cost of a rule. To calculate the full cost of an implemented rule one would need to know the sum of compliance burden, implementation burden, the cost of rule formulation, and the opportunity costs. Nor is compliance burden the amount of resources *required* to meet the rule, but the amount the complying organizations actually *expends*.

People or organizations seeking to comply with rules may expend either more or less resources than are actually needed to meet the rule. In complying with a rule, why would anyone spend *more* money than actually required? In some instances, more resources may be spent because the complying individual or organization favors the functional objective of the rule; thus, a sort of voluntary contribution. In still other cases, extra expenditure of resources might be to achieve some personal object of the rule. For example, a recently chastised firm might spend more resources on environmental clean up than required simply because it wishes to take out advertisements trumpeting the firm's good works. The favorable publicity may boost sales.

In some cases, overcompliance (or undercompliance) is a matter of poor prediction. One of the themes developed throughout this book is that *rules are predictions of human behavior and often go awry because of human indeterminacy.* In creating and implementing a rule we are saying, in effect, "If a rule requires behavior x, under conditions j (or holding conditions constant), the result will be outcome y." All rules entail behavior assumptions and predictions. Sometimes the rules are very simple and the predictions simple. But the more complicated the behaviors required and the more complex the assumptions, the more likely our implicit predictions will fail. Assessing compliance burden is only one of many crucial issues relating to the fact that rules predict behavior. The effectiveness of rules and the red tape generated from rules both relate to the predictive character of rules. In later chapters we return to this crucial issue.

Rules entail not only a compliance burden but, in most instances, an implementation burden. There are some rules that are self-implementing, but most entail at least some level of energy and resources, even if nothing more than posting a sign. In many instances, the implementation burden and compliance burdens are born by different organizations. Thus, when a state environmental agency regulates, the agency may bear an implementation burden, while the regulated business may bear the compliance burden.

> *Implementation burden:* total resources actually expended in implementing a rule

The implementation burden may have even more impact on bureaucratic behavior than the compliance burden. In an experimental study of bureaucratic discretion and control flowing from rules, Scott (1994) found that subjects who were making decisions about simulated welfare cases were much more affected by the intensity of the rules (his term for compliance burden) than by the number or percentage of formal rules. The rule implementers were willing to substitute their discretion for organizational rules when it was relatively easy (from a rule compliance standpoint) to do so and were much less likely to use discretion when the compliance burden increased.

RULE DENSITY AND RULE INCIDENCE

From the perspective of the managers of organizations, the critical issue often is not the compliance burden associated with any particular set of rules and regulations, but the compliance burden required for all the rules, regulations, and procedures to which the organization is subject. While regulators tend to think only about the rules they impose, managers think about the resources they can bring to rule compliance in general. Whether the rule is from OSHA or EPA may make little difference and, indeed, managers may not even know the origin of some rules. The concept of *rule density* relates to this issue of aggregate rules and the resources required.

> *Rule density:* total resources devoted by the organization to complying (i.e., compliance burden) with all its rules (i.e., its rule sum), as a percentage of total resources available to the organization

Using rule density and compliance burden concepts helps in thinking about the implications of bureaucratization for management theory. Figure 4-1 depicts the relationships among total organizational resources and total compliance burden with differing rule densities calculated from a line dividing the X axis (total resources) and Y axis (total compliance burden). If one takes total resources as a reflection of the volume and "energy" of organizational activities, one can consider the implications of combinations of total resources ("energy level") and total compliance burden ("bureaucratization level").

The chief lesson of the model depicted in Figure 4-1 is that each organization has a finite set of resources which can, in principle, be used in a number of different ways. These resources are the organization's

FIGURE 4-1   RULE DENSITY TYPOLOGY

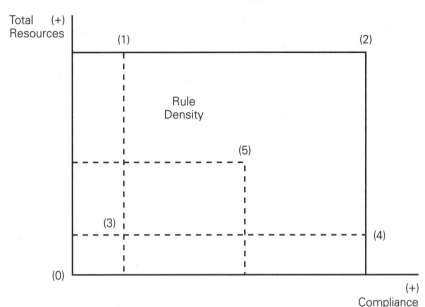

1 = High Energy/Low Bureaucratic
2 = High Energy/High Bureaucratic
3 = Low Energy/Low Bureaucratic
4 = Low Energy/High Bureaucratic
5 = Medium Energy/Medium Bureaucratic

Source: From Barry Bozeman, "A Theory of Government Red Tape," *Journal of Public Administration Research and Theory* 3, 3 (1993). Reprinted by permission of Transaction Publishers. Copyright © 1993 by Transaction Publishers; all rights reserved.

energy. Just as the human body consumes resources and uses calories (burns energy), organizations use their resources and burn energy. If a high percentage of the organization's energy is devoted to complying with rules, less is available for achieving other tasks.

We can speculate about the implications of the organization types corresponding to the various levels of energy and compliance (the legend under Figure 4-1). Thus, a high energy/low compliance organization likely has few external controls. This is not inherently good or bad. The extent of control should depend on the nature of the organization's missions and its interdependence with other organizations. Similarly, we can speculate that a low energy/high compliance organization is the classic overworked, overcontrolled bureaucracy. It has relatively few resources but many formal demands put on it. The general point is that considering the organization's energy level compared to its compliance requirements can give us some insight into its ability to take on new tasks and its potential for change.

RESEARCH ENCOUNTER: COMPLIANCE RESOURCES REQUIREMENTS VERSUS COMPLIANCE BURDEN

Rules require a given level of resources for compliance, but that does not mean that the needed resources will be actually be expended. Rules may be ignored entirely or organizations may comply only in part. In some instances rules are ignored because the organization is unaware of them. This is particularly likely with small organizations subject to a large number of externally imposed rules. Let us consider an example. Several years ago, Syracuse University researchers were asked to do a study of hazardous waste policy compliance for the New Jersey Hazardous Waste Citing Commission (Bozeman, Deyle, and O'Leary, 1987). New Jersey state officials felt that large firms were generally in compliance with state requirements (and when they were not it was often possible to determine noncompliance). However, they were less confident that so-called small quantity generators were in compliance with state regulations. The Syracuse team's task was to determine the degree of compliance among firms classified as small quantity generators. Small quantity generators include, for example, gas stations, printers, dry cleaners, and automobile body and paint shops. Analysis revealed that the quantities of dry cleaning chemicals, automobile batteries, printer's ink, and such produced by the small quantity generators added up to worrisome levels. Moreover, the great majority were unfamiliar with more than a small fraction of the state hazardous waste regulations.

The compliance problem was straightforward, but not easily remedied. Many of the small quantity generator firms had as few as three or four employees. Even though a knowledge of the regulations was in their self-interest (fines being substantial), the small companies had insufficient time and personnel to seek out and understand the many regulations to which they were subject. From the regulator's standpoint, there were too many small quantity generators, and too few state environmental agency officials, to permit frequent, easy, and adequate communication between the environmental bureaucracy and the thousands of small quantity generators. The *behavior requirements* were high, the *compliance resources* requirements were high, the *implementation burden* was (potentially) high, but the *compliance burden* was low. Most companies were simply unaware of the rules. There was little burden because there was little compliance.

A final consideration is rule incidence: the persons affected by a rule. In public finance and taxation, an important issue, in addition to the amount of a tax, is exactly who ends up paying it. Rule "incidence" is a similar concept. It is the number and types of persons who "pay" for the rule by complying with it, enforcing it, expending resources it requires.

Rule incidence: the number and types of persons affected by a rule, regulation, or procedure

Regardless of the potential importance of the propositions about under- and overcontrol, rule density, or rule incidence, these issues are *not* issues of red tape. Red tape occurs not because of the number of rules but when rules consume resources and fail to achieve objectives.

BUREAUCRATIC PATHOLOGY: RED TAPE CONCEPTS

If compliance burden is, roughly speaking, the direct cost of a rule, *rule efficacy* is the direct "benefit" of a rule. As is the case with compliance cost, there may be impacts that are not direct. Often rules provide benefits to some purpose other than the functional object of the rule. For example, fuel economy rules tend to have not only energy savings benefits but the reduction of harmful emissions.

Rule efficacy: the extent to which a given rule addresses effectively the functional object for which it was designed

This definition of the benefit of rules is not one enabling much precision. Many rules have an extremely murky functional object. Certainly, there is no requirement that the functional object be clear-cut or universally agreed upon. Indeed, it is often the case that the functional object is open to diverse interpretations. The classic example of an ambiguous rule in the public sector is the injunction to "rule in public interest." More than a few regulatory statutes include broad language instructing regulators to act in the public interest. Walter Lippman (1955: 4) defined the public interest as what we would choose if we "saw clearly, thought rationally, and acted disinterestedly and benevolently"—a stringent set of requirements. In most cases, however, the functional object of the rule is more concrete than that.

Usually, measuring rule efficacy presents problems. Generally, the simpler the rule, its ecology, and its functional object, the easier it is to measure rule efficacy. Back to our recurring example: If we develop a no smoking rule, put up a sign implementing the rule, and then measure incidence of smoking (or, alternatively, air quality) before and after the rule implementation, we can probably get a satisfactory index of rule efficacy. Sure, it is possible that a convention of nonsmoking Mormons will come through the airport and confound the results a bit, but the before-after measure would probably be useful nonetheless. Most cases aren't so simple. Consider the case of the state-mandated inspections of automobile catalytic converters (see pages 74–75). The functional object of the rule is enhanced air quality. But so many factors can affect air quality that any attempt to evaluate results by tracking ambient air quality is unlikely to shed much light on the effectiveness of the inspections. Nor do we know much from the number of inspections or even the number of inspections failed. Such factors as variance in the stringency of the inspection and garage owners' profit-motivated "false positives" come into play. Even if we were able to come up with an entirely satisfactory measure of rule efficacy, the determination of the compliance burden of state-mandated inspections is inordinately complicated. For example, how does one value the literally thousands of hours citizens devote to inspections, hours that would have otherwise been devoted to leisure and work?

The red tape concept does not take a rigid cost-benefit perspective on rules. It is, in some circumstances, useful to think of red tape as rules with net negative cost-benefit ratios. But given the enormity of measurement problems and the ubiquity of rules that are truly odious and provide no benefit, the concept of red tape presented here is extremely conservative—rules with *no* benefit.

RED TAPE DEFINED: "NO REDEEMING SOCIAL VALUE"

Two red tape concepts are presented here; each has some range of utility. One definition, *organizational red tape*, assumes that effects are unitary. The other, *stakeholder red tape*, assumes that a rule may be red tape for one set of stakeholders, but functional for another. The theory developed here is based on two definitions of red tape—one an authority-based definition and centering on the organization implementing the rule, the other stakeholder-based.

> *Organizational red tape:* A rule that remains in force and entails a compliance burden for the organization but makes no contribution to achieving the rule's functional object

This red tape concept has the advantage, an important one, of not viewing the amount of rules as identical to red tape, thus dispensing with the confusing notion of "good" red tape. A central assumption in the organizational red tape concept, one that should be made explicit, is that it is contingent on the relationship of the rule to the functional object. The functional object is defined in terms of an authoritative, official statement of purpose. That official statement can come from the organization or an authoritative controller of the organization (e.g., a parent organization, a superordinate government bureau, and a legislative or judicial body). But each formal rule has a formal statement of purpose.

A potential drawback of the authority-based definition of red tape is that it fails to note that rules can have very different meanings and impacts for different stakeholders. Thus, what may seem to an organizational client or customer to be useless red tape may seem to a manager an important work-processing rule.

In some cases, there are analytical and practical advantages to viewing red tape as subject-dependent. Thus, a second definition of red tape, a subject-dependent concept, focuses on stakeholders.

> *Stakeholder red tape:* A rule that remains in force and entails a compliance burden, but serves no objective valued by a given stakeholder group

WHICH CONCEPT?

From the standpoint of research, the organizational red tape concept is more practical. It is less complex, it is based on a formal statement of the purpose of the rule, and it is more amenable to measurement. Stakeholder red tape is particularly useful when analyzing coalitions of interests in organizations or when the focus is not on the organization as unit of analysis. But stakeholder red tape leads quickly to complexity, often so much complexity that explanations of rules' impacts become almost impossible. Given the central premise that human indeterminacy and unpredictability are among the most important issues in assessing the effects of rules, we can see the virtual impossibility of predicting outcomes for diverse sets of stakeholders. But if stakeholder red tape is not the easy concept, it has some value as an ideal construct.

Revisiting Waldo's (1946: 399) view that "one man's red tape is another man's system," one might well conclude that stakeholder red tape has more face validity than organizational red tape. But the more stakeholders, the greater the problems in sorting out stakeholder red tape. In a government organization, one might expect at least the following stakeholder types:

- Parent agency
- Political superiors (e.g., Congress)
- Central management agencies (e.g., Office of Management and Budget)
- Interorganizational partners (both public and private sector)
- Clients and clientele groups
- Intraorganizational coalitions

A rule that is red tape for one group within a category may not be red tape even for another group in that same category. Thus, the category "intraorganizational coalitions" may include such diverse sets as the psychologists in the personnel department, the cohort of younger middle managers, and employees interested in innovation and change. Each of

TABLE 4-1   RULES AND THEIR CONSEQUENCES—ORGANIZING THE CONCEPTS

WHAT?	HOW MUCH?	WHO?	TO WHAT EFFECT?
Rules a) Behavior requirements	Compliance Burden	Rule Incidence	Rule Efficacy
b) Implementation mechanisms	Implementation Burden	Rule Ecology	Rule Density
c) Enforcement provisions			Red Tape
Functional Object of Rule			

these coalitions may have unique sets of values and different functional objects to be served (or not served) by the organization's rules and procedures. What this means, from the standpoint of researching red tape, is that comprehensive and valid measurement of a stakeholder concept of red tape is inevitably a prodigious task, so much so that organizational red tape may well be the better hope for developing researchable constructs. In the remainder of this book, the term *red tape* refers to organizational red tape.

Since the concepts presented in this chapter are in some cases new ones, some relationship to simple questions may be useful. Table 4-1 organizes several of the most important concepts according to the questions they address with respect to rules and their effects: "What," "How Much," "Who," and "To What Effect?" Armed with a set of concepts that allow us to discuss rules, red tape, and their components and consequences, we turn in the next chapter to the primary concern of this book—the *causes* of red tape.

CONCLUSION

Organization theory uses terms in so many different ways that it sometimes seems that up is down and left just another word for right. But in this book, when we use the term red tape the meaning will not be far removed from the ways in which people normally talk about it. Red tape is bad. It is not an aid to accountability or a means of ensuring participation. Rules that appropriately hold organizations accountable may not be popular with the people constrained by them but they are not red tape. Nor is red tape the same has having a great many rules. The amount of rules is formalization and the level of formalization may tell us little or nothing about the amount of red tape. Many rules do not imply effective rules. Few rules do not imply effective rules.

An important subtext, one developed further in later chapters, is that the number of formal rules needed in one type of organization may be quite different than is needed in another type. Some organizations require few rules and need to maintain a high level of autonomy to further their mission. Organizations that prize creativity and innovation may need few rules. Some organizations may be "self-regulating" if there are strong professional norms followed and those norms are compatible with the organization's mission. Other organizations need extensive rules. This is likely the case, for example, with organizations charged with providing specifically mandated services on an equitable and standard basis. Thus, in assessing whether organizations' rules are red tape or not, the judgment cannot be made apart from a knowledge of the objectives the rules seek to serve. Rules that are observed but that do not further the objective qualify as red tape. The fact that we do not like particular rules does not qualify them as red tape. The fact that we dislike the objective the rule serves does not qualify the rule as red tape. Red tape is a pathology, one involving the waste of resources. The waste of resources in complying with red tape pertains not to bureaucratic requirements and controls but to the formulation and implementation of rules that, for one reason or another, do not work.

Why would anyone formulate rules that do not work? Would even the most misanthropic bureaucrat make work for others to no purpose? The next two chapters deal with one of the most intriguing mysteries of organization theory—how good purposes are dashed.

Before turning to the causes of red tape, we should make note of the glossary at the end of the book. This chapter presents many new terms. This focus on developing a language to talk about red tape and bureaucratic pathologies may seem a bit taxing. But there is a need for greater precision in talking about bureaucratic problems. Without some more precise terminology we tend to mix together all our dissatisfactions with organizations and management in ways that make it difficult to get to the bottom of problems.

RULES "BORN BAD": RULE-INCEPTION RED TAPE

Red tape only seems an act of sabotage. In most cases, the worst organizational outcomes spring from the best intentions. How do rules, regulations, and procedures crafted to further organizational objectives end up as red tape?

Some rules are "born bad." They are red tape right from the start. Some rules that were once functional transform into red tape: "good rules gone bad." In this chapter we distinguish between *rule-inception* red tape and *rule-evolved* red tape. Rule-inception red tape refers to rules that are red tape at their very beginning. Rule-evolved red tape is red tape that occurs as once useful rules become less useful, either because of changes in the need for the rule or changes in the execution of the rule. The focus in this chapter is rule-inception red tape.

RULE-INCEPTION RED TAPE

Rules begin as red tape if, at their origin, they meet the requirement specified in Chapter 4—having a compliance burden while not addressing a legitimate, official purpose (functional object). The question leaping out is: "Why would *anyone* establish a rule serving no useful purpose?" Yes, this is a puzzle, but a puzzle one may solve with just a bit of reflection.

In the first place, the red tape criterion focuses on legitimacy in socially or organizationally sanctioned objectives. Many rules are created by people who do not have in mind the best interests of society, an institution, or an organization. Self-serving rules are not easy to establish in the full light of day, but are much easier to develop in relative obscurity. Often rules are cloaked in symbols or apparently pure motives to hide self-serving origins. No one actually says "here is a rule we shall observe because it will enhance my power," but, nonetheless, many rules serve only a self-aggrandizing function.

While one should never underestimate venality as a cause of bad rules, it seems likely that most rules, even ones that are bad rules at the outset, do not originate from narrow self-interest but from failed attempts to serve the collective interest. In all likelihood, the red tape and inefficiency occurring as a result of self-serving rules is much less than the red tape created to forestall self-serving behaviors. No less a bureaucrat (and politician) than Elliot Richardson, former attorney general, notes that "the critics need to be reminded that much of what they dislike most about government—the complicated regulations, the red tape, the costly layers of supervisors—is the direct consequence of distrust in government" (Richardson, 1996: 27). This echoes Kaufman's (1977: 59) conclusion that the combination of distrust and democracy causes "the profusion of constraints and unwieldiness of the procedures which afflict us."

Instances of rule-inception red tape are many, but the causes relatively few. The following is a categorization of causes:

1. *Incorrect rule forecasts*: Rule-makers' assumptions about the relation of means to ends turn out wrong.
2. *Illegitimate functions*: Rules are self-serving and do not promote a legitimate, sanctioned purpose.
3. *Negative sum compromise*: Rules are a compromise, serving more than one objective, none well.
4. *Overcontrol*: Rules established for managerial control and accountability impose so much control that the business of the organization and its clients is impeded.
5. *Negative sum process:* The adage "you can never have too much democracy" proves wrong; process gets in the way of accomplishing core objectives.

INCORRECT RULE FORECASTS

Many dysfunctional rules have their origins in misunderstanding of the relation between means and ends. In a great many instances the reason for the inefficacy of rules is simple—persons designing the rules have insufficient understanding of the problem at hand, the relationship of the rule to the perceived problem, or others' likely application or response to the rule. The fact that this occurs so often should not surprise anyone; forecasting human behavior is inordinately complex.

Every rule contains, implicitly or explicitly, a forecast about human behavior: "If we implement Rule X, Behavior Y will occur." At the time of origin, there is only a forecast, not a proof, because there is no valid, in-context evidence. The fact that the rule worked a certain way in another organization may be useful supporting evidence but not a valid test of the forecast. The implementation of the rule provides, in a sense, a test of the forecast. Considering the hazards and inherent uncertainties of forecasting (Helmer and Rescher, 1959), it should come as no surprise that rule forecasts are often proved wrong.

Some rules entail easily understood patterns of causation and, thus, apparently less risky rule forecasts. Let us say, for example, that an organization located in a dense urban area wishes to help reduce traffic congestion. Among possible options: changing work hours to nonstandard ones. The causal reasoning would be simple enough:

1. Workers cause traffic congestion arriving and leaving at the same time.
2. Our workers will be required to arrive and leave at a different time than others.
3. Therefore, traffic congestion will be reduced.

Acting on this reasoning, the organization might develop a rule requiring half of its employees to arrive at 10:30 A.M. and depart at 6:30 P.M. Now let us use some of the concepts developed thus far to analyze the rule. The *functional object* of the rule is reduction of traffic congestion. The *rule forecast* is that changing arrival and departure hours will decrease congestion. The *compliance burden* might include, among other possibilities, the inconveniences born by the employees and the problems of coordinating work activities among employees arriving and leaving at different times. The rule is judged *red tape* if it does not accomplish the functional object. If it accomplishes the functional object it may or may not be a "good rule," but it is not red tape. How might it be a "bad rule" but not red tape? One possibility would be that the coordination costs entailed from employees arriving at different times prove enormous. Thus, the functional object is served—reducing traffic congestion—but at too high a price.

Even in this relatively simple example, the rule forecast might prove wrong. Perhaps the change in work hours would mean that fewer employees would use public transportation because its scheduling focuses only on rush hours. Or the mixing up of employees' work hours might cause the break-up of car pools. The point is that all rule forecasts, even seemingly simple ones, involve uncertainty and thus susceptibility to incorrect rule forecasts (Reason, 1990). In many instances the causal assumptions underlying a rule forecast are extremely complicated (Kerwin and Furlong, 1992), especially in cases where there are numerous spillover effects and unanticipated consequences pertaining to the rule's functional object. Doubtless, much red tape results from incorrect rule forecasts and the failure to adjust the rules in the face of contravening evidence.

Incremental learning, perhaps public administration's most significant contribution to theory (e.g., Simon, 1957; March and Simon, 1958; Lindblom, 1959), is often ignored in rule making and implementation. Decades ago, March and Simon (1958: 141) provided a metaphor to compare "optimal" decision-making to "satisficing," the difference between "searching a haystack to find the *sharpest* needle in it and searching the haystack to find a needle sharp enough to sew with it." But for the most part, March and Simon were focusing on decisions and actions taken within single organizations. Implementing a set of rules at one level of government (e.g., federal) to be diffused throughout the scores of agencies at another level (e.g., state) and having an impact on millions of citizens, is more akin to searching for the sharpest needle at the bottom of the ocean. Without a compass, some metal detectors, and a willingness to listen to orientation readings, there's not much chance that it will be found.

It is not particularly difficult to envision the factors likely to lead to incorrect rules forecasts. The most important issues have to do with the complexity and interdependence of the forecasts and the extent to which redundancy and "back up" are built in. If the desired outcomes can be achieved even when some predictions turn out incorrect or when some systems fail, then the likelihood of red tape occurring from incorrect rules forecasts is reduced. Interestingly, the study of redundancy in high reliability systems may have something to teach us about promulgating effective bureaucratic rules. LaPorte and colleagues' studies of high reliability organizations, such as air traffic controllers and nuclear power plants, provide lessons about predicting organizational outcomes in "tightly coupled" organizations and missions with little margin for error (LaPorte and Consolini, 1991; LaPorte and Thomas, 1990). LaPorte and Consolini (1991: 28) observe that high reliability organizations must be "alert to surprises or lapses that could result in errors small or large that could cascade into major system failures from which there may be no recovery." This is not so different from large-scale implementation of regulatory rules—the ability to expect *and accommodate* surprises is equally critical for insuring that rational plans for systems of bureaucratic rules do not go awry once implemented in the messy real world.

ILLEGITIMATE FUNCTIONS

Rules should serve a legitimate, organizationally or politically sanctioned functional object (depending on whether the organization is public or private). In the public sector, the organization (agency) is not the sole provider or arbiter of legitimacy. Superior executive agencies, legislative bodies, and judicial authorities and, ultimately, the electorate determine legitimacy. In the private sector the case is not as different as it might seem, as private firms are subject to public laws. Indeed, the legitimacy of corporations owes much to the state and its licensing and chartering procedures. Business organizations with high degrees of "publicness," external control, and constraint by political authorities (Bozeman, 1987), must look not only to themselves and to stockholders as sources of legitimacy. Thus, while the sources of legitimacy do vary considerably between public and private sector, they are not wholly different. Nevertheless, it is accurate to say that, in general, legitimacy is internal and organizational with private firms but external and extra-organizational with government firms.

Regardless of the *source* of legitimacy, a rule serving an individual's or group's self-interest, but no legitimate function for the organization, qualifies as red tape. There is a compliance burden produced, but no legitimate functional objective is served—the definition of red tape used here. Thus, if an employee in the accounting division sets a rule requiring additional reporting on travel reimbursement forms for the unsanctioned purpose of expanding his or her knowledge base and organizational power, the result is, by definition, red tape.

The problem presented by illegitimate functions red tape is determining "legitimacy." *Defining* legitimacy is not so difficult (see Gawthrop, 1969; Bozeman, 1987), but, except in the easiest cases, such as illegal acts, *measuring* legitimacy presents problems. If one breaks the law there is usually no difficulty determining illegitimacy. But generally determinations of legitimacy are much more complicated. Motivation often poses difficulties. Official actions are often cloaked in legitimacy while serving illegitimate functions. High-minded rhetoric often accompanies self-serving deeds. But how do we know? How do we judge legitimacy when entangled in motive?

Negative Sum Compromise

Decisions about rules often reflect compromise. In some instances a rule may be established that serves so many diverse objectives that a considerable compliance burden is sustained but none of the objectives is achieved. Rule-makers seek to do too much and end up doing little or nothing. Often rules built on overly elaborate compromise serve too many masters. One recalls the old saw about an elephant being a horse put together by a committee.

It is easy enough to think of examples of large-scale public policies to illustrate negative sum compromise. More than a few of the laws

---

BUREAUCRATIC ENCOUNTER:
MOTIVE AND LEGITIMACY IN POSTAL RULES

To illustrate the complexities of sorting through motive, and the relation of motive to illegitimacy in rules, let us consider a dispute between the U.S. Postal Service and the Postal Rate Commission (McAllister, 1993). Upon assuming the postmaster general position, one of Marvin Runyon's highest priorities included getting rid of overly complex regulations and unnecessary rules. This goal certainly seems inconsistent with a set of procedures released concerning visits by postal rate commissioners to U.S. Post Office facilities.

The Postal Rate Commission is an independent board that regulates various aspects of the Postal Service, most importantly the price of postage. At some points the relationship between the Postal Service and the Postal Rate Commission has been a bit rocky and, during Runyon's term, it was rockier than usual.

Runyon set forth guidelines, some six pages of guidelines, mandating just how and when the members of the Postal Rate Commission and their staff may visit postal facilities. One rule required written permission for visits, another prohibited video taping and photographing during the visits. One even forbade commissioners asking questions of postal employees. The commissioners were irate. Commissioner John Cruthcer wrote a letter to the *Washington Post* complaining that the new rules "appear to me to be a thinly veiled effort to control our access to operational knowledge, or worse than that, thought control" (McAllister, 1993: A-15). Shortly thereafter, Mary Elcano, the Postal Service's top lawyer, wrote a letter to the chair of the Postal Rate Commission, George Haley, assuring him that the new rules were part of "an affirmative program to make tours available to the commission." The thrust of the rules, according to another postal official, was to ensure that there was no unauthorized contact between the Postal Service and the Rate Commission during periods in which there were on-going postal rate proceedings.

The rules and procedures in the Postal Service example might well be interpreted as serving no other function than allowing the postmaster general to vent his ire—an illegitimate function and abuse of authority. *Or* the rules might be a conscientious effort to help define the proper boundaries between the regulator and the regulated and, thereby, to increase confidence in the propriety of regulatory proceedings. Whatever one feels about the case (and there may be interpretations beyond these two), the issue really boils down to the postmaster general's *motives* in the regulation. Sometimes the line between vindictiveness and proper delimiting procedures is not just thin, it is as invisible as one's state of mind.

---

passed each year by the U.S. Congress seek to serve too many interests. But let us consider an example within the realm of the regulatory bureaucracy. In many instances, energy policy, environmental policy, and economic development policy are hard to disentangle. Some state government agencies have simultaneous responsibilities in the three policy arenas. Let us assume that a state government energy agency is interested in stimulating the industrialized (prefabricated) housing market in order to promote energy efficiency. One finds quickly that there are significant and often unpredictable spillovers in the areas of pollution and economic development policy. While most industrialized housing currently available represents great energy efficiency improvements over the exiting housing stock, many of these energy savings are due to the fact that the houses are well sealed. Another way of saying "well sealed" is "poor ventilation" (Bayer, 1990). The result is that prefabricated buildings are especially prone to so-called "sick building syndrome" (Kriess, 1993). The public manager's task, in such an instance, is to set standards for industrialized housing that will, at the same time, take advantage of energy savings and provide for adequate ventilation at a cost that will permit the industry to develop and be competitive with stick-built homes. Thus, at least three conflicting cardinal values must be juggled—energy efficiency, ventilation, and construction and materials cost. Not surprisingly, regulations serving multiple, conflicting values often result in the realization of none. In such cases, rules expand with no objective served and, thus, red tape emerges from combined good intentions.

NEGATIVE SUM PROCESS

In many organizations, unmitigated faith in participation and out-of-control "democracy" becomes a source of red tape. Not only is there an attempt to make sure that all relevant parties participate, but those who have nothing to add and who wish to be left out are, through formal rules and procedures, required to participate. Thus, rules that enhance process can take the value of participation to such an extreme that it serves no purpose.

Gordon Kingsley (1998) notes another source of negative sum process, one aiming less at democratization than sheltering the organization from political enemies. Kingsley conducted research in a state agency whose chief mission is funding research and development projects. The agency had important political enemies in the state legislature. The director of the agency, a savvy politician himself, took steps to protect the agency, mandating extensive procedural controls on new project approval. This guaranteed that program managers would not unilaterally approve projects that would draw fire from the legislature. The tactic seemed to work, but at a cost. One of the program managers interviewed by Kingsley reported on the downside of an effective political strategy (paraphrased below):

> All these new procedures for approving projects have gotten the politicians off our back. There was a time when we weren't sure what might offend some legislator. Some lowly project manager could

---

BUREAUCRATIC ENCOUNTER: HOW MANY PH.D.S DOES IT TAKE TO FILL A VENDING MACHINE?

University faculties are a great place to look for negative sum process. Donald Z. is a professor on the faculty of the public affairs program of Midwestern University. It is a high quality program with a good reputation but it is also generally viewed as one of those relaxed environments where there are many smart, able people who seem not to produce much research, even with low teaching loads. According to Donald Z., who recently joined the faculty of Midwestern University, the explanation may lie in negative sum process.

He described the situation as follows (this is a paraphrase of an actual conversation):

> When our new department chair arrived we were excited about the fact that she was committed to participative governance. Now we would be pleased to have a little more benevolent dictatorship, maybe even malevolent dictatorship. Nothing gets done here without a meeting, a plan or policy, a vote, and usually multiple votes. If we wanted to put Snickers bars in the vending machines and take out the Milky Ways, we would set up a committee, develop a departmental snack replacement policy, and have a vote. We have committees for everything, but the committees don't have any authority. The whole faculty considers every little point that comes up, including ones that some of us don't care about at all. Not having tenure and being about fifty years away from retirement, I really don't want to be involved in setting the rules for awarding of professor emeritus designation. When I'm not teaching I need to be off doing research. But I go to meeting after meeting all week. Most are silly. Still, I feel that I have to go. Most of the people on this faculty here are super friendly and might think I was a jerk if I didn't show up for meetings. Also, they're going to be voting on my tenure. The fact that most of them aren't very productive doesn't stop them from voting against others who produce as little as they do.

Naturally, others may have a different perception of the circumstances and a more positive view of the meetings. But the point is that participative management, implemented thoughtlessly and ending up with pointless rules, can lead to "participative" red tape.

approve a project that would for some silly reason, like a poorly thought out project title, get political bigwigs all riled up. Now we have them in our tent. But it has sure come at a high cost. There used to be a day when I could walk into this place on Monday, talk directly to my boss, and have a research project approved by Friday. I also had the authority to make changes to the contract when I thought it was in the best interest of the project. Now it takes an average of nine months to get a project approved going through innumerable internal and external review boards. And maybe I have the authority to buy doughnuts in the morning and change the coffee filter.

AUTOCRACY AND PARTICIPATORY RED TAPE AS A TRADE-OFF

When it comes to participative procedures and the rules flowing from them, organizations and clients sometimes choke on too much of a good thing. But how does one set the proper balance? When do participative procedures become red tape? The simple answer is that participative procedures become red tape when no organizational value is served but there is a compliance burden. The key to the balance issue is knowing when legitimate organizational values are no longer being served and, in turn, the key to this knowledge is a good understanding of the values. Some might argue that participation is an end in itself, but this is a dicey position. Participation is a value-without-limit only so long as one ignores the costs of foregone opportunities. If one values time for activities other than participation (and, of course, everyone does), then participation must be set against those other values. Participation serves many values, including a more harmonious work place (Angle and Perry, 1981), improved information for decision-making (Coursey and Bozeman, 1990), "buy-in" for the implementation of decisions (Nutt, 1984), and greater satisfaction with one's work (Cherniss and Kane, 1987). But *how much* participation is needed to achieve these and other important values varies according to the organization, its functions, the decision context, organizational history and culture, and even the individual. Nevertheless, certain simple diagnostics can be suggested to help determine "how much is enough participation?" First, if a large percentage of potential participants are passing up opportunities to participate, there may be too many opportunities. When attendance at democratic meetings begins to decline, negative sum process may be the culprit. Second, persons who, in the sign-off line (i.e., individuals needed to approve new rules or decisions), begin to take their time in signing off or to show limited knowledge or interest in the contemplated rules or actions, one suspects negative sum process. Third, when a significant percentage of an organization's rules are *about* rules and rule making, there is greater hazard for negative sum process.

OVERCONTROL

The most common source of rule-inception red tape, overcontrol may be the most difficult source of red tape to weed out. Unlike some sources, overcontrol is neither inadvertent nor incidental. Overcontrol goes to the heart of management and governance. It arises from the depths of political culture via limited government norms and public distrust of authority, but also from the shallows of particular managers' insecurities.

Managerial and political control are important values and usually legitimate ones. But overcontrol is quite common. Given the differences in cause and effect between "political overcontrol" and "managerial overcontrol," they deserve separate treatment.

MANAGERIAL OVERCONTROL

Generally, managerial control objectives result in internal rules and managerial overcontrol results in internally derived red tape. Few question the need for management control. Managers' responsibilities for obtaining organizationally sanctioned objectives necessitate developing tasks and rules ensuring that subordinates will take coordinated actions to achieve the objectives. Even in organizations with limited hierarchy and strong participation norms, some degree of managerial control remains vital. The issue, again, is one of balance. Too much managerial control is no less stultifying than too little.

With too little control the organization cannot achieve coordination and effort is expended to little purpose. With too much managerial control, initiative is crushed, too much time is devoted to control and reporting, and tasks serving organizational objectives get deflected. Exerting *appropriate* levels of control and formalization is crucial to organizational effectiveness. Unfortunately, it is never easy to determine just how much control to exert or which activities should be formalized and which should remain discretionary.

One of the less-explored topics in management research is guidelines for formalization. Clearly, rules cannot cover every contingency and, thus, the "informal organization" is inevitably important. The informal organization, under some circumstances, can even "preserve the organization from the self-destruction that would result from literal obedience to the formal policies, rules, regulations and procedures" (Dubin, 1951: 68). But one of the most common responses to uncertainty and ambiguity is seeking control through formalization. Formalization and red tape are not the same thing. But they are closely related. It simply makes sense that organizations that are more rule-bound have a higher likelihood of generating red tape.

The organizational psychology of overcontrol holds much interest for organization theorists and managers. There is no shortage of ideas as to why it is that managers sometimes strive mightily to control the uncontrollable and to overcontrol when effectiveness requires delegation of power. Perhaps, as Thompson (1961) maintains, managerial overcontrol results from the inherent ambiguity of managerial work in bureaucracies, especially in public bureaucracies. Perhaps Downs (1967) is correct that all bureaucrats maximize self-interest and usually perceive control as in their self-interest. But whatever the reason, and however unfortunate the consequences, to manage *is* to control (Landau and Stout [1979] notwithstanding), and usually to overcontrol.

POLITICAL OVERCONTROL

Managerial overcontrol plagues almost all organizations, but so does political overcontrol. Private organizations as well as government agencies are subject to political overcontrol. Many of the "unnecessary rules and regulations" industry officials never tire of complaining about are political overcontrol; but in many instances, industrial officials' complaints really are more about the disjunction of private interests and public ones. Political control of business enterprise certainly is appropriate and even the most enthusiastic adherents of the market will, if pressed, acknowledge that at least some government-imposed rules and regulations are needed. If nothing else, they wish to protect against predatory business practices of competitors. Absent externally imposed rules and regulations, unsafe working conditions would abound, industrial pollution would remain unchecked, insider trading would wreak havoc, dangerous products would be foisted off on unwitting consumers, industrial espionage would be at new heights, the necessary ingredients of market efficiency could not be achieved. Unconvinced of the need for political controls? A quick review of 1920s business history gives a good idea as to the workings of unfettered commerce (Chernow, 1998). Vogel (1996) argues that many spheres of government activity arose directly in response to particularly egregious corporate abuses.

When not taken to the extreme, complaints of business and public agencies about undue political controls often have much validity. It is always difficult to sort out self-interested carping from valid complaints about red tape, but it is not so difficult, on a case-by-case basis, to identify red tape aimed at political overcontrol. Let us consider two examples, one of which is, in retrospect, easily identified as political overcontrol, another which was, at the time, widely alleged as overcontrol but now is generally accepted.

First, let us consider the case of the surgeon general's warning about the health risks of tobacco products. When initially introduced, a great many people, not just the tobacco industry, decried these rules as intrusive government interference and red tape. While there were few informed citizens who disputed the health hazards of tobacco, research had not at that time produced a smoking gun (pardon the pun). One reason is that much of the research was done by the tobacco industry and was proprietary. Recent revelations show that the tobacco industry was well aware of the effects of smoking, despite contemporary complaints to the contrary. The carping about unneeded regulations and red tape can, in hindsight, be dismissed as self-serving hypocrisy.

Sometimes allegations of unreasonable rules and red tape have a clear ring of truth. Bureaucratic overcontrol is such an easy target of ridicule that it has given rise to a new genre of popular nonfiction, best embodied in John Kohut's (1995) provocatively titled *Stupid Government Tricks: Outrageous (But True!) Stories of Bureaucratic Bungling and Washington Waste*. Among Kohut's entertaining snippets:

> In 1988, the Tennessee Valley Authority dropped its employee suggestion program because its cost was much greater than the savings developed under the program. Among other problems, the program produced a two-inch-thick handbook specifying rules about who and what could be included in the program to qualify for bonuses for good suggestions.
>
> The director's office of the National Park Service, in 1994, issued a memo to seventy-nine senior officials instructing them in the art of drafting letters, including 1. Please do not split infinitives. Adverbs should go before the infinitive. 2. Please eschew the word "issue."
>
> The *Federal Personnel Manual* gives explicit instructions on how to put a name on a file folder. "According to the rules, the name should appear: "LAST NAME (comma) SUFFIX (Jr., Sr., etc.) (comma) (space) FIRST NAME or INITIAL (space) MIDDLE NAME(s) or INITIALS(s)." (Kohut, 1995: 83)

The Heritage Foundation, a conservative Washington-based "think tank" has specialized in documenting government overcontrol. The Occupational Safety and Health Administration (OSHA) is one of their favorite targets. One publication (Moloney, 1996) featured the story of the owner of an Evanston, Illinois, doughnut shop who was nearly put out of business after an OSHA inspection. The inspection of her thirty-person bakery resulted in fines for such infractions as failing to warn employees of the hazards of household dishwashing liquid.

Obviously, bureaucratic overcontrol happens; it is a problem and an easy target of humor. But if one considers the literally millions of directives implemented each day, is it possible to avoid an occasional lapse or excess? Does the isolated anecdote, no matter how biting, really tell us much about the functioning of bureaucracy? OSHA is an excellent case in point. Unquestionably, OSHA sometimes implements rules that seem nitpicking and, unquestionably, many people in business do not like OSHA and its rules, whether nitpicking or not. But consider some of the following OSHA accomplishments (Occupational Health and Safety Administration, 1995):

- OSHA's cotton dust standard has nearly eliminated deaths from brown lung disease.

■ Standards for lead reduced blood poisoning in battery and smelting plants by two-thirds.

■ Overall, within the three years after an OSHA inspection that results in penalties, worker injuries and illnesses dropped by an average of 22 percent.

Since OSHA was formed in 1970, the overall workplace death rate has been cut in half (OSHA, 1995). While no one knows exactly what percentage of that reduction is attributable to OSHA, common sense tells us that at least some significant percentage is likely due to regulation. When one considers that more than 6,000 U.S. citizens die annually in workplace injuries and that workplace injuries cost the U.S. economy more than $110 billion per year, then the issues of workplace regulation should not be trivialized, even if there is some demonstrable overcontrol.

OVERCONTROL AND ILLEGITIMATE FUNCTIONS: A RED TAPE TRADE-OFF?

Two sources of red tape, political overcontrol and illegitimate functions, stand in complex relation to one another. Much political overcontrol comes from overzealous and ultimately ineffective efforts to forestall illegitimate functions. It is not too much an overstatement to say that virtually any highly visible and egregious abuse of authority leads inevitably not only to political control efforts but to overcontrol. Often the "cure" is more costly than the "disease."

Let us consider an example of a painful cure resulting from a painful disease. Say the words "Stanford's yacht" and most university researchers wince. Stanford University returned $500,000 to the federal government after a federal audit determined that Stanford had billed the government for, among other things, depreciation on the university's yacht, and furnishings and flowers in the Stanford president's residence (*Christian Science Monitor*, 1991).

A General Accounting Office Report (GAO, 1995) reviews the copious legislation Congress created in the aftermath of the university indirect cost accounting scandals. Without going into details about such arcane issues as the 26 percent cap on federal reimbursement for indirect cost under Circular A-21 (a topic best left to accounting mavens), let us simply note that Congress's terrible swift sword plunged deep. Today, any university researcher who submits a grant proposal to a federal agency finds that the scientific ideas and the description of the research to be performed is only a small fraction of the paperwork required.

The university accounting case is interesting because it is so typical—big administrative oaks from (relatively) small oaks of incompetence or indiscretion. It is also interesting because the red tape implications are not clear-cut. It is surely the case that, in 1991, university accounting was lax. Today's accounting is much more thorough. In many universities the accounting division is growing faster than almost any other unit. University accounting has improved and federal dollars have been saved. But at what cost? If we assume that university-based scientists developing research proposals for the federal government (the primary source of funding for university science) previously spent 5 percent of their proposal-writing time on forms and paperwork and now (after new regulations) spend 20 percent, what is the cost in terms of reallocated human capital? Federally sponsored university research is the chief source of basic research in the United States (Crow and Bozeman, 1998). If one believes that basic research contributes greatly to technological innovation and economic growth (e.g., Solow, 1957; Mansfield, 1991), then the shift of researchers' time from developing ideas to developing accounting assurances may be a bad bargain.

Given the strong likelihood that illegitimate uses of authority will lead to overcontrol, is there any way to prevent the use of a chainsaw when a scalpel is required? Perhaps not. So much of policymaking is driven by "big events," the problem is even more fundamental than political control. Big, unpredictable events drive funding, policy agendas, and power shifts among political interests. If there are urban riots, urban policy makes it to the forefront. If there is a public health crisis, such as massive food poisoning, then public health moves to the agenda. The need for policy solutions may have been just as great before the big event, but the big event puts the need on the agenda. One could pick almost any policy domain and witness a similar phenomenon—big event leads to policy deliberation. This is no less true when the big event is corruption, malfeasance, or some other form of illegitimate function and, indeed, the tendency may be even more pronounced.

One way of guarding against rules that are an overreaction to illegitimate functions is to be aware of the tendency. Government-wide policymaking responses may be a virtually inexorable response to illegitimate functions magnified by the media. Nonetheless, individual organizations have the option of being more deliberate and evenhanded in organization rule making. In the smaller scale of organizational rule making it may be possible to perform an implicit cost-benefit analysis that at least alerts one to potential for overcontrol. Simply providing an honest best guess to the question "will this set of rules be even more harmful than the behaviors they are designed to control," reduces likelihood of disproportionate response.

FEDERAL PROCUREMENT: AN ILLUSTRATION
OF RULE-INCEPTION RED TAPE

There is no better crucible than procurement policy for stirring up red tape controversies. We continue to hear tales about $400 Defense Department hammers and contractors using government funds to buy Red Sox tickets for clients. These occurrences suggest that rules are too few or ineffective—probably the latter since *Federal Acquisition Regulations*, the bureaucratic purchasing bible, now amounts to 744 pages of statutes and procedural codes. At the same time as egregious abuses occur, the controls also result in a litigation nightmare where virtually every large-scale contract award is challenged, many successfully, at the cost of millions of dollars in legal fees and administrative overhead.

Rather than focusing on the seemingly endless problems of procurement policy, let us consider an example of just one part of the problem, procurement challenges. As reported in *Business Week* (Lewyn, 1993), the U.S. Air Force's attempt to buy 300,000 personal computers tells us much about today's legalistic procurement system. In May, 1991, the computer industry was licking its chops at the prospect of $1 billion sales of computers. The Air Force, for its part, was equally excited about the prospect of replacing its outdated 80386 chip computers with the latest state-of-the-art. The outcome? By mid-1993 nothing had happened and the Air Force was purchasing, under an earlier order, overpriced 80386 machines because it had been unable to steer successfully through the rip tides of purchasing requirements.

This is a red tape story resembling hundreds of others, but there is a different twist here. When the Air Force announced the procurement, it announced at the same time that it would be operating under new, improved procurement rules. The Desktop IV proposal, as the procurement was designated, entailed relatively simple, uncluttered guidelines—making award challenges more difficult—and mandated a shorter request for proposals that was intended to discourage losers from appealing on the basis of insignificant details. Also, unlike most procurements, bidders could submit only a single, nonnegotiable proposal with no revisions. Each of these changes is among the reforms that critics (Kelman, 1990; Gore, 1993b) of the federal procurement process have urged as a means of diminishing the number of procurement challenges.

The Desktop IV saga began in May 1991, when the Air Force announced its acquisition of 300,000 personal computers, at the same time specifying its new, streamlined procurement procedures. From among twenty-two bidders, an award was made in November, 1991, to CompuAdd and Sysorex Information Systems. As soon as the winners were announced, the losers complained that their proposals had been rejected on minor technical grounds, including leaving a section blank rather than specifying "not applicable," and, in another case, failing to specify the price of a single spare part. In January, 1992, after review of these and similar complaints, the General Services Administrations Board of Contract Appeals canceled the award.

In April, 1992, the Air Force started over, requesting new bids. In September, it made an award to Zenith Data Systems, a division of the French corporate group, Groupe Bull. This time the losers lodged complaints about the award to a company substantially foreign-owned. While the case was not straightforward, the political heat was immense as members of Congress got into the act on behalf of losing companies located in their districts. In December, 1992, after ten days of hearings and 4,000 pages of documents, the GSA canceled this second award. The Air Force tried to save this one, splitting the order between Zenith Data and U.S.-based Government Technology Services and arguing that while Zenith Data is foreign-owned, its computers are domestically produced. CompuAdd and Electronic Data Systems challenged, arguing that Zenith Data was selling foreign-made monitors and that the Air Force should have been awarded to more than two companies. The contract was suspended awaiting resolution and, in the meantime, the Air Force continued to purchase computers under its old contract, forged in 1989, at a price far above the prevailing market price for the archaic technology.

THE MORAL OF THE STORY?

This story resembles many others; the only novelty is the sincere (though obviously inadequate) attempt at the beginning to reduce the usual procurement red tape and to streamline the process. But what is the moral to this story? As in most cases of red tape assessment, there is room for disagreement. Arguably, this is not even an instance of red tape but an unfortunate by-product of the federal government's legitimate need to protect the vendors from arbitrary decisions by bureaucrats obsessed with details. The minutiae involved in the first challenge seems to support this view. However, the details with which the bureaucrats seemed to be obsessed were legislated procurement rules. It was only the interpretation that was in dispute.

Given the thousands of procurement rules and regulations on the books, one might be hard-pressed to sort out rules "born bad" from functional rules. But there is one good starting point—the 1984 Competition in Contracting Act (this overview draws extensively from Kelman, 1990). In an effort to forestall bias in the letting of contracts, the 1984 Act transformed the appeals process. A more formal trial-like process, one that is adversarial with legal rules of procedure and discovery requirements, replaced a largely informal process with a single channel of administrative appeal. In addition to GAO, the GSA Board of Contract Appeals was created and began to hear challenges. Most important, the GSA Board operated not under the conservative "burden of proof" rules that the GAO had used for years (under which protesters had to demonstrate bias) but under a more lenient "preponderance of evidence" test. As a result, whereas the GAO has ruled in favor of the protester about 10 percent of the time, the GSA ruled for the protester about half the time. What this means, of course, is that the probabilities are such that a company that has already invested $1 million or more in a proposal process has little to lose, and often much to gain, by protesting any large-scale, big money award. In for a penny, in for a pound.

We can consider the results of the red tape created by the 1984 Competition in Contracting Act in terms of the sources of rule-inception red tape. This seems a classic case of *incorrect rule forecast*. There simply was insufficient understanding of the onslaught of problems that would result from the attempt to ensure against inequity and vender bias. As mentioned previously, every rule that is formed involves, at least implicitly, a forecast of behaviors that will accompany the rule. The forecasts, such as they were, turned out to be incomplete.

There is also some reason to believe that *negative sum process* was involved in this rule-inception red tape. There was such a concern with guaranteeing process that there was inadequate attention to the costs of that guarantee. One might take the extreme position that any degree of vendor favoritism is intolerable, regardless of the price paid to eliminate it. Absent that extreme view, this would seem to be a case of negative sum process, sacrificing effectiveness for the sake of process.

If there is a single problem that seems to pervade procurement rules, it is *overcontrol*. There is too high a rule density and the reason is the obsession with control. Consider Kelman's (1990: 89) criticisms of procurement policy:

> To achieve good substantive performance in a changing world, an organization design relying heavily on rules of any sort becomes increasingly inappropriate. Many of the judgments that public officials make are too specific to the situation to be put into rules.

Kelman goes on to point out that the rules are made to promote equity, efficiency, and integrity but performance and quality rarely have a place in the mix. While one might argue that his prescription—providing more discretion to public managers—risks "sweetheart deals" and corruption, these exist under the current rule-bound system. (Incidentally, Kelman moved from Harvard to become President Clinton's procurement policy expert at the Office of Management and Budget, getting the chance to introduce many of his ideas under the aegis of the National Performance Review).

BUREAUCRATIC ENCOUNTER:
REAL WORK, PAPER WORK, AND OPPORTUNITY COSTS
IN THE DEPARTMENT OF HUMAN SERVICES

To illustrate rules' opportunity costs let us consider the case of a recent crisis in social work record-keeping in Washington, D.C. (Castenda, 1993). As a result of decades of poor record-keeping, district-area social workers found themselves under a court order to catch up. In 1989, the American Civil Liberties Union sued the D.C. Department of Human Services, contending that shoddy record-keeping and case reporting had created enormous problems for the city's child-welfare system, including children living in crowded or even unlicensed foster homes. There appeared to be insufficient ability to keep track of cases, due, in large measure, to inadequate record-keeping. Children were getting lost in the system.

The court mandate compelled the department to review and update files on more than 3,000 children in foster care or under home supervision. The paperwork associated with the task was formidable—one of two detailed questionnaires, one fifty-two pages long, and the other twenty-three pages. Despite the burden involved, there was no great outcry that the information required was excessive. As one of the lawyers for the ACLU pointed out "a child's life depends on the information in the file. Social workers change assignments; emergencies occur; the agency needs a record of the child." (Castenda, 1993: B2). The problem was one of opportunity costs.

The people charged with filling out the paperwork were caseworkers. The service providers were also the recorders. At the time, there were 180 social workers in the department and the neglected or abused child cases alone had mounted to more than 1,300. The work is complicated by the fact that there is a 20 percent turnover in social workers each year, meaning that the record-keeping is, at the same time, vital and difficult to complete. As a result of the vast increase in paperwork requirements, there has been a diminution of time devoted to actual casework. As one former social worker noted, "[t]he social workers' schedule is not as open to work with families and kids because of the amount of time they are required to spend in court and doing paperwork because of the court order" (Castenda, 1993: B2).

Does this case illustrate a problem of red tape? There is considerable compliance burden, and enormous opportunity costs. However, the rule compliance serves a legitimate, organizationally- and socially-sanctioned function.

Much of rule-inception red tape begins in efforts to control the uncontrollable. In other cases, however, it results from a failure to perform even an informal cost-benefit analysis of the cost of controls. Millions of dollars of controls resulting in thousands of dollars of fraud and abuse savings is rarely a good investment, even in the most politically-charged atmosphere (see Darby and Karni, 1973).

HIGH COMPLIANCE AND HIGH OPPORTUNITY COST RULES

This book employs a stringent red tape definition. High cost rules do not qualify as red tape, not so long as they continue to achieve a legitimate functional objective. Nevertheless, rules "born costly" sometimes generate more harm than rules "born bad." Rules born costly entail a substantial compliance burden and considerable opportunity costs.

Up to this point, we have not directly considered *rules' opportunity cost*. In connection with rules, we can use the term opportunity costs in its traditional usage: "the cost of using resources in terms of the value of the best alternative good these resources could have produced" (Apgar and Brown, 1987: 393). The implication for organizational rules is that it is important to consider not only the compliance burden (cost) and benefits associated with a rule, but also the benefit that might have been obtained had the cost spent in compliance been spent on some other activity.

The issue of the opportunity costs of rules is really one of management policy and strategy. To say that a rule is not red tape, is not to say that it is a good rule. In many instances, a rule that serves an important function may do so at too high an opportunity cost. As such, it might be a poor rule, but not red tape. Some bad rules are red tape, some are not. As the Washington D.C. social-work case and the Stanford University yacht case show, it is sometimes difficult to distinguish between a poor rule and a good rule accompanied by high compliance and opportunity costs.

CONCLUSION

Sometimes red tape is "built in." Rule-inception red tape occurs as a result of a flaw present right at the beginning. One of the most common flaws is an understandable one. If we view rules as a forecast, then rules' effectiveness falls prey to the poor predictive ability of human beings—especially when those predictions involve other human beings. Human behavior generally surprises, and when a rule requires a complex web of interdependent human behaviors we should not be astonished if the rule generates red tape.

Red tape is usually inadvertent and often a result of the best of intentions. However, red tape sometimes occurs because officials wish it to occur. Bureaucracies inevitably involve the meshing of organizational and individual goals. In the most favorable circumstances the individual's personal goals and the organization's goals are highly compatible. Sometimes, however, these become out of alignment. In some cases, this disjunction between personal and organizational goals occurs because the individual is more ethical or public-spirited than the officials who control the organization are. This may lead to whistle-blowing, resignation, or, perhaps more common, a demoralized employee. In other cases, the individual sets aside the organization's goals in favor of personal ones. This can lead to a number of problematic outcomes (e.g., embezzlement, low work productivity) of which the creation of red tape is only one. Red tape usually occurs when the individual seems to have something to gain by constraining others' behavior. The gain may be as little as a twisted satisfaction in watching a social services client submit to the individual caseworker's bureaucratic power. Other times, the gain may be more tangible than psychological, such as using red tape to buy time to cover one's mistakes.

Perhaps the most complicated source of red tape is overcontrol. By this point it should be clear that determining whether a rule is or is not red tape is often a judgment call. Judgment calls are particularly difficult when they involve attempts to exert control. There is no ironclad means of determining when control has become overcontrol. There are some guidelines we can use, however, as we look for possible overcontrol. One of these is to consider the underlying rationale and historical context for the controlling rules. Rules generated after a perceived abuse often have the effect of killing a fly with a sledgehammer.

In sum, there are some good reasons for bad rules. In some cases, rules are born bad. They never have a chance to be socially productive, good organizational citizens. In the next chapter we see that even when officials promulgate good rules serving good objectives, the rules can still turn up later as red tape.

RULES "GONE BAD":
RULE-EVOLVED RED TAPE

This chapter focuses on the ways in which good intentions go awry. The "devolution" of functional rules to red tape can be caused by characteristics of the organization making the rule or by the individuals enacting the rule. Often it requires many people acting in concert to turn a good rule into red tape. We know relatively little about why and how good rules turn into bad ones. While studies of decision-making abound (for an overview, see Hickson, et al., 1986), and studies of rule-making are available, if less common (e.g., Kerwin, 1994), studies of rule change remain scarce.

We shall see that the change of effective rules into red tape mimics natural processes. Just as natural systems, ranging from our bodies to the universe itself, tend to "run down," so do rules wear out. It may seem odd that something as intangible as a rule can actually wear out from use. (This notion of worn-out rules brings new meaning to the saying that rules are made to be broken.)

THE EVOLUTION OF RULES

Rule change is a different social process from rule creation, responsive to different social and political factors. There is remarkably little empirical evidence about processes of rules change. In one of the few formal studies of rules change, an exhaustive study of more than one hundred years of organizational rules developed and implemented at Stanford University, Zhou (1993) found differences between rule-founding rates and change rates. Founding rates were largely due to historical period effects, but didn't relate to organizational complexity, changes in organizational learning, or government policy change. Rule founding seemed chiefly related to organizational crises of various sorts, consistent with organization theorists' (e.g., Cyert and March, 1963) views that rules serve as means of coping with uncertainty. By contrast, rates of rule change were relatively stable across historical periods and seemed more a function of organizational learning processes, particularly problem detection and correction.

Before discussing ways in which organizational rules become red tape, we consider two features of organizations that make them vulnerable to rule-evolved red tape. "Organizational phantoms" relates to the fact most people work under organizational rules created by persons no longer with the organization. "Organizational entropy" is the tendency for organizational and management systems to "run down" or disintegrate.

ORGANIZATIONAL PHANTOMS

One fascinating aspect of bureaucracies is the linkage of the organization's "living" with the organization's "dead." If we include among the "dead" not only the literally dead, but former organizational members who have retired or taken other jobs, we can speculate that *most* of the internal rules under which organizations operate were created by people no longer working there. In the absence of frequent revisiting of organizations' rules, regulations, and procedures, these phantoms hold much power (as the State Energy Agency case on pages 108–109 demonstrates).

Organizational phantoms pose an obvious problem and an obvious solution, albeit one rarely used. By occasionally reviewing organizational rules and asking "why do we do this, does anyone know?" the phantoms can be exorcised. A more formal and intensive approach—the "red tape audit"—is discussed in the concluding chapter.

ORGANIZATIONAL ENTROPY AND THE DISINTEGRATION OF SYSTEMS FOR RULES-BASED BEHAVIOR

During the 1950s heyday of general systems theories, there was much enthusiasm about the notion that a single unifying theory—systems theory—could be applied across the sciences, including the social sciences. Many organization theorists were quite enthusiastic about the prospects of systems theory for understanding organizations (for an overview, see Scott, 1987). For a number of reasons, most having to do with the explanatory weaknesses of systems theory, systems theories of organizations did not come to much. But there is at least one concept from systems theory that has some utility, at least as a metaphor, for understanding processes of change in organizations, including organizational rules.

> ### BUREAUCRATIC ENCOUNTER:
> ### RED TAPE EXORCISM AT THE STATE ENERGY AGENCY
>
> As research director of a medium-sized, northeastern consulting and research firm, Sarah B. was the principle investigator on a contract to conduct an intensive, multiyear evaluation of a state government agency. An unexpected result of this project was a close encounter with organizational phantoms.
>
> The State Energy Agency's mission is to fund research and development (R&D) projects, chiefly in energy- and environment-related fields. The agency is a quasi-government organization, retaining many of the rights of a business firm. In examining the rules and procedures of the agency, Sarah and her colleagues discovered one particularly controversial rule—a recoupment clause. Under the recoupment clause the Energy Agency has the right to recoup its investments from the R&D contracts it provides to industrial firms and private individuals. Thus if the agency, say, provides a contract to a small company for the development of (to use a real example) radio frequency lumber drying technology, the agency can, at the beginning of the project, write a recoupment provision into the contract. The agency's legal division tailors the recoupment provision to the particular project.
>
> Interviewing Energy Agency personnel, Sarah found some disagreement about the recoupment clause, its effects, and its desirability. But most did not like it. A few, especially those in the legal department, said the rule safeguarded the Energy Agency against "undue enrichment." According to this view, it is the agency's mission to provide public funding for energy and environmental technology development, but it is decidedly not the agency's mission to take public money and allow entrepreneurs to use it to get rich.
>
> The many opponents of the recoupment clause had two basic arguments. First, why *not* make people rich? If new businesses are started, those businesses will hire people, usually citizens of the state in which the agency operates, and the businesses as well as the new workers will contribute to the state's economic growth, including paying taxes. By this view, "undue enrichment" is an oxymoron. Indeed, the proponents could even point to the economic development mission included in the Energy Agency's enabling legislation. Second, does the agency really want to be in the foreclosure business? The recoupment provisions provide legal rights for the Energy Agency to take property if contracted repayments are not forthcoming. But many of the projects are high-risk, and individuals and companies come to the Energy Agency because they cannot get money from more conventional sources such as banks. In general, those willing to accept the more extreme recoupment clauses (a good "return on investment," in the view of the legal department) are those most desperate and with fewest funding alternatives. In at least a few cases in the past, the only collateral offered was personal property. While the agency had always had the good sense to refrain from exercising its option on homes and other personal property, who needs this legal sword of Damocles hanging over their head?

BUREAUCRATIC ENCOUNTER: RED TAPE EXORCISM AT THE STATE ENERGY AGENCY (CONTINUED)

Moreover, during the entire history of the State Energy Agency, only two or three (of several hundred) projects funded by the agency had produced licensing fees or royalties in excess of $10,000.

After performing an audit analysis, Sarah determined that the costs of implementing the recoupment clause had, over the years, far outweighed the revenue returned. By almost any standard it seemed a bad rule. Yet the rule had been in place for many years, with increasingly harmful effects. Why?

Sarah's research team set out to see if the rule could be repealed, and the first step was to interview Energy Agency personnel to find out more about the history of the recoupment rule. The first two people she interviewed, two program managers, indicated that the rule was a favorite of the current agency head, Mr. Cane, and that he had originated it some time ago. When Sarah interviewed Mr. Cane she found that his views about the rule were much more ambivalent than she had been led to believe. At the end of the interview Mr. Cane said, "I guess I really should have gotten rid of that rule, but it was a favorite of my predecessor, Dr. Issak, so I didn't want to come right in and change it."

Dr. Issak had returned to the nearby university from which he had come to the Energy Agency. Sarah drove the few miles to his office. Interviewing Dr. Issak, Sarah got much the same story. Mr. Issak didn't feel strongly about the rule but *his* predecessor, the agency's founder, Mr. Adam, had established the recoupment rule and he, Dr. Issak, had not quite gotten around to changing it. "It seemed relatively innocuous," Dr. Issak said, "so long as we didn't do something foolish like seize some poor guy's bank account."

There had only been three agency heads (the agency was founded in the early 1970s), and the founder, Mr. Adam, was alive and well. Having retired recently, he was getting set to move to Arizona, but, at the time retained his apartment only two blocks from the Energy Agency. Sarah joined him for lunch and asked about, among other things, the origins of the recoupment rule. Mr. Adam's response: "I don't really remember who started that damned fool thing—I think it was some under-worked lawyer in our legal division—but I never liked and should have gotten rid of it before I left. You mean to tell me they *still* write in those recoupment clauses? I'm surprised they can even get anyone to take their money with those kinds of conditions."

To a remarkable degree, rules are created by *organizational phantoms*. Particularly in the case of large organizations and old organizations, the creators of rules get lost in organizational history. Sometimes the rules they leave are like organizational poltergeists, rumbling around in the attic and corridors, stirring up trouble. Usually the troubles are small ones, for if the troubles are big ones, current organizational members more often change or overturn the rule.

Entropy is a concept borrowed from physics and it pertains to the tendencies of physical systems, whether microbiological organisms or solar systems, to "run down." In general, energy is lost in systems as the connecting rods that hold systems together begin, over time, to disintegrate.

If we think of organizations as systems of social interaction whereby individuals generate resources, use resources, and cooperate to achieve shared goals—a common definition of organizations—then we see that the bonds of organizations are almost always tenuous. Organizations are held together not by gravitational pull or subatomic forces, but by such changeable and even volatile "bonds" as shared interests.

More than most physical and social systems, organizational rules are prone to entropy. To a large extent, this is due to the weakness of the bond holding the system together. Effective implementation and compliance with rules depends upon an extraordinary chain of events, each of which has potential to alter the weak bond of shared interest. Given a "good rule," the good rule must be effectively communicated and effectively administered. Compliance with the rule assumes not only an understanding of the rule, not only a shared interest, but also a shared (or at least symmetrical) perception of the instrumentality of the rule. All this is required just for the *possibility* of effective compliance.

After one understands the rule, evaluates its expectations, and then decides to comply, there are still the following prerequisites: (1) sufficient personal ability to meet the requirements of a rule (illiterate individuals may *wish* to take the written test to obtain a driver's license but wishing doesn't get it done); (2) sufficient resources to comply (the compliance burden cannot exceed available resources, no matter how high the value of the functional object of the rule). The prerequisites for stable and effective implementation and compliance with a good rule are enormously stringent. The possibilities for entropy, for the weakening of the already weak bond, exist at every point.

RULES TO RED TAPE: REASONS FOR RULE-EVOLVED RED TAPE

There are several processes by which rule-evolved red tape occurs. These include the following:

- In *rule drift*, the rule itself is changed (though not formally).
- In *implementation change*, there is no change in the content or basis of the rule, but in the way it is executed.
- There may be a *change in the functional object* of the rule, rendering the rule unneeded or less effective.

- The rule and its implementation may stay the same, but some external change can undermine the rule's efficacy; that is, there is a *change in the rule's ecology.*

- *Rule strain* occurs as the sheer number of rules increases, with a corresponding increase in compliance burden, until the marginal benefit from rules becomes less and less, and then negative.

- *Rule incompatibility* occurs as new rules are promulgated that may be effective but, at the same time, undermine the effectiveness of old ones.

Each of these putative red tape culprits is discussed in the following sections. Later in the chapter, an overall explanatory model is presented showing how "good rules go bad."

RULE DRIFT

All rules, including galling ones, are divided in three parts: the behavior required, the implementation mechanism of the rule, and the enforcement conditions. Rule drift occurs when the meaning and spirit of the rule get lost in organizational antiquity as contemporaries inadvertently change the rule or its meaning.

Organizational phantoms are a major culprit in rule drift. Sometimes individuals enforce rules or comply with them without having any idea why the rule was formulated or what function it serves. Perhaps the need for the rule no longer exists. Rules may be observed ritualistically even if there is no understanding of the manifest purpose of the rule. Indeed, mysterious rules may even be venerated ("that's just the way we have always done things here...") for the stamp of organizational peculiarity or legend they confer.

Rule drift is not always a matter of the length of time that has passed since the rule's origins. Other factors that may be related to rule drift include personnel turnover (in the case of internal rules), changes in client composition (for external rules), and the reorganization of organizations and programs. Furthermore, rule drift interacts with other red tape causal processes. Particularly troublesome is *interaction between rule drift and rule strain.* As more and more rules are added to the organization, particularly over a relatively brief time span, usually less attention is given to communicating the rules' content and objectives. In such cases, there is high potential for inadvertent change in the rules content.

Rule drift is particularly likely in cases where rules are enacted only infrequently. Rules enacted by the same people within the same context over brief, regular periods are likely to be rules that will preserve content. The familiarity of frequently enacted rules reduces the likelihood of unwitting change. Rules that are special occasion rules are generally more likely to be misapplied in any of several ways, including change in content. This explains, in part, why emergency procedures, rules that are vital by definition, are so often poorly enacted. Rule drift often occurs because of lack of familiarity with the rules' content, which, in turn, is explained by a lack of opportunity for enactment. Thus, nuclear "events," space station docking accidents, and natural disasters are often compounded as rules infrequently executed are poorly executed.

It is not only the frequency of rule enactment that explains rule drift; the number of people interacting affects rule drift. If the same one hundred people enact a rule one hundred times each day, there is limited likelihood for drift. But if it is enacted one hundred times each day by one hundred *different* people, there is much greater likelihood for rule drift. Indeed we can think of rule drift in terms of a simple equation:

pRule Drift f([nE] [nA]), where the probability of Rule Drift is a function of:

nE = the number of occasions of rule enactment over time, and

nA = the number of people administering the rule.

This point can be expressed in another way as well. Figure 6-1 is a four-celled graphic that presents a rule-enactment typology relating the number of rule-enactment occasions to the number of persons enacting the rules. Rules may be enacted with more or less frequency. If a large number of persons are enacting the rules, then rule enactment is "distributed;" if few people are enacting the rules, rule enactment is "concentrated."

FIGURE 6-1   RULE ENACTMENT TYPOLOGY

 # Rule Enactments/Concentration of People Enacting

(H,L) ***Frequent/Concentrated*** [Auditors]	(H,H) ***Frequent/Distributed*** [Welfare Eligibility Determinations]
(L,L) ***Infrequent/Concentrated*** [Parole Review]	(L,H) ***Infrequent/Distributed*** [Election Administration]

Each of the four types has particular meaning for predicting rule drift. In the infrequent/concentrated case we have few people enacting rules rarely. We can go back to the case of a nuclear plant accident as an illustration. However, there are many other instances of relatively unimportant rules being implemented infrequently by a few. Indeed, some rules are enacted infrequently *because* they are relatively trivial.

Least troublesome is the frequent/concentrated case—relatively few people enacting rules frequently. There is little reason to expect rule drift in such cases. This does not suggest that administration is necessarily efficient in such cases. Those enacting the rule may become bored with their jobs, with the result that less attention is given to the implementation of the rule. But even in such cases there should be a good understanding of the content of the rule and little reason to predict a shift in the rule's behavioral requirements. A simple example in this category is the case of air traffic controllers. The rules are usually clear-cut and well understood and, by all reports, usually well-executed. The persons executing the rules understand them and, thus, the content is not altered through drift. When there are problems it is not from rule drift, but from fatigue, poor communication and implementation of the rule, or some other such source.

The highest threat for rule strain is the infrequent/distributed case—rules enacted infrequently but by many people. The classic case would be large-scale civil emergencies, such as natural disasters. The infrequent distributed case is particularly important for rule drift and, in general, a particularly acute problem in the evolution of functional rules into red tape.

An extended case is presented at the end of this chapter, examining problems that can occur when many complex rules and procedures rarely implemented must be implemented during crisis conditions and by officials from diverse jurisdictions. The problems in the aftermath of Hurricane Andrew, at the time the greatest natural disaster in U.S. history, illustrate the tendency of rules to disintegrate in the face of calamity.

IMPLEMENTATION CHANGE

Sometimes rule content changes in undesirable ways and creates red tape; in other cases there is no change in rule content but a change in the rule's implementation. For one reason or another, individuals begin to implement the rule in a different manner. Naturally, not all changes in rule implementation are red tape, some are sensible and functional adjustments to changed circumstances or unique features of special cases. But when the change undermines the achievement of the rule's functional object, then changes in implementation can transform a working rule into red tape.

In cases of rule drift, the content changes; whereas in cases of change in implementation, the content stays the same. But from a practical standpoint it is often very difficult to sort out the difference between the two. Probably the most common changes in implementation have to do with the amount of discretion with which the rule is applied. Most rules *assume* that some discretion will be used in their application. For most rules it is neither possible nor desirable to specify all the possible conditions to which the rule should apply. Nor is it possible in most cases to specify exceptions. Discretion often saves us from ourselves and gives us a way out of obviously ridiculous circumstances that rule-makers did not foresee.

One similarity between rule drift and implementation change as sources of red tape is that they are sensitive to many of the same causes and interpretation. Thus, the rule enactment typology previously introduced for rule drift is relevant for change in implementation. Similarly, both problems are often a function of rule complexity.

Let us consider an example of change in implementation, one that (in terms of the typology) relates to a frequent/distributed quadrant of the typology. For simple rules, the fact that many people are enacting the rule is not likely to lead to dysfunctional change in implementation. Thus, in Washington, D.C., cab drivers are required by rule to provide a receipt to all riders requesting one. This is a simple rule, easily understood, and easily enacted in essentially the same way by thousands of cab drivers. But Washington cab drivers implement much more complex rules for fare calculation. The basic fare structure is itself unusual and relates to the number of geographic zones required to take the passenger to his or her destination. On top of this, there are fare rules related to peak traffic hours, the number of passengers, and whether waiting is involved. There are also special fees related to airport routes. This greater complexity might lead to limited change in implementation if there were only a few cab drivers, each with scrupulous personal ethics and long experience. But when there is turnover among the cab drivers and the rules are complex, the likelihood for benign change in implementation (and, for that matter, malignant fare cheating) is intensified.

Implementation change is not only one of the most common sources of red tape but also a particularly nettlesome one. Often, there is no easy remedy. Effective management requires initiative and discretion. Effective management also requires attention to the rules and stability in their administration. There is a rich literature (e.g., Gruber, 1987; Leazes, 1997; Wamsley and Wolf, 1996) in public administration and political science on the inherent conflicts among the values of administrative efficiency, discretion, stability and fairness in application of rules, and ability to deal sensibly with exceptions and special needs. The boundaries among these values are rarely clear and it is often not easy to develop rules-of-thumb. Thus, implementation change is worrisome because it is required for good management, but it is also a source of red tape. When managers exercise discretion or bend rules, it is rarely clear whether the consequence will be red tape or a needed adjustment of the rules.

Sometimes instances of change in implementation have nothing to do with the exercise of discretion. A particularly common form of change in implementation is *misapplication of rules*. Misapplication of rules can occur for any of a variety of reasons. Sometimes rules are difficult to interpret or apply because they have been written poorly and, thus, quickly evolve into red tape. Sometimes the purpose of the rule has never been clearly communicated to the person charged with enforcing the rule. Sometimes the persons expected to comply with the rule do not understand the rule or its purposes.

Rules must be thought of as, essentially, communication events. This does not mean that rule-makers must communicate directly with each person charged with implementing the rule or with each person affected by the rule. But it is vital to communicate the purpose the rule is supposed to serve (its functional object) if there is to be any long-range hope of effective implementation. Further, if the functional object is clearly communicated, it is more likely that changes in implementation will be positive, self-conscious changes. The failure to communicate the primary purpose of rules is one of the most important sources of red tape and certainly one of the most important reasons for individuals perceiving red tape when, in fact, the rule serves a legitimate function that is simply not apparent.

CHANGE IN THE FUNCTIONAL OBJECT

Sometimes the functional object of the rule changes in ways that render the rule obsolete or otherwise useless. There may no longer be a need to achieve the objective of the rule, but the rule remains in place nonetheless, with compliance burden intact.

Let us consider a simple example. The City of Oakdale requires each of its agencies to issue each year a strategic plan with a twenty-year planning horizon. The functional object of the rule is that the city council should have information about each agency so that it can make wise decisions about allocation of resources to agencies. But the City of Oakdale Office of Public Statues and Monuments has just been dismantled by the city council and all operations terminate at the end of the fiscal year. Requiring the Office of Public Statues and Monuments to provide a strategic plan would be red tape because the functional object has changed—there is no need for a long-range plan for an agency with a short-range future.

In this simple example the likely culprit is habituation. That is, there are routines in bureaucracy and politics, and these routines are powerful and seem to take on a life of their own. Bureaucratic organizations work according to routine and seasonal requirements. It is now the end of the fiscal year, so it is time to spend money; it is now the end of the planning cycle, so it is time to develop this year's strategic plan. Often old habits take time to catch up with new circumstances.

In many instances problems with change in the functional object occur as a result of organization phantoms That is, the rule's objective was set up by others no longer with the organization; the objective has been lost along the way, the rule remains. The functional object is obscured, the rule compliance behavior, much more visible, remains.

CHANGE IN THE RULE'S ECOLOGY

Even if the rule's functional object does not change, circumstances may occur that mitigate the rule's usefulness. For example, a rule requiring carbon copies of memoranda makes little sense if almost all communication is via electronic mail on a computer-based local area network. In this case, the rule's ecology would include the organization's adopted communications technology. This is a simple example of ecological change transforming a rule into red tape, but the situation is often similar for broader, more significant rules embedded within a much more complex ecology.

An example of changes in rule ecology occurred recently in a bizarre locale: outer space (Cowen, 1994). Space commerce began slowly in the 1960s with communications satellites and grew steadily until it had encompassed a number of fields, including space manufacture of metal alloys, pharmaceuticals, and electronic materials or, in short, any product made more easily or cheaply under weightless conditions in orbit. The problem is that the makers of tariff and customs policy never gave much thought to products emerging from outer space. As Tony Calio, then deputy administrator of the National Oceanic and Atmospheric Administration (NOAA), observed, "Customs laws were fine when they first started, but no one anticipated producing products in space. And space, like the high seas, is considered beyond the national borders" (Cowen, 1994: A4). Finally, rules changed so that products made by U.S. companies in space were not taxed as imports. But, as often happens, the rules' ecology changed and, for a while, left the rules behind.

In all likelihood, certain classes of rules are more prone to harmful effects of change in ecology. The culprit is not, of course, the change, but the continuing existence of the unmodified, suddenly useless rule. Change does not create red tape, failure to adapt creates it. If those affected are close at hand and communication is more frequent, it is more likely that the flaws in the rule will be swiftly communicated. Thus, a university department chair producing the carbon copy rule will quickly hear from the faculty when the rule is no longer functional. But a state legislature enacting the same rule might get word a bit later. The greatest difficulty of rules keeping up with the world will be in those instances where those setting the rules and those implementing them are far removed in time, status, and geography.

RULE STRAIN

Organizations with high-rule density often create strain and inefficient use of resources. Rules that are "good," but too abundant, can have a net negative effect. Five good rules may be within those capabilities, ten good rules may, simply because of limited compliance capability, cause the organization or individual to interpret and apply rules less effectively. To put it another way, red tape may be caused by organizations having compliance and implementation burdens that cannot be met with existing resources. This deficit in resources leads to shortcuts or lip service to rules with the result that rules, even when they have strong content and are directed appropriately toward a legitimate functional object, may be transformed into red tape.

While rule strain may occur in any of a variety of ways, a particularly perverse possibility is that it may occur as a result of efficiency-based strategies, downsizing and "right-sizing." When already lean personnel rosters are further cut, with no concomitant reduction in workload, the capacity to meet compliance requirements may be taken beyond the critical point. If the organization controls the preponderance of its rules— that is, if they are internal in their origin—then it may have the flexibility and the good sense to cut back compliance burden. But in cases—as with most government agencies—where the preponderance of rules are external in their origin, there is particularly high potential for rule strain and red tape.

Rule strain is not always associated with personnel decrements. Often it is simply a matter of more and more compliance and implementation burden with no increment in resources. The term "unfunded mandates" refers to the setting of requirements by one level of government to be performed by another, but with no additional resources provided. The problem finally became so critical that the congressional Republicans included it as part of their "Contract with America."

New requirements do not *inevitably* lead to rule strain, only if the new requirements are net additions to compliance and implementation burden. If organizations have freedom to meet new requirements by shedding some previous work activities, thereby freeing up additional resources, then rule strain can be avoided. Usually public agencies do not have this freedom.

RULE INCOMPATIBILITY

Rules often build one on top of the other. If rules are inconsistent or at cross-purposes their net effect may be damaging (even if particular rules remain effective with respect to their functional object). *Rule incompatibility* means that rationality added to rationality may sum to irrationality. This is not a matter of the volume or density of rules (as in rule strain), but the incompatibility of rules.

Let us consider a simple example of rule incompatibility. It is reasonable for an organization to have a rule requiring that employees log each telephone number on long-distance calls. Despite the time and trouble required, if personal use of long-distance is becoming a major expense, the logging rule may be justified. Similarly, it is reasonable to establish a rule that all long-distance telephone callers use an assigned dialing code keyed to an individual calling account. What makes no sense is to have both rules in force at the same time.

In some cases, rule incompatibility is not so easy to judge—especially those rules at a higher policy level. There are many "incompatibilities" in public policy that may seem inefficient, illogical, or just plain stupid, but that are simply conforming to a set of political rules that may be internally rational. Let's get back to our no smoking example, but at a "high policy" level. Perhaps the classic example of policy incompatibility is to provide huge subsidies for tobacco farmers and, at the same time, mount government-sponsored antismoking campaigns. This seems the height of rule irrationality until we recognize that the rules serve different constituencies and political rationality.

A MODEL OF RED TAPE ORIGINS

Taking the disparate concepts and propositions presented thus far, we can connect them in a rudimentary model explaining the development of rules into red tape. Figure 6-2 depicts a theory of red tape origins. Distinguishing between rule-inception and rule-evolved red tape, the pictorial shows how objectives may be defeated by bad rules forecasts, problems with the rules themselves, and problems with implementation. Each of several rule-inception and rule-evolved threats is presented. In the next chapter, we consider the model in connection with this question: "Do government organizations have more red tape than private organizations?

FIGURE 6-2   A MODEL OF RED TAPE ORIGINS

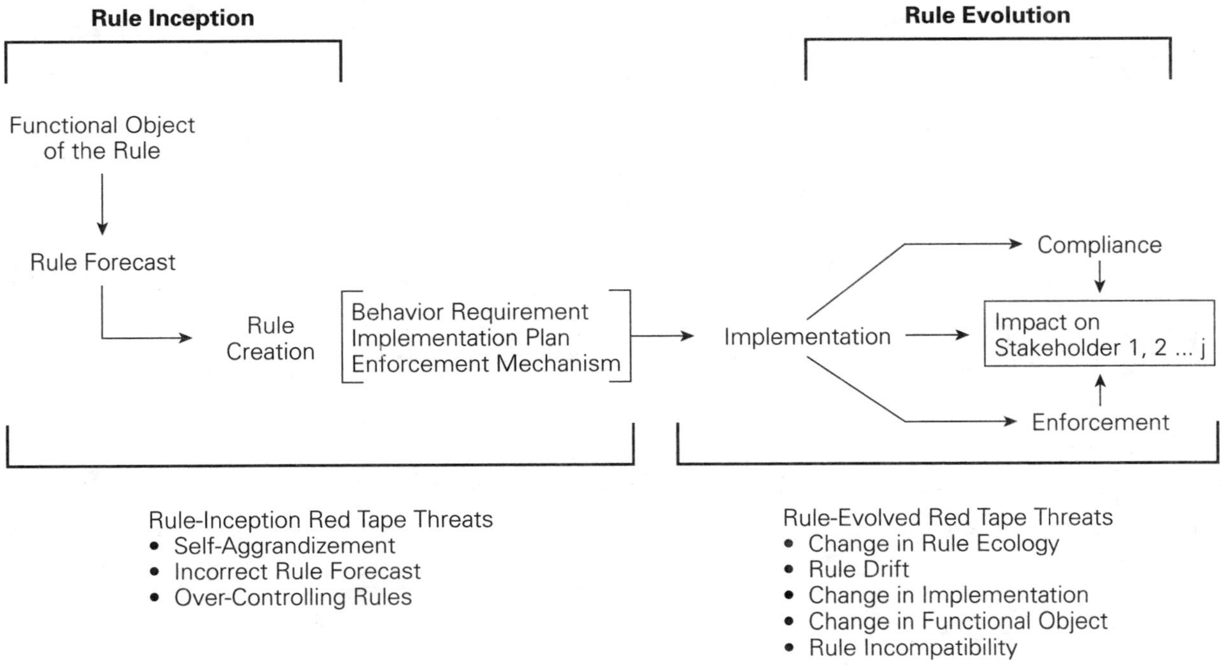

Rule Inception

Functional Object
of the Rule

Rule Forecast

Rule
Creation

Behavior Requirement
Implementation Plan
Enforcement Mechanism

Implementation

Rule Evolution

Compliance

Impact on
Stakeholder 1, 2 ... j

Enforcement

Rule-Inception Red Tape Threats
• Self-Aggrandizement
• Incorrect Rule Forecast
• Over-Controlling Rules

Rule-Evolved Red Tape Threats
• Change in Rule Ecology
• Rule Drift
• Change in Implementation
• Change in Functional Object
• Rule Incompatibility

BUREAUCRATIC ENCOUNTER:
RED TAPE AND HURRICANE ANDREW

Hurricane Andrew approached the Miami, Florida, area on Monday, August 24, 1992. The Federal Emergency Management Agency (FEMA) responded well to evacuation, the first phase of disaster preparation. More than 750,000 people were evacuated by the time the hurricane struck (Anderson, 1992). Hurricane Andrew made landfall in Dade County, Florida, in Homestead, just south of Miami. Because of the successful evacuation and the hurricane's path away from the crowded areas of Dade County, only twenty-five lives were lost (Davis, 1992). Nonetheless, Homestead was devastated. FEMA Director Walter Stickney said "the hurricane has caused more destruction and affected more people than any disaster America has ever had (Slevin and Filkens, 1992: 1A)."

The second phase of disaster response began as the storm moved into the Gulf of Mexico. In this phase, FEMA failed miserably. Desperately needed food and water were stuck in traffic jams of evacuees returning to Miami. There were too few national guard personnel and those that were there lacked sufficient equipment for communication about housing in the disaster area. There was no plan that could be activated without formal requests from the local emergency response units, who were victims themselves. This lack of preparation meant that the details of relief had to be worked out on the fly.

Over 250,000 people were left homeless, without food, water, or any way to care for themselves. Just eight hours after the hurricane, Lawton Chiles, Governor of Florida, toured south Dade County in a helicopter and described it as looking "bombed out" (Leen and Freedberg, 1992).

FEMA and the Federal Response

The Federal Emergency Management Agency has 2,800 employees, quite small by federal agency standards, working in its Washington headquarters and its ten regional offices. Because of its small size, FEMA does not actually provide many services in case of large disaster. It coordinates other federal and state agency disaster relief efforts. FEMA has no authority to order the other agencies to act and has no budget to reimburse other agencies for their actions.

When a catastrophe strikes, the standard sequence of events is as follows. The governor of the affected state may ask the president to declare an emergency or disaster if, in the governor's judgment, state and local resources are inadequate. The FEMA staff set up a regional headquarters, then survey the area to assess needs of the affected area. The director of FEMA then receives an assessment of the disaster from the regional office and makes a recommendation to the president on whether or not to declare a disaster.

After Andrew hit, the federal response to cleaning up the disaster began

| BUREAUCRATIC ENCOUNTER: |
| RED TAPE AND HURRICANE ANDREW (CONTINUED) |

quickly. Early Monday evening, President Bush arrived and toured the area with Governor Chiles. They toured the area in a jeep, posed for photographs, but never got to the hardest hit sites. In a press conference, President Bush declared there will be "27 agencies of the government ready to help in any way that the federal government can." Local Florida reporters who had seen the damage were excluded from the press conference. On Tuesday morning the first FEMA mobile hospital arrived in south Dade County. The second medical team arrived around noon, because the feds had been unable to find a transport plane. Less than twelve hours after opening, the federal hospital was out of surgical supplies. New supplies took five hours to arrive. The National Guard noted that at 9:20 A.M. the U.S. Army had been briefed "on the current situation."

The Army Role

The U.S. Army told the Florida National Guard, "Florida has not requested any support from other states or federal agencies, nor do we project a need." Over 18,000 Airborne troops were put on alert on Monday. They stood ready to assist as needed. Generally, the military is involved in civilian disaster relief only in catastrophic situations. Until three days after the hurricane struck Florida, the U.S. military was not involved in any significant way.

The Red Cross

Congress chartered the Red Cross in 1905 to aid in disaster relief. Its role is to coordinate disaster relief and provide trained volunteers to support that effort. This puts the Red Cross in the position of coordinating federal agencies and other volunteer agencies. The Red Cross disaster relief center lacked generators large enough to run the computers that were supposed to track supplies, provide damage assessments, and make note of calls for aid. In the absence of computers, record-keeping and data management were performed by hand.

After Andrew hit, less than a third of the 1,000 area Red Cross volunteers showed up for work. Often, untrained walk-ins served as replacements. Response teams were so overwhelmed that victims were having to make appointments to apply to get aid. To further complicate matters, the National Red Cross from Washington, D.C. took over the Dade County chapter on the Wednesday after the storm, adding to confusion over the chain of command.

Where Is the Cavalry?

The Florida National Guard statement that "Florida has not requested any support from other states or federal agencies, nor do we project a need," did not fit the view held by Dade County officials. By Monday evening, the

---

BUREAUCRATIC ENCOUNTER:
RED TAPE AND HURRICANE ANDREW (CONTINUED)

County knew it was in deep trouble. County officials met with FEMA and told them what was needed. The FEMA officials were taking notes. Local officials begged for supplies but neither FEMA nor the Army quartermaster was sure who had responsibility. Everyone had an evacuation plan, but no recovery plan existed for state, local, and federal agencies.

On Tuesday, the weaknesses of the food distribution network were starting to show. By Thursday they were glaring. The 78,000 meals provided by the Red Cross and Department of Agriculture were not in South Dade but stuck on the crippled Florida highways. On Thursday afternoon the Guard was given the job of delivering items to distribution centers for approximately 650,000 people. Lines were the longest anyone had seen. Demand was so massive that it seemed nothing was getting into South Dade. Donations were coming in from around the country and no one was effectively coordinating the distribution efforts.

By Friday morning, those involved in the relief effort were beyond exhaustion. They were feeling abandoned by the rest of the country. Where was the logistical effort used to support the military in the Gulf War? Further frustrating the local relief workers, Elizabeth Dole, the head of the Red Cross, was on television telling the world that the aid was being delivered and that things were just fine.

Enter Kate Hale

Kate Hale was Dade County's emergency operations director. A Flint, Michigan, native, she moved to Florida for the weather. Her responsibilities included evacuation and disaster-response planning. Arguably, her successful planning and execution of the largest evacuation in U.S. history saved hundreds of lives. On the other hand, she bears some responsibility for the lack of an integrated plan to provide supplies to victims of the storm.

By the third day of the hurricane's aftermath, almost all of which she spent on the phone pleading for assistance, Kate Hale walked into the pressroom and told a cameramen: "I want this live." She proceeded to lecture Washington (Slevin and Filkins, 1992). "Enough is enough. Quit playing around like a bunch of kids.... Where in the hell is the cavalry? For God's sakes where are they? We are going to have more casualties because we are going to have more people dehydrated." Hale's eyes brimmed with tears, "We need food, we need water, we need people down here. We're all about ready to drop, and the reinforcements are not coming in fast enough." She also blasted the National Guard. "We need a better National Guard down here. They do not take orders from me, they take requests from me.... I am not the disaster czar down here. President Bush was down here. I'd like him to follow up on the commitments he made."

Hale got the attention of the White House. Within hours Secretary of

BUREAUCRATIC ENCOUNTER:
RED TAPE AND HURRICANE ANDREW (CONTINUED)

Transportation Andrew Card was named as Bush's representative. He promised that the army would fill the void and noted that, after all, Governor Chiles had requested the troops only two hours earlier.

Governor Chiles had a different version, arguing that he and his aides repeatedly asked for help, beginning just a few hours after the hurricane moved on. In a face-to-face meeting with an Army colonel, the governor's staff requested Army field hospitals and engineering support, though the governor did not put it in writing. "If they had wanted written requests, we, I'm sure, would have complied," said Herndon, Chiles' chief of staff. "We didn't feel we had the time to write out written requests and invitations."

The White House had yet another version of events. Since no formal request came, the president didn't order a massive troop call-up. The 18th Airborne Corps was on alert, but President Bush did not activate them until after Hale's blowup. Lt. Gov. Buddy MacKay blamed "chains of command in the military." Other sources familiar with the snafu said, "the Governor didn't say the magic word."

Kate Hale blamed the damage assessment that was provided by the governor's office on the Monday after President Bush designated Florida a disaster area. With a better idea of the damage, and in writing, top officials might have acted sooner, she said. According to Hale, "apparently this whole thing is dependent on little pieces of paper."

Questions

1. Some media accounts of the many and diverse bureaucratic problems associated with emergency assistance in the aftermath of Hurricane Andrew summarize the problems as "red tape." Considering the concepts of red tape introduced in this book, just what parts of the mismanagement (if any) seem to have been caused, in part or in whole, by red tape?

2. Given the inherent difficulties involved in rules in the "infrequent/distributed" category—rarely enacted but with many having responsibility—can rule drift be anticipated and can steps be taken to guard against it?

3. Do the notions of "normal bureaucracy" and "bureaucratic pathology" make sense in instances of unique events such as a natural disaster? If not, what standards can we employ for judging the effectiveness of bureaucracy in such cases?

Source: This case was written with Andrew Kleine and Stan Larmee, then graduate students at the University of Michigan's Institute for Public Policy Studies.

CONCLUSION

Figure 6-2 provides a brief summary of the major points developed in this chapter and the previous one. The model distinguishes between two sources of red tape; red tape caused by flaws inherent in the rule from the beginning (rule-inception red tape) and problems presented after the rule's formation (rule-evolved red tape).

In examining the rule inception part of the model we also note once again several key points about rules. Generally, they begin with a functional object. Someone, acting in an official capacity, believes that a rule can help achieve an organizationally sanctioned objective. Whether doing so consciously or with little awareness, the rule formulator makes a rule forecast, tying provisions of the rule to expected behaviors. Often the rule is "born bad" because those forecasts are unrealistic. Indeed, problems may occur even earlier with the functional objective. If the objective is extremely unrealistic there may be no rule that can achieve it.

Moving to the next part of the model, we note the three elements shared by all rules: behavior requirements, an implementation plan, and enforcement mechanisms. Red tape (and many other bureaucratic problems) can occur coincident with flaws in any of these aspects of rules. Three of the most common sources of rule-inception red tape are self-aggrandizement, the setting aside of organizational objectives in favor of personal ones, poor forecasts of behaviors entailed in the rule, and a desire to control the uncontrollable.

If a rule has been formulated and implemented and has survived these formidable birthing hazards, red tape may nonetheless lie in wait. Any of several factors may conspire to transform a well-functioning rule into red tape. The execution of the rule may be problematic or the environment within which the rule operates may change in ways that undermine the effectiveness of the rule. The meaning and significance of the objective that the rule was created to serve may itself change.

No organization is red-tape proof. However, there seem to be certain cases in which we can expect particularly high red tape potential. If the rules are more complex and require more "tailoring," it is likely that the quality of rules will not easily be preserved. If organizations operate in a highly changeable environment, but have limited opportunity to reexamine or evaluate rules, red tape potential is high. If organizations are highly interdependent and subject to multiple, crosscutting rules created by other organizations—watch out! Interestingly, these characteristics describe many public organizations. In the next chapter we consider whether public organizations have more red tape or just more accountability.

GOVERNMENT RED TAPE

7

Government bureaucracies *seem* to have more red tape—but do they really? Is red tape truly the bane of government? Or is the supposition of massive government red tape just another element of antigovernment rhetoric?

Most scholars interested in the issue of government red tape go along one of two paths. Those more sympathetic to the public sector (e.g., Kaufman, 1977) explain that government's commendable emphasis on public accountability often has the unfortunate side effect of red tape. The apologists, many of whom are political scientists, tell us that actions that may fly in the face of economic efficiency often look more rational from the standpoint of political efficiency. Critics, often economists working within a market failure or property rights model (Chapter 3), tell us that the public sector's absence of a "bottom line" seals the fates of inefficient government bureaucracies. Usually privatization is presented as the only viable solution to government's red tape and inefficiency.

Both the accountability and the "bottom line" explanations have some merit, but neither has a monopoly on the truth about red tape. Each explanation works better as the answer to a more general question: "What are the important differences between public and private organizations?" Indeed, the question of red tape's relation to sector is wound through and around the question of differences between public and private organizations.

Why should we care whether public organizations have more red tape? In the first place, the seemingly perpetual government reform efforts assume that government is, in general, inefficient and, specifically, a fount of red tape. What if these assessments were wrong? The reinvention labs would seem a little foolish. What if the assessments are right? Would it not be useful to know *why* government has more red tape before we set out to reform?

There is an even more deep-seated reason to be concerned about government's red tape and inefficiency. The United States is steeped in a free market ethos that begins with the assumption that government should provide goods and services only in cases of "market failure." When there is no reason to suspect market failure, government should, the reasoning goes, get out of the way and let the market do its magic. However, if government, laboring as it does in the arid fields of market failure, has no more red tape than private organizations, then the meaning of market failure may require some reexamination.

Another reason to be concerned about government red tape is that it is our shared burden. While we can, sometimes, change our portfolio of government services by moving to another city, we have only one federal government in the United States. It is a monopoly provider in many areas of life. If private organizations create red tape, their clients and ultimately their employees and stockholders may suffer. If public organizations create red tape the suffering is likely more widely distributed.

RED TAPE AS A PIECE OF THE "PUBLICNESS PUZZLE"

Is it the institution of government that causes red tape? Is it interaction with government that causes red tape? Do private organizations that have more dealings with government have more red tape than private organizations that have little truck with government? These questions cannot be addressed apart from the "publicness puzzle": the extent to which organizations, public or private, are affected by external political control (Bozeman, 1987). After discussing some theoretical reasons why the public status of organization might have bearing on organizations' levels of red tape, we turn to some empirical results for studies examining red tape in public and private organizations.

PUBLIC-PRIVATE DIFFERENCES IN RED TAPE

Is government ownership an inherent cause of red tape or is red tape simply correlated with government ownership and caused by other factors? This turns out to be quite a complicated question and we shall not entirely resolve it—but it must be asked. As we shall see later in this chapter, the research evidence (e.g., Pandey and Bretschneider, 1997; Bozeman and Kingsley, 1998; Bozeman, Reed, and Scott, 1992) shows that government organizations typically have more red tape than do private organizations. The results must be approached with caution. In some cases, the measures of red tape are based on perceptions and, thus, it is possible that the perceptions do not match reality. Indeed, many have noted the disjunction between perceptions and objective measures of red tape (e.g., Pandey, 1995; Pandey and Kingsley, 1995; Bozeman and Crow, 1991). Further, studies comparing levels of formalization between public and private organizations have generally found modest differences (Rainey, 1997).

Even if there is a genuine tendency for greater red tape in government, this does not prevent some private organizations from having more red tape than similar government agencies. There are many government organizations with little red tape and private organizations with a great deal. This implies that red tape is not an inexorable consequence of government ownership. In all likelihood there are few *inherent* attributes of government organizations causing red tape.

GENERIC RED TAPE: AN EXTERNAL CONTROL MODEL

Some of the factors leading to red tape are as relevant to private as to public organizations. Two primary causes of red tape in all organizations are (1) high degrees of external control, and (2) large numbers of diverse stakeholders. When these factors are present in any organization, government or business, more red tape is usually the result. Figure 7-1 presents an external control model of red tape, one as applicable to private as to government organizations. In the figure, a plus indicates a factor facilitating the likelihood of red tape; a minus is a factor inhibiting red tape.

FIGURE 7-1   EXTERNAL CONTROL MODEL OF RED TAPE

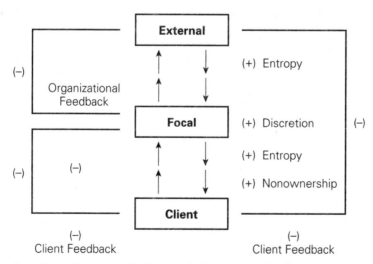

The reasoning behind the model is as follows. An organization's (in the figure, the "focal organization") red tape potential increases with number of organizational entities and subunits developing rules to be implemented by the organization. There are several reasons to expect this. First, there is an increased opportunity for use of discretion in rule application (and, thus, an increased opportunity for misapplication). Second, the chances are greater that there will be entropy affecting the communication of rules and their results. Finally, when there is a high degree of external control there is likely to be a decreased sense of ownership of the rules on the part of the organizational unit in charge of implementation.

In Figure 7-1, the plus signs imply a positive association with red tape, the minus signs imply that a factor is associated with less red tape. Thus, client feedback means less red tape and entropy means more red tape. As the figure implies, managers can take steps to reduce the impact of external control on red tape. The key to reducing red tape is effective communication between the organization formulating and requiring rules and the organization actually implementing them. Thus, if communication is more frequent, of higher quality, and in both directions (rather than just edicts from above), the likelihood of red tape is reduced.

We can think of rules as having an underlying probability distribution representing the propensity for rules to become red tape. As mentioned previously, if there are more rules, then there are more opportunities for mistakes in application and a greater burden in keeping track of rules and their implementation. Generally, the more rules and regulations affecting an organization, the higher the likelihood of rules beginning as red tape (rule-inception) or being transformed into red tape (rule-evolved). More rules and regulations do not inevitably mean more red tape, but more rules make red tape more likely.

The "probability distribution" (i.e., propensity to red tape) changes when the rules come from the outside. With externally imposed rules and external control there is greater chance for slippage. Distance (geographic but also organizational, cultural, and temporal) undermines the ability to monitor. In most cases it is actually expected that some local discretion will be used in the interpretation and application of externally imposed rules. While that use of discretion is vital, it also leads to red tape for all the reasons described in the preceding chapter.

A factor not previously mentioned is more psychological than organizational—ownership of the rules. Generally, individuals more eagerly embrace rules they have had a role in developing or, to a somewhat lesser degree, those developed in their organization by people known to them. Externally imposed rules are much more likely to be misunderstood, resented and, ultimately, undermined. Typically, retribution for undermining externally imposed rules is less likely.

If there are close ties between the organization imposing the rules and the organization governed by or implementing the rules, then the rules are likely to be better understood and less likely to seem capricious. Just as important, if the rules themselves are seriously flawed (rule-inception red tape) the flaw can be detected more quickly and remedies provided. Similarly, rules imposed on organizational clients are less likely to result in red tape if the clients or customers have close ties with the organization and frequent opportunities for effective communication.

EXTERNAL CONTROL AND GOVERNMENT RED TAPE

The external control model presented in Figure 7-1 is as applicable to private as to government organizations. When business organizations have high degrees of external control, they also have a greater likelihood of red tape. But there are inherent attributes of government organization that lead to high degrees of external control and, in turn, a higher propensity for red tape. Particularly important factors are government's *sovereign political authority*, and governments' *breadth of mission*.

POLITICAL AUTHORITY AND PROCEDURAL SAFEGUARDS

While political authority affects private organizations and can even be exercised by private organizations acting in proxy, sovereignty belongs to government. This is the *only* absolute difference between government organizations and private organizations with high degrees of publicness (Bozeman, 1987). In the United States and many other nations, sovereignty carries with it legitimate coercive power of such force that citizens inevitably demand sharp constraints on officialdom and safeguards, usually procedural ones, against abuse. This is one of the chief points in Kaufman's (1977) analysis of red tape and he is quite correct in noting that these procedural safeguards lead to the proliferation of rules, regulations, and procedures.

A set of rules protecting citizens from official abuse is not red tape. However, a set of rules devised to protect citizens from official abuse, but not meeting that purpose, may be red tape. One of the reasons government has more red tape is that it has voluminous rules designed to protect citizens from the illegitimate uses of the legitimate powers of government and, sometimes, the rules simply do not work. Other times (as in the "Stanford yacht" case), the cure is as costly as the disease.

Using the concepts developed to explain the origins of red tape, we can say that there are certain causes of red tape that are particularly likely to arise in the case of procedural safeguards. The havoc wreaked by *organizational phantoms* often targets procedural safeguards. Since procedural safeguards generally do not reflect the mission objectives of agencies they are less likely to change frequently and less likely to be reviewed. This means that procedural safeguards have often been produced long ago in response to crises or abuses forgotten long ago. Due to organizational phantoms and the slow pace of rule change, rule *drift* is common in the case of procedural safeguards, as is *change in implementation*.

Perhaps most important, however, is *rule strain*. In many instances the sheer number of procedural safeguards, many of which are quite specific and detailed, produce an extensive compliance burden and, for organizations with limited resources, a high rule density.

Rule incompatibility often occurs with procedural rules. As governments seek to downsize and to privatize, costly procedural rules often contradict one another. In much of the federal government's "reinventing" rhetoric the apparent objectives are very much at odds with procedural safeguards. For example, "streamlining purchasing practices"—a worthy goal—can be translated as "reducing procedural constraints."

BREADTH OF MISSION

Another inherent attribute of government that leads to increased red tape is the nature of government policy missions. Generally, interorganizational linkage is associated with red tape (as indicated previously). In the private sector, interorganizational linkages typically occur among autonomous organizations seeking mutual economic advantage. In government, interorganizational linkages often seek to achieve broad policy missions that transcend the linked government organizations and, thus, the linkage is qualitatively different. This qualitative difference means that linkage mechanisms require a different sort of interorganizational "glue"—glue that can easily turn out to serve as the adhesive to red tape.

In a competitive market, the success of one firm at the expense of another firm in that same industry is not only expected and tolerated but often seen as beneficial to the industry and the economy as a whole. The competition between firms leads, presumably, to better products and stronger firms. However, if the goal-attainment success of one government organization comes at the expense of another government organization working in the same "policy industry," there is no presumption that a higher good is served. Instead, the presumption is that government organizations are counterproductively working at odds with one another. Why would this inherent difference in government organizations lead to red tape? Simple—working at cross-purposes is presumed in competitive private firms, but is the very definition of red tape in government organizations: compliance burden without social benefit.

In sum, there is little reason why government organizations *must* have more red tape than private organizations, but there are several good reasons why there is a stronger likelihood of red tape in government. The balance of values in government management is such that accountability and fairness are often just as important as efficiency and performance. The need for enhanced accountability and the need to insure fair and, in most cases, equitable treatment require control mechanisms different in degree and kind from ones used in business. These controls do not always lead to more red tape, but sometimes they do. If we think of rules—especially controlling rules—as having an "underlying probability" of turning into red tape, then more rules will likely mean more red tape. When these rules are complex and when they are imposed from the outside, the probabilities become greater.

RESEARCH ON RED TAPE AND PUBLICNESS

After years of neglect, red tape research has become a more popular topic, especially among public administration researchers. Until the 1990s about the only empirical study addressing red tape was Buchanan's (1975) analysis. In this pioneering study, the results confounded usual expectations about greater red tape in government. Buchanan's findings showed that private sector managers expressed greater adherence and commitment to rules than did their public sector counterparts. Since Buchanan measured red tape with formalization scales it is not clear that this early work is comparable to more recent studies distinguishing between formalization and red tape.

A continuing difficulty of red tape studies is developing appropriate and useful measures of red tape. To a large extent, measurement flows from method. Since most research studies of public agencies' red tape have been based on survey research and questionnaires, the choice of measures is generally limited to the type of data that can be collected quickly and conveniently in survey instruments. This means that many of the concepts of red tape developed in this book are not employed in previous empirical studies because they do not lend themselves to measurement by questionnaires. Much of the theory and many of the propositions presented here are better tested by qualitative, case-oriented, and historical approaches.

The growth and decline in research topics is never a random process. In the case of red tape studies, it is easier than usual to explain the growth. A number of public administration researchers self-consciously set out to develop data that would be useful in the analysis of public sector organizations. As a result of this collaboration in the National Administrative Studies Project, empirical research on public organizations and, specifically, red tape has grown substantially during the past decade.

THE NATIONAL ADMINISTRATIVE STUDIES PROJECT

In 1992, a consortium of researchers at the University of Denver, Florida State University, University of Georgia, Ohio State University, and Syracuse University, met and agreed to gather data from matched public, private, and nonprofit organizations. The researchers focused on, variously, personnel systems (Wittmer, 1991), organization structure and goals (Lan and Rainey, 1992), ethics (Wittmer and Coursey, 1996), decision making (Coursey and Bozeman, 1990), and red tape (Rainey, Pandey, and Bozeman, 1995). The unifying objective was to understand differences between public and private organizations.

Questionnaire data were developed from a variety of sites and from hundreds of organizations, under the common framework of the National Administrative Studies Project (NASP). While the NASP data attempted to be representative of a wide range of organizational types and functions (see Bozeman and Rainey, 1998), other data were pooled with the NASP data. These other projects focused on topics as diverse as research and development laboratories (Bozeman and Crow, 1992; Bozeman and Crow, 1998), management information systems organizations (see Bretschneider, 1990), and organizations subject to the air emissions environmental regulations (see Bozeman, Kingsley, and Dehart-Davis, 1998). Each of these projects had much in common with the more general NASP data, including an ability to compare public and private organizations and a focus on red tape, generally measured in identical ways. The result is a broad basis for comparative research on red tape.

RED TAPE IN PUBLIC ORGANIZATIONS: RESEARCH RESULTS

Studies of red tape are still much less common than studies of formalization and organizational structure, but research is becoming more plentiful. Table 7-1 (on pages 134–135) provides a summary of red tape studies, almost all questionnaire-based studies.

In reviewing empirical results we ask just two critical questions: "Do government organizations have more red tape than private organizations?" "Why?"

(1) Do Government Organizations Have More Red Tape? Yes. But the issue is more complicated than it might seem. Almost every study (Buchanan, 1974, being in part an exception) finds that government agencies have more red tape than private organizations. This finding is more consistent than one might expect given the diversity of samples and measures of red tape. Government organizations take more time to perform core missions (Bozeman, Reed, and Scott, 1992; Bozeman and Crow, 1991), have more people required in sign-offs and approvals (Bozeman and Kingsley, 1998), and have higher levels of perceived red tape (Rainey, Pandey, and Bozeman, 1995). One interesting exception—private organizations have a higher incidence of "bureaucratic personalities," people who feel the need for more rules (Bozeman and Rainey, 1998).

Despite considerable convergence of findings, the issue of government red tape is complicated. In the first place, once one controls for a variety of factors, including government financing and other measures of external control, the difference between government and private organizations' red tape is much more modest (Bozeman and Bretschneider, 1995). That is, organizations with strong external control tend to have more red tape. It makes little difference whether the controlled organization is public or private. But since government organizations tend to have more external control, they also tend to have more red tape.

A second complication is that the degree of sector-based difference in red tape depends greatly on the *type* of red tape. Generally, government organizations have higher degrees of perceived red tape (e.g., Pandey, 1995), but this may be a self-fulfilling prophecy. Indeed, one study shows (Bozeman and Crow, 1991) that in some organizations there is a *negative* correlation between perceptions of red tape and objectively measured (time for core activities) red tape. This finding was for a subset of high performing R&D laboratories, suggesting that those who have a low tolerance for red tape are particularly likely to be aware of it and to perceive that there is more red tape than is actually the case.

Bretschneider's imaginative approach to measuring red tape (e.g., Bretschneider, 1990; Bretschneider and Bozeman, 1995; Pandey and Bretschneider, 1997) raises another issue. Is it even appropriate to take direct measures of red tape without first factoring out the size, function, and institutional setting of the organization? Is not the real issue the level of red tape in relation to truly comparable organizations? By looking at within-group variances in red tape it may be possible to come up with findings that are more useful for bureaucratic reform. There is no reason to expect that a large, public regulatory agency will have the same level of red tape as a small, private R&D laboratory. While NASP studies have to some extent tried to develop reasonable function-based comparisons between the sectors, the validity of comparisons is always an issue in examining market-based vs. "market failure" organizations.

(2) Why Do Government Organizations Have More Red Tape? Not surprisingly, researchers have done better answering question 1 than question 2. Comparison is always easier than causal explanation. But the evidence suggests that government organizations, when they do have more red tape, such as in personnel administration (Baldwin, 1990; Bozeman, Reed, and Scott, 1992), have more red tape because of external control efforts. Such evidence as has thus far been

TABLE 7-1   RED TAPE RESEARCH FINDINGS

STUDY	DATA	MEASURES	FINDINGS
Buchanan (1975)	Questionnaire data from nonmatched convenience sample of public and private managers	"Structure salience scale": the extent to which managers feel constrained by rules	Private sector managers feel more constrained than public managers do. Explanation: rules have different effects on lower and upper management in the respective sectors
Rosenfeld (1984)	Questionnaire data from public managers working with community development bloc grants	Questionnaire items on the sum of government guide lines, procedures, and forms perceived as excessive or unwieldy in effects on decision making	Concerned with measuring levels of red tape more than providing explanations
Baldwin (1990)	Data from public and private sector personnel managers	"Formal" red tape measured as perceptions of burdensome personnel procedures; "informal" red tape refers to constraints created by external sources such as the media or public opinion	Higher levels of red tape among public managers, with respect to personnel administration
Bozeman, Reed, and Scott (1992)	Questionnaire data from 1,341 directors of Research and Development laboratories in public and private sectors	Items pertaining to the amount of time required for core organizational activities including hiring, firing, circulating research products, purchasing equipment, beginning a new project	Variance in red tape according to government, university, industry setting. Government status affects red tape, but so does communication with government agencies and reliance on government agencies for budget resources. Sector affects red tape in equipment purchase and personnel, but not in release of research products or beginning new projects
Bozeman and Crow (1991)	Same as Bozeman, Reed, and Scott (1992)	Items pertaining to the amount of time required for core organizational activities	Technology transfer activities do not increase levels of red tape. Government laboratories have higher levels of red tape than universities or industry

Study	Data/Sample	Method/Measures	Findings
Pandey and Kingsley (1995)	From matched, dispersed samples of the National Administrative Studies Project (NASP), n=365 managers NASP	Questionnaire items measuring perceived red tape	Perceptions of red tape are strongly related to alienation which, in turn, relates to levels of employee motivation
Rainey, Pandey, and Bozeman (1995)	NASP	Items pertaining to the amount of time required for core organizational activities; items measuring perceived red tape	Public and private managers differ not only with respect to "objective" red tape but also perceived red tape, with public organizations being higher in each case
Bretschneider and Bozeman (1995)	State government program managers (n=1637) responding to national survey by National Association of State Information Systems	After examining ranges and variances for number of weeks required to perform core tasks (as in Bozeman, Reed, and Scott, 1992), computed red tape measure as a residual score	Government organizations consistently experienced greater procedural delays, but differences are related to degree of external influence. The *distribution* of delays is quite similar in public and private sector
Pandey and Bretschneider (1997)	Same as Bretschneider and Bozeman (1995)	Same as Bretschneider and Bozeman (1995)	Whether organizations see computer technology as a means to reduce red tape depends on the existing level of red tape and the perceived level of importance of information technology to the organization's mission
Bozeman and Rainey (1998)	NASP data	Questionnaire items pertaining the reported need for more or less rules and regulations; task delay measures; measures of perceived red tape	Personality factors, especially alienation, play a strong role in perception of need for more rules and regulations. The number of layers of organizational authority affects perceived need for more rules
Bozeman and Kingsley (1998)	NASP data	Questionnaire items related to risk-taking; task delay measures; measures of perceived red tape	Organizations with higher level of red tape and formalization have less risk-taking propensity. Risk-taking is accounted for by goal clarity and expectation of reward for good performance

**RESEARCH ENCOUNTER:
MEASURING RED TAPE**

*C*onsider the imaginary memorandum below and decide which of the several suggested red tape or efficiency measures seem most useful for improving performance. Which measures seem valid indictors of performance? Does any one best capture the organization's level of "red tape?"

**Acme Associates
3501 Bandito Boulevard
Beltway City, Maryland 42305**

"We Crunch Data to Your Specs!"

January 18, 2000

To: Cornelius Case, Executive Director, Interfaith Action Alliance
From: Dr. Adrian Acme, President
Re: Results of Management Effectiveness Study

Acme Associates is pleased to assist Interfaith Action Alliance (IAA) in its effort to improve its management effectiveness. As agreed, we began by developing measures of organizational performance (provided below). Then you will convene a "stakeholder panel" to assess possible red tape and develop ideas for improved efficiency.

The measures presented below are "benchmarked" against similar religious-affiliated social services organizations, including Catholic Charities, Salvation Army, and Unitarian Outreach. These organizations are quite similar to IAA with respect to services delivered, funding levels, number of personnel, and characteristics of clients. To preserve anonymity, we provide data from these organizations under the labels "Organization A," "Organization B," and "Organization C."

In considering the data, it is important to remember it is up to you and your stakeholders to determine the relative importance of each of these measures. My firm takes no position as to which of these measures has the greatest significance.

1. Ratio of case worker personnel to administrative support personnel:

    IAA: 4 to 1
    "A":   3 to 1
    "B":   5.5 to 1
    "C":   4 to 1

2. Average number of "sign offs" required for initiating services to a new client:

    IAA: 6
    "A":   3

"B":   2
"C":   None (at discretion of caseworker)

3. Weeks taken to hire full-time personnel:

   IAA: 8
   "A":   3
   "B":   3
   "C":   5

4. Weeks required for final contract with State Division of Social Service after award has finally been agreed upon:

   IAA: 18
   "A":   6
   "B":   4
   "C":   6

5. Costs per client, per fiscal year (total budget, all sources, divided by number of clients served):

   IAA: $1,754
   "A":   600
   "B":   647
   "C":   1,109

6. Percentage of professional employees responding "agree" to questionnaire item "Compared to similar organizations with which I am familiar, this organization is less flexible and has more red tape."

   IAA: 15%
   "A":   18
   "B":   25
   "C":   31

7. Percentage of organization's clients responding "agree" to questionnaire item "This organization seems too inflexible and has too much red tape."

   IAA: 17%
   "A":   17
   "B":   19
   "C":   9

Thank you for your confidence in my organization. It has been a pleasure to work with you and your excellent staff. Please find enclosed our bill for services rendered. We hope to receive payment in two weeks (your organization's average is six weeks).

obtained (e.g., Bozeman and Bretschneider, 1994; Bretschneider and Bozeman, 1995; Bozeman and Loveless, 1987), suggests that when government and business organizations are subjected to similar levels of external political control they tend to have similar levels of red tape. Using delays as a partial measure of red tape, studies using different data sources (Bozeman, Reed, and Scott, 1992; Bozeman and Bretschneider, 1994; Bretschneider and Bozeman, 1995) found that private organizations with stronger ties to government exhibit more red tape. This suggests that it is not government ownership that is the chief causal agent, but the exercise of external political authority.

CONCLUSION

While such reform efforts as the National Performance Review have taken care to sort out the red tape from procedural safeguards and accountability mechanisms, other reform efforts seem mainly concerned with making government go away. Red tape cutting requires a scalpel, not a meat ax. In their frenzied enthusiasm for red tape cutting, some zealots and political opportunists portray all rules and regulations as red tape. If there is any single point to this book it is that nothing is accomplished, either in understanding or reform, by lumping together all rules and regulations as just so much red tape. To put it another way, the issue of cutting red tape is clearly separable from conservative political agendas seeking a rollback of government functions.

In some cases, there are sound reasons for numerous rules. In others, just a few rules may entail a great deal of red tape. Some organizations are hamstrung by red tape and other organizations are undercontrolled, having *too few* rules and regulations. Any effort to, for example, "cut red tape by 10 percent across government" is poorly informed. All rules are not created equal.

Whether "limited government" is defined as downsizing or a revolutionary paring back of almost all functions of civilian government, the cutting of rules and regulations is often a convenient means to an end. For better or worse, many government functions are *defined* by the promulgation of rules and regulations and "reform" realized by cutting rules and regulations willy-nilly is often little more than a thinly disguised attack on the functions of government. To be sure, there are government activities that should be reviewed and assessed. But it is better to do so in open policy deliberations than by means of "neutral" government reform. Government reform of any sort is inevitably political, but the danger comes when politics are masked.

How do empirical findings relate to these normative concerns? First, showing that red tape is not a "natural" concomitant of government but, instead, a consequence of external control, brings some light to decisions allocating functions among sectors and to decisions about privatization. If contractors deliver a service previously provided by government but the level of external control stays the same, there is no reason to expect a reduction in the level of red tape.

Especially noteworthy in today's climate of privatization of government functions and "hollowing out" of government is Meyer's (1979a) suggestion that attempts to privatize public sector goods and services may actually serve as another source of red tape. Red tape stems from the documentation and other administrative requirements that are attached to federal funds as a means to ensure compliance with federal guidelines. If these continue, red tape is likely to follow the interorganizational ties.

Finally, red tape may well be inextricably related to the character of the political system, particularly the distribution of authority. The fragmentation and dispersion of authority created by the U.S. Constitution ensures extensive rules and procedures, and, thereby, increases the likelihood (i.e., the "underlying probability distribution") for red tape. Dispersion of political authority to contractors may do little to decrease the incidence of red tape, at least so long as there is an interest in retaining high levels of accountability and control.

Before moving to possible remedies for red tape, we consider in the next chapter an application of some of the concepts and ideas presented here. The extended case is in the field of air pollution policy—a regulatory arena in which red tape charges and counter-charges merit some systematic inquiry.

RED TAPE
AND ENVIRONMENTAL POLICY

The trench warfare among red tape cutters, accountability insurers, and policy activists is perhaps greatest in environmental policy. Despite the complexity of environmental problems and proposed solutions, the battle lines come easily into view. On the one side, environmentalists make the irrefutable argument that nothing is more important than environmental preservation because all life depends upon it. On the other side, industry and economic growth advocates make the equally irrefutable point that environmental policy is inevitably a trade-off between the values of environmental preservation and other values such as economic growth, jobs, housing, and public works. One trade-off is especially relevant to our purposes: "How can environmental objectives be achieved efficiently and effectively, with minimal red tape?"

No one disputes the considerable compliance costs of environmental policy. However, there are many debates on environmental policy's effects on other values such as accountability, economic growth, and social equity. The crosscutting values of environmental policy make it an ideal focus for students of red tape and bureaucratic pathology.

This chapter uses the concepts and theory developed in this book as a lens for examining air pollution policy. The specific policy examined is Title V of the Clean Air Act Amendments of 1990. By applying to a single case many of the ideas developed in the preceding chapters, the possible uses for red tape theory are highlighted. Ultimately, the test of any theory or model is its utility. Ideas may prove useful in explanation, a strin-

Note: This chapter was written with Leisha DeHart-Davis. The chapter draws from two related works: Bozeman, DeHart-Davis, and Kingsley, 1999; Bozeman and DeHart-Davis, in press.

gent utility test. Sometimes ideas are useful because they help us organize our thinking about a topic. In other cases the utility of ideas comes from their ability to suggest hypotheses or interpretations. Given these utility tests, let us see if red tape theory has value for understanding the regulatory thicket of air permitting policy.

ENVIRONMENTAL POLICY AS A BALANCING ACT: LEGISLATIVE BACKGROUND OF THE CLEAN AIR ACT AMENDMENTS

The Clean Air Act Amendments of 1990 include a provision, Title V, requiring states to implement an air quality permitting program that will ultimately involve detailed regulation of as many as fifty thousand U.S. businesses. The purposes of the air quality permitting program are manifold, but the chief assumption is that increased information will lead to reduced air pollution. The routes to this end are diverse. One pathway for use of the information is by citizen participation, at least so long as citizen and not just industry groups are heard (Golden, 1998). The framers of the legislation, many of whom were lawyers who had experience representing citizens' groups, believed that the truth will, indeed, set you free, so long as that truth is publicly available. They assumed that with the increased information available under Title V, private citizens and citizens groups would bring suit against local polluters. Later, we return specifically to this assumption as we examine the premises of Title V.

Another assumption is that state permitting programs will be improved as a result of enhanced information about companies' air emissions. There is also hope that the companies will become more integrated into state information and policymaking systems and become better and more cooperative corporate citizens. Significantly, the permitting system does *not* set pollution standards or limits.

The controversy about the cost of Title V permitting has been heated. Most costs come from filling out extensive permits. These permits, some of which fill a good sized box, require companies' personnel time and often involve significant consulting expenses. Industry groups have alleged that the ultimate cost will be in the billions of dollars. Title V also has its strong advocates, and not only at the U.S. EPA. Debates about the merits of Title V permitting inevitably move from questions of costs to a question of implementation.

Early in most Title V discussions the term *red tape* makes an appearance. Questions about red tape are rarely formulated with any precision. Indeed, most observers fail even to distinguish between compliance costs and red tape. The key question of compliance costs is: "What quantity of resources are required for achieving the behaviors specified in regulations?" The question of red tape is: "What degree of inefficiency, duplication, and wasted effort is likely to follow?"

In this chapter we use the concepts and theory thus far developed in the book and apply them to the case of Title V permitting. While the approach here involves legal analysis of some statutes and records, findings from interviews are also introduced. Government officials, industry experts, consultants, political staff, and others were interviewed in connection with a research project (Bozeman and DeHart-Davis, in press; Bozeman, Kingsley, and DeHart-Davis, 1999) and many of these interviews are used here. We begin with a bit of environmental policy history.

FEDERAL AIR QUALITY POLICY
PRIOR TO THE 1990 CLEAN AIR ACT AMENDMENTS

The federal government entered the air quality policy arena in the 1950s, with funding for research to study sources and impacts of poor air quality (Air Pollution Control Act of 1955). Explosive growth in automobile ownership and highway travel drove Congress to expand this funding in the 1960s to include automobile pollution research (Motor Vehicle Act of 1960).

Congress laid the groundwork for national air quality standards in the 1963 Clean Air Act, when it authorized the establishment of scientifically based air quality criteria to guide state air quality policies (Clean Air Act of 1963). States were not required to adopt the criteria, but federal officials could convene state and local pollution regulators when exceeding the criteria led to interstate pollution-endangered health or welfare. These conferences theoretically provided the basis for federal abatement action. Ultimately, however, the act spurred less than a dozen conferences and only one enforcement action (Percival, et al., 1992: 761).

Congress enabled direct regulation of air pollution in 1965 and 1967, with laws requiring states to adopt air quality standards, directing the identification of air quality regions, enabling standards-setting for automobile emissions (Motor Vehicle Air Pollution Control Act of 1965 and Air Quality Act of 1967). By 1970, federal officials had defined less than one-third of the air quality regions and no state had set complete standards for any pollutant (Bryner, 1995: 99).

The slow pace of federal enforcement, combined with political pressure from consumer advocacy groups, propelled the Clean Air Act of 1970 (Percival, et al., 1992: 763). This statute took a more aggressive approach than its predecessors did, in an effort to "protect and enhance the public health and welfare and the productive capacity of its population." (42 U.S.C. 7401a, 1970). The act replaced state air quality standards with national standards based on the criteria documents. States were required to issue state implementation plans that brought poor air quality areas into compliance by 1970. If a state's plan was inadequate, the newly created Environmental Protection Agency (EPA) was empowered to design and implement a plan. EPA was also directed to set nationally uniform emissions limits for the new major stationary sources of air emissions (hereafter, "sources").

The 1975 deadline for achieving federal standards and enforcing state plans came and went, with thousands of sources still not in compliance (Bryner, 1995: 101). Considering the act's previous track record, Congress undertook another round of amendments in 1977 that targeted *nonattainment* areas (those not meeting air quality standards) of the country that had failed to meet federal standards (42 U.S.C. 7401b, 1977). The law required new standards for existing sources and cutting-edge technology and emissions offsets for new sources. Nonattainment areas were given until 1982 to achieve federal standards, a deadline that came and went with no further progress toward achieving the nation's air quality goals (Percival, et al., 1992: 765).

THE POLICY SETTING: TITLE V AND THE CLEAN AIR ACT AMENDMENTS

Prior to the 1990 Clean Air Act Amendments, industry compliance with air quality regulations was characterized by confusion and ambiguity over standards, negotiated compliance agreements between industry and regulators that sometimes informally rewrote state plans, and lack of political will by the states for pursuing aggressive enforcement. Confusion often stemmed from the complexity and inaccessibility of state implementation plans. The state plans served as a blueprint for how the state would achieve federal air quality standards. The plans included details about hundreds of regulations to which industrial sources were subject. Determining applicable requirements was a challenge because states rarely distributed their plans and, even if they could, applicable requirements were buried in hundreds of pages of regulatory detail (Novello, et al., 1995: 39).

Title V of the Clean Air Act Amendments of 1990 greatly extends permitting requirements among businesses emitting substantial amounts of any of nearly two hundred pollutants. Title V impinges on many aspects of firms' strategy and day-to-day allocation of resources.

The implementation issues involved in Title V vary a great deal from state to state. There are differences according to preexisting permit programs, number and type of "sources" (i.e., facilities with air pollution emissions); staff and resources devoted to Title V, and the political climate for environmental policy and business. In the case of the State of Georgia, for example, the State of Georgia's Department of Natural Resources (GNDR) has been issuing permits since 1973, having issued some 11,000 permits for more than 3,500 facilities.

The information required under each permit is considerable and includes general facility information, a description of processes and products, emissions-related information, air pollution control requirements, defined operational flexibility, compliance plan, and compliance certification. Additionally, sources must retain compliance records for five years, during which time they must be available for inspection upon request.

One major issue for companies confronted with Title V requirements is whether to seek status as a "synthetic minor." The Synthetic Minor rule of the 1990 Clean Air Act exempts from Title V permitting those companies that restrict their potential emissions below threshold levels triggering Title V permitting requirements. Sources may restrict potential emissions by implementing innovative prevention technologies, traditional end-of-the-pipe controls, or production ceilings. In exchange for restricting potential emissions, stationary sources undergo a simpler permitting process that requires less detail in application, less record-keeping, less monitoring and reporting, and lower permit fees.

TITLE V IN CONTEXT

The 700-page Clean Air Act Amendments of 1990 has been called "one of the most complex pieces of regulatory legislation adopted, and one of the most impenetrable" (Nickel, 1991: 18–22). In addition to the national permit program, the act addressed several important deficiencies in previous legislation. The act imposed new requirements for areas out of compliance with air quality standards (Title I, Part D), a new program to control hazardous air pollutants (Title I, Section 112), an acid rain control program (Title IV), and new controls on mobile sources and the fuels they burn (Title II, Part C). Each of these provisions is important to the nation's environmental future, but it is Title V that best serves as a specimen for red tape researchers' microscopes.

Title V begins by directing EPA to establish regulations within one year of the act's passage that outline the minimum elements to be contained in state operating permit programs, including permit application requirements, monitoring and reporting requirements, and a permitting fee structure (CAA § 502[b]). States, in turn, must propose their permit programs based on those regulations in a written plan to EPA within three years of the act's passage (CAA § 502[d]). The legislation empowers states to collect fees for permits. The fee money goes directly to administering new permit programs (CAA § 502[b]). The law also specifies that states submitting inadequate plans or failing to administer approved plans may face loss of federal highway funding or restrictions on industrial growth (CAA § 502[d]) and § 179[b]).

While much of the Title V language directs EPA and the states, the provision also specifies requirements that directly affect permitted sources. Major sources of air pollution, defined in the act as companies emitting certain amounts and types of pollution (CAA § 502[a]), must submit a compliance plan and application for an operating permit to the state. The deadline for this submission is twelve months after the state permitting program has been approved by EPA (CAA § 503[a][c]). Facility permits must detail all regulations with which the source must comply, include a minimum six-month reporting requirement, and specify inspection, monitoring, and certification approaches (CAA § 504). EPA is empowered to veto those permits that do not conform to the act or to the state implementation plan (CAA § 502[i]).

Significantly, the act also criminalizes certain violations associated with Title V permitting. Sources that knowingly violate their permit conditions face fines and imprisonment of up to five years (CAA § 113[c]1). Failure to report, misrepresentation of permit or monitoring information, and tampering of monitoring equipment may induce a fine or two years imprisonment (CAA § 113[c]2). This part of the act led to the gallows humor of companies identifying responsible officials as "designated felons."

The act's citizen suit and criminal penalty provisions are integrally linked to permit enforcement. Title III enables citizens to sue states or EPA in U.S. District Court to enforce specific permit requirements applicable to individual sources (CAA § 304). Citizens groups have had problems filing suits against companies because of limited data or access to data about emissions. Title V rectifies these problems by providing for the collection of compliance data and centralizing air emissions source's requirements in one publicly available document. Citizens can seek civil penalties against noncomplying sources, the proceeds of which go to "beneficial mitigation projects which are consistent with this Act and enhance the public health or the environment" (CAA § 304[g]2).

The citizen suit provisions of Title III are important to understanding legislative purpose (Bozeman and DeHart-Davis, in press). The framers of the legislation assumed that empowering citizens would have the effect of more intensive and effective monitoring and, in turn, companies wishing to avoid the spotlight of public hearings would take steps to voluntarily reduce pollution. (Later in this chapter we return to consider the underlying logic of the citizen action provisions of the legislation).

TITLE V IMPLEMENTATION

Title V implementation has been a controversial and often difficult process. The first step required EPA to promulgate regulations for state operating permit program design. As required by the regulatory review process, EPA first submitted draft regulations to the Office of Management and Budget. The President's Council on Competitiveness reviewed this draft. The council was established by the Reagan administration to reduce regulatory burden on industry. The council, seeking to simplify, proposed over one hundred changes to the draft regulations. One significant change was to allow minor permit modifications to be accomplished with a simple notification to the state. Another was to exempt permit revisions from public review (Bryner, 1995: 196). Congressional staff intimately familiar with the original legislation regarded the proposed rule changes as "substantially weaker than those mandated by Congress" (House Subcommittee on Health and the Environment, 1991: 2).

The controversy over Title V implementation has continued well past the final rule publishing. Industry, state, and environmental groups have sued EPA over nearly sixty parts of the final rules (Novello, 1995: 1). EPA has responded by re-proposing the most controversial aspects of the final rules, dealing with operational flexibility at facilities, with subsequent re-proposals due in 1996 (Federal Register, 1994: 44460). In addition, the agency has released two white papers, nonbinding and nonregulatory guidance documents that increase the states' flexibility in implementing requirements (EPA, 1995; EPA, 1996). But even if the changes have increased flexibility, they have introduced some confusion and a view that the rules of the game are being invented while the game is underway.

TITLE V PERMITTING AND SOURCES OF RULE-INCEPTION RED TAPE

The Title V case serves as an excellent illustration of many of the points developed in this book. While considered in depth, the case does not draw fully from red tape theory. Indeed, it is unlikely that any single case would, because no single policy would likely include all of the antecedents of red tape. But many of the causes of red tape are already evident in Title V.

INTERVIEW DATA

Title V has not yet been fully implemented, yet there is an extensive legal trail. Thus, the data for this analysis include the statutory and documentary evidence available. In addition to the paper trail, we examine data (see Bozeman and DeHart-Davis, in press) from interviews with key informants knowledgeable about Title V. Those interviewed include congressional staff, political executives, and lobbyists who were present at the beginning, helping shape the Clean Air Act Amendments and Title V, specifically. EPA officials interviewed included those charged with reviewing states' Title V permits. State government officials were interviewed, including those responsible for designing and implementing Title V programs. Further data come from scores of industry personnel, both environmental professionals and "designated felons," the persons who have ultimate responsibility for firms' compliance and who are, according to one of the more controversial elements of Title V, subject to criminal prosecution if their permit information is deemed fallacious.

KEY CONCEPTS AND THE TITLE V CONTEXT

While a number of propositions of red tape theory can be examined within the Title V context, a more elementary but still quite useful approach is to simply consider the terms of the theory in connection with the case. We start with the most fundamental concept, the rule.

THE RULE

Red tape theory assumes all rules have *behavioral requirements, implementation mechanisms,* and *enforcement provisions.* Table 8-1 (on page 148) gives the major statutory content for each of the rule elements and an early assessment of the *stability* of the respective rule elements.

The early history of Title V shows remarkable instability and rapid evolution with respect to both its behavioral requirements and its implementation mechanisms. This instability seems to have implications for red tape and Title V's ability to achieve the *functional objects of the rule.*

Functional Objects of the Rule   The following excerpt from the Clean Air Act Amendments provides a succinct formal explanation of the functional object of the Title V rule:

> The Title V permit program will enable the source, States, EPA, and the public to understand better the requirements to which the source is subject, and whether the source is meeting those requirements. Increased source accountability and better enforcement should result. The program will also strengthen EPA's ability to implement the Act and enhance air quality planning and control, in part, by providing the basis for better emission inventories. (*Federal Register*, Vol. 57, no. 140, July 21, 1992: 32251)

The objectives of Title V, as with so many broad rules, are not precisely defined. Title V received less attention than other elements of the Clean Air Act Amendments (CAAA). One congressional staff member who participated in the design of the legislation observed, "Title V was the drudgery work. Members [of Congress] cared about specific environmental issues, others were worried about particular industry interests and

TABLE 8-1 RULE ELEMENTS TITLE V

RULE ELEMENT	STATUTORY CONTENT		STABILITY
Behavioral Requirement	*State level:* design program in accordance with Part 79 regulations, including setting criteria for permit applications, securing authority to charge fees, adequate enforcement personnel and funding, permit enforcement, and public participation	*Firm level:* Deadline of one year past state program approval for turning in permit application; targets sources based on emissions levels	Both firm—and state-level requirements have changed considerably since CAA passage. High potential for instability
Implementation Mechanisms	Programs, once approved are implemented by the states through permit application requirements and established public hearings processes; implementation funded in part by fees assessed		Lack of standardization among state programs, high potential stability of within-state implementation
Enforcement Provisions	Civil penalty of $10,000 per day for sources' noncompliance; criminal prosecution authority via states' attorneys general for fallacious permit applications and knowing violations of permit conditions or filing requirements. EPA retains enforcement authority for states without approved programs. EPA sanctions against the states include a highway funding cutoff and a 2-to-1 offset ratio for new and modified sources with no submittal because of program disapproval		Enforcement provisions have remained stable, high potential for enforcement instability

local utilities' allowance.... There were not a lot of people stirring up things on permitting." (Personal interview, March 22, 1996).

The congressional testimony regarding Title V is only a small fraction of the testimony for more controversial aspects of the CAAA. Nor was there substantial consensus among the parties who designed and directly influenced the legislation. One particularly well-informed observer, who was a staff member for Congressman Henry Waxman (D-Cal.), then chair of the Energy Committee's Subcommittee on Environment and Public Works, was asked about his perceptions of Congress's intent for Title V:

> They wanted to improve enforcement. Congress had the metaphor of 'balancing the budget,' looking for the most efficient way to do it. They felt there was about 80 percent compliance out there, but wanted to

pick up more emissions sources without increasing the standards. [The other objective was citizen participation.]... Before, the citizen supervision standards in clean air had not worked, in clean water they had. Could we design something that was effective from the standpoint of citizen supervision? Citizens' access to the information would give pressure for industry to be in compliance. (Personal interview, March 22, 1996)

In the Senate, a major actor was a staff member for Senator Durenburger, focusing especially on CAAA air toxin legislation. This staff member remarked that Title V, despite the ultimate costs passed along to states and industry, did not receive a great deal of attention.

Lee Thomas [former Administrator, USEPA] had given [Congressman] Dingle an air toxins bill which included *a little thing about permitting* [author's emphasis], built on the model of the Clean Water Act. The permit title is really just an expansion of that memo from Lee Thomas. It was not something from the business community, but for EPA who saw problems ... in terms of fragmentation and wanted one piece of paper to rationalize ... what they were expected to do. (Personal interview, March 21, 1996)

Rule Implementation There are at least fifty-one authoritative rule implementers for Title V, each of the states and EPA. Actually, it is many more than fifty-one because in some states there are municipalities and regional governments with implementation authority. In most respects, EPA should not be viewed as a single entity, given the vast differences among EPA regions with respect to political culture and approaches to implementation (Church and Nakamura, 1993).

There are vast differences among the states with respect to their views of Title V. As this is written, less than half the states have completed initial implementation of Title V permitting programs. There are many factors that explain states' degrees of receptivity to the program. Generally, states that had extensive source permitting programs before Title V tend to see less benefit. States with an extremely strong probusiness regulatory environment see less benefit. Of course these differences among the states were at the heart of the Title V rationale. As one congressional observer noted, "There is [sic] great differences in states' political will for enforcement, but under Title V if the states don't do it, EPA can walk in." It is not clear, however, that this is a palpable threat given the resource limitations of EPA and the political turmoil that such a "walk in" would entail. An important policy instrument question is this: If the regulatory problem is differences among implementers' effectiveness, can the problem be resolved by new and better-codified rules? If the problem is implementation approach, not rule, then what is the likelihood that the problem will be addressed by new rules?

COMPLIANCE

There has never been much agreement as to the likely compliance burden of Title V permitting. The National Association of Manufacturers compiled estimates of costs for facilities obtaining permits and concluded that for a small source emitting a single pollutant the costs would be $2,000 to $5,000; for small to medium sources with multiple pollutants the average would be $15,000. Adding costs related to sampling, monitoring tests, and public hearings costs for a small to medium business might range from $30,000 to $85,000. But not everyone believes these figures. As one knowledgeable EPA official noted, "Much of this is just beltway posturing; groups saying it would cost $20–30 billion per year to implement based on their projection of continuous monitoring and several implausible assumptions."

Georgia industrial officials interviewed provide highly variable figures but, on average, are close to the estimates of the National Association of Manufacturers, the leading trade group for manufacturers. Perhaps some of the more useful estimates come from consulting firms hired for "turnkey" permit applications. According to one experienced consultant who works for a company that has done hundreds of permit applications, the "price [for a turnkey permit] can range from $25,000 to $500,000 depending upon facility complexity." He estimates that the average price for the firms (generally large ones) contracting with his company is $100,000 for a 75–100 emission point facility employing about three hundred people. This does not, of course, include the labor costs of companies' personnel who work with the consultants on gathering permitting application data.

It is not yet possible to derive even a good "ball park" estimate of the total costs to industry of implementing Title V. But given the many thousands of sources under the Title V major source umbrella, even low estimates add up to tens of billions of dollars. The sheer magnitude of regulatory activity means that questions of compliance burden, resources, and implementation burden are vital.

Compliance Resources and Compliance Burden   A question often important in regulatory policy (but not usually asked this way) is: What is the discrepancy between compliance resources (the amount of resources required to fully comply with a rule) and compliance burden (the amount actually expended)? In many instances, the key is to ensure that compliance burden is not much less than compliance resources. In Title V, the "gap" problem may well go both ways. As is normally the case, some sources will likely seek shortcuts by, in this instance, providing rough estimates, avoiding precise tests, and using extrapolation techniques (rather than actual sampling) for permit application data. But

---

RESEARCH ENCOUNTER:
ESTIMATING COMPLIANCE COSTS

In a questionnaire-based study of Title V (Bozeman, Kingsley, and DeHart-Davis, 1998), a number of approaches were used to estimate the compliance costs for hundreds of sources in five states. One of these, perhaps closest to market-based reasoning, examined the costs to sources of "turnkey" consulting contracts. Turnkey permitting means simply that consulting companies do all the needed measures and calculations and fill out all the forms required for Title V permitting. By examining the cost of turnkey permits (as reflected in the amount spent on consultants) we can estimate Title V costs.

Arguably, the market is a useful indicator of the cost of Title V compliance. It we assume that the amount spend on consultants' turnkey permitting services captures most of the cost of compliance, then the methodological problem is to extrapolate those companies using turnkey services to those not using them.

We began by noting that the companies' per capita costs of those using turnkey services is, on average, $82.72 per employee. We then adjust for the costs of company employees' work with consultants, $31 per capita for companies using turnkey consultants. Using this measure, the costs of Title V are estimated at about $114 per employee. This measure can be refined to include such factors as: the companies' employee costs as a percentage of business costs; scale effects for company size; per capita consultant costs at various scale thresholds.

A possible flaw in this approach is that the findings may not be representative. Not all companies used consultants and the ones who did not were systematically different from the ones who did. Smaller companies sometimes had insufficient funds to employ consultants and the larger ones had their own in-house expertise. But the findings seem useful, especially after statistical adjustments are made to compensate for the unrepresentativeness of the companies using consultants (see Bozeman, Kingsley, and DeHart-Davis, 1998, for details on extrapolation and statistical adjustments).

---

there is also the problem of "overcompliance," especially in small firms that have not been permitted before. There are two especial factors that may give rise to overcompliance (i.e., a compliance burden greater than required compliance resources). First, there was a great deal of initial confusion about the exact nature of the requirements and what pollutants at what levels were covered. There was no consistent answer until EPA published two lengthy "white papers" giving greater detail and, by some interpretations, backing off somewhat on the stringency of requirements. Firms who filed permit applications before the white papers may have overcomplied. One environmental manager in a medium-sized firm estimated that she would have spent 30–40 percent less time on her company's permit application if she had prepared it after the release of the white papers rather than before (personal interview, February 1996). In this case, the instability of the behavioral requirements of the rule seems to have penalized early compliers.

A second factor that may lead to overcompliance is the so-called "designated felon" provision of Title V. The inclusion of criminal penalties may well lead responsible officials to overcomply. In one small (seventy-five employees) flexible packaging company, the responsible official (the second ranking official in the firm) indicated to us that for the past several months more than 50 percent of his time had been devoted to compliance. One of the consultants interviewed (Bozeman, Kingsley, and DeHart-Davis, 1997), an individual who had been involved in more than one hundred Title V permits, indicated that overcompliance is the norm among his customers.

Implementation Burden Rules are costly not only for those complying but often for the government agency charged with implementation. While estimating the implementation burden for Title V is of some import, the fact that most states have granted the authority for state environmental agencies to retain permit fees means that the implementation burden is offset by the ability to retain fees. Indeed, in some states, environmental agencies are highly motivated by the fees. An air quality official in New Mexico reported that the Title V permitting program had allowed his agency to hire several new personnel and that the permit fees have been a considerable boon for a small agency (personal interview, May 10, 1996). But an individual representing a state air pollution administrators' association expressed ambivalence about the fees. Whereas the state agencies enjoy having resources from the fees, they have some concern that the fees will become more important than implementation and enforcement.

One can think of compliance burden and implementation burden as two distinct and independent dimensions (Table 8-2). Title V seems a "High, High"—a significant resource drain on the regulator and the regulated entity.

ASSESSING TITLE V'S RULE INCEPTION RED TAPE

Previously, we distinguished between red tape embedded in rules creation (rule inception) and red tape that evolves from rules originally functional (rule-evolved). Since Title V has not been fully implemented, this analysis focuses chiefly on rule-inception red tape. The two sources of rule-inception red tape most important for Title V are incorrect rule forecasts and overcontrol.

TABLE 8-2   COMPLIANCE VERSUS IMPLEMENTATION BURDEN

RESOURCE DRAIN	COMPLIANCE BURDEN	IMPLEMENTATION BURDEN
Both	High	High
Regulating Agency	Low	High
Regulated Entity	High	Low
Neither	Low	Low

INCORRECT RULE FORECASTS

Every rule contains implicit or explicit assumptions and forecasts about human behavior and often-incorrect rule forecasts lead quickly to red tape. Title V has layers-within-layers of rule forecasts. Depending on the layer one chooses, one can begin with relatively general forecasts such as the following:

> Providing additional information to the states will lead to improved compliance.

Or one can focus on an inner layer and examine a somewhat more specific forecast such as the following:

> Including criminal penalties for sources' responsible officials will lead to greater attention to Title V and, ultimately, greater compliance.

We can also distinguish rules forecasts that are more explicit and less explicit. Explicit forecasts can be easily derived from a reading of rules and their statutory context, but implicit forecasts, while not always difficult to discern, at least require some interpretation. An example of an implicit forecast easily derived from interviews but not easily derived from a reading of the Title V statutory bases is as follows:

> The authority for EPA intercession (takeover when a state does not implement a program) will prove a sufficient threat to result in timely and technically suitable permitting programs in the states.

The largely implicit assumption central to Title V is that many states have been dragging their feet in implementing significant source permitting programs, and that greater EPA involvement will enhance states' programs.

A CASE IN POINT: PUBLIC PARTICIPATION AND PUBLIC INFORMATION

Clearly, the tangle of interdependent assumptions and of implicit and explicit forecasts entailed in Title V is sufficient to employ an army of logicians simply to specify and sort them out. This means that incorrect rules forecasts, a prime culprit in rule-inception red tape, is a serious threat. Even rules with the best of intents can turn out to be red tape if the behavioral logic upon which the rule depends is found to be wanting.

For a simple illustration, let us focus on just one aspect of Title V— public participation and public information. This is just one element of Title V but certainly illustrates the difficulties of achieving policy objectives through rule making. The behaviors required for public participation to have an effect on air pollution control seem more clear once the forecast is laid out.

A straightforward statement of the rule forecast is as follows:

> Providing greater access to information on the part of the public will enhance sources' compliance.

Since red tape is measured as departure from the rule's functional object, we reexamine a statutory summary of the Title V's functional object:

> The Title V permit program will enable the source, States, EPA, and the public to understand better the requirements to which the source is subject, and whether the source is meeting those requirements. Increased source accountability and better enforcement should result. The program will also strengthen EPA's ability to implement the Act and enhance air quality planning and control, in part, by providing the basis for better emission inventories. (*Federal Register*, Vol. 57, no. 140, July 21, 1992: 32251)

By this statement, public understanding is key. Indeed, it is no less important an instrumentality than EPA oversight or states' enforcement prerogatives. As one EPA official indicated, "Title V is really only two things: government in the sunshine and good information infrastructure." (Personal interview, U.S. EPA, April 10, 1996). To better understand thinking about the role of public information, we can consider the commentaries provided by officials who helped put together the legislation and who have responsibility for its implementation.

Most persons interviewed agreed that there had been many successful citizen-initiated law suits concerning water pollution but very few concerning air. It was assumed that if the information provided were sufficient, citizen lawsuits concerning air pollution would increase and, more to the point, the threat of lawsuits would give industry pause. The branch chief in the EPA Office of Enforcement, one of the officials responsible for coordinating CAAA enforcement across the nation, sees value in the citizen information provisions of Title V:

> A major accomplishment in Title V is the citizens' provision, which we can enforce at the federal level. If EPA cannot enforce state limits, and then citizens cannot enforce state limits.... Some states give citizens standing to sue for enforcement, but some don't. If citizens don't

have standing or access to information, then they don't have a foot in the door. Access to information is much easier at the federal level because we have broad statutory powers under the Act to request information from sources if we suspect compliance problems. (Personal interview, March 3, 1996)

An EPA lawyer who has been involved with Title V permitting from the inception of the legislation describes the value of the public information provisions as follows:

[Before Title V] ... much of the interaction had occurred between a source and its regulating authority, an interaction that was not subject to public scrutiny. Title V changed all that by letting the public in on all these questions. The issue of how much public notice is needed has been hotly debated. A key policy question is what really is the benefit of exposing all of this to the public? Does the public care? How would an economist quantify the benefit of public review? The interim effect is that a source may be more careful in preparing its application. It would be tremendously helpful for the EPA to know (the effects of public scrutiny on the representatives of regulated sources). (Personal interview, April 10, 1996)

If we consider the rule forecasts in Table 8-3, we see that even this simple model is dependent upon several implicit expectations. There is

TABLE 8-3   RULES FORECASTS FROM CITIZEN INFORMATION PROVISIONS

I. Increased citizen information will lead to greater source compliance assuming the following conditions pertaining to citizen suits:
    A. The information gathered by state agencies is, indeed, readily available to the citizens.
    B. Citizens are aware that the information is available.
    C. The information is available in a form that is usable.
    D. Citizens are sufficiently attentive and can mobilize.
    E. Citizens have the financial resources for law suits.
    F. Citizens have adequate legal expertise at their disposal.
    G. The courts are receptive to the citizen suits (rule on standing).
II. ...And assuming the following conditions pertaining to source officials' behaviors:
    A. Sources are aware of the fact that information provided to state agencies is available to citizens.
    B. Sources are more likely to take care with their permitting information and compliance behaviors because of the availability of information to citizens.
        1. The threat of lawsuit is palpable.
        2. The threat of lawsuit is a deterrent (rather than, say, a welcome opportunity for legal challenge).
        3. In the absence of a compelling need to consider lawsuits, the source is motivated by some other factor (e.g., need to keep a "clean" public image) related to availability of information.
    C. Assuming motivation, sources will have sufficient knowledge and resources to improve information reporting and compliance.

no single valid interpretation of the rule forecasts inherent in any rule or set of rules. Since significant rules are almost always formulated by groups of individuals, particular members of the group may have unique forecasts and assumptions. Indeed, it is well known (e.g., Lindblom, 1959) that much of public policymaking proceeds on the basis of consensus about means rather than ends. Thus, it is often the case that policies are put together based on agreement about means, not ends, with conflicting notions about the likely results of the means pursued.

Assessing the vulnerability of these rule forecasts requires no great exercise in logic. The interdependence of many of these forecasts greatly increases the likelihood that events will not conform to behavioral expectations implicit in the rule. One key to understanding the weakness of the forecasts is the joint dependence of behavioral assumptions about citizens and source officials. If *either* party acts against expectations, the rule forecasts may be thwarted.

Clearly some forecasts are more problematic than are others, though determining the plausibility of *any* of these forecasts is a matter of subjective judgment (Bozeman, 1977; Helmer and Rescher, 1959). Thus, for example, the forecast that "the courts are receptive to the citizen suits" seems highly likely given the clear guidelines provided in the statute. But many of the forecasts rest on more dubious behavioral claims. One approach to understanding any explanation is the method of "alternative plausible hypotheses" (Huck and Sandler, 1979). Let us consider just one, the forecast that "citizens are sufficiently attentive...." Let's consider the case for the most direct alternative plausible hypotheses:

> *Citizens are not sufficiently attentive, because....* Other possible explanations of inattentiveness: low salience; attentiveness by the "wrong" persons (those who lack feelings of efficacy); episodic, unsustained attention; attention at the wrong point in time; attention to the "wrong" issues (i.e., ones not covered by Title V, such as truck traffic on new plants).

The best argument, to this point, for this alternative hypothesis is the lack of previous citizen action in the air pollution domain. If the attentiveness was due to anything other than a lack of information (and access to information) then the rule forecast (and interrelated forecasts) fails. The rule forecast, in light of the empirical evidence of previous inattentiveness, becomes "citizens *who have not been attentive* to air pollution issues *will become attentive* when provided requisite information." If this questionable proposition proves incorrect, the entire behavioral edifice of the Title V citizen participation provisions crumbles.

Arguably, the rule forecasts of the citizen information provisions of Title V are highly vulnerable. They are vulnerable because of the interdependence of the forecasts more than because of the implausibility of any of the individual forecasts. Even if we subjectively assigned a .90

probability to each of the individual rule forecasts, their interdependence means that the primary behavioral claim—that increased citizen information will lead to greater source compliance—is assailable. For present purposes, two issues need addressing: First, why promulgate a rule with such dubious logic? Second, what are the red tape implications?

Why Implausible Rule Forecasts? There are two primary explanations of this and probably most implausible rule forecasts. First, the overall complexity and general intractability of social systems is well known and well documented (Hempel, 1968). The task of formulating efficacious rules dependent upon the occurrence of complex, poorly understood events is simply a formidable task. A second point, though, has more direct practical implications. Many rules, including ones that have stringent behavioral and compliance requirements and prodigious compliance resource needs, are not well thought out. If we consider the possibility that the entirety of Title V was little more than "a little thing" emanating from a Lee Thomas memorandum, then it is likely that any particular provision received limited attention (certainly less than would be required for mapping out the logical trail of the assumptions built into one provision). A mighty regulatory oak has begun to grow up from the Title V acorn, an oak that will be paid for with billions of dollars in sources' compliance. However, the persons drafting CAAA were, appropriately, attentive to an entire forest of oaks, with limited time and resources to devote to a single acorn, no matter how fecund that acorn.

Red Tape Implications Red tape flows from rules forecasts when the forecasts turn out to be inaccurate and, from the standpoint of compliance behaviors, in the "wrong" direction. If the behaviors do not occur along the trajectory forecast, then there is great potential for the expenditure of resources (compliance burden) that have little or no impact on the achievement of the rule's functional object. Thus, let us assume that a given state agency invests considerable resources in building a database that has the express purpose of facilitating citizen access to information. If there are, in fact, no citizens using that information then the *implementation burden* associated with the agency's action can be judged as pass-through red tape flowing from the statute and EPA to the agency. The resources have been committed and the functional object of the rule has not been achieved.

RED TAPE AND "OVER-CONTROL"

Another major cause of red tape is overcontrol. Organizational theorists have documented (Thompson, 1961; Dubin, 1951; Downs, 1967) the tendency of managers and public policymakers to try to reduce uncertainty through exertion of inappropriate, and ultimately ineffective, levels of control. The field of environmental policy and regulation is particularly prone to this behavior because many of the behaviors which policymakers are interested in constraining are discrete and highly dispersed. Policymakers seek control over thousands of toxins for hundreds of thousands of sources. Moreover, the delegation of authority to the states has some potential to enhance control but also has much potential to provide for unstable and inconsistent patterns of control. Title V permitting is highly subject to overcontrol and red tape could come about in several ways. Let us consider just a few particularly vulnerable areas.

Overcontrol of High Performers   Sometimes the issue is less "how much control?" than "how much, directed at whom?" One of the primary EPA motivations behind Title V is to encourage states to develop better permitting and information systems. One EPA official observed the following:

> A large part of Title V is about having [the states'] files straightened out. It may seem like a small thing and mundane, but if you don't have it, you're in trouble. In many states there has [sic] been years of procrastination, but now they have to clean out the attic. It's not always deviousness or rapacity, but inertia and a lack of state resources in permitting. (Personal interview with EPA enforcement official, April 1996)

While this analysis certainly fits many of the states, no one fails to recognize the vast differences among the states. For example, in California the permitting system in place before Title V met or exceeded expectations of Title V (personal interview with air quality consultant, February 1996). It seems likely that California and other states that had already made great strides in their permitting systems will expend resources that do not serve the functional objects of Title V. Thus, "high performers" who are overcontrolled experience red tape.

Herded Cats Herding Cats: Diversity among Implementers
Herding cats may be easier than trying to control hundreds of thousands sources. But Title V is more difficult than herding cats; a more apt metaphor is herded cats herding cats. The fifty states vary tremendously in their commitment to Title V and, more generally, to clean air, at least as opposed to sometimes competing values such as economic development. Even if the states were all willing and eager partners, obvious variations in local political culture, relations between the regulated and the regulators, particular environmental problems, and, of course, levels of enforcement and administrative resources, would ensure inconsistent implementation. When implementation is *sure* to be inconsistent, highly

detailed controls—as opposed to general guidelines—set standards that cannot be met. Red tape is a likely result. This does not mean, incidentally, that there is necessarily a suitable alternative to highly detailed regulations; it may be that in some instances red tape is a sort of "waste by-product" of the policy production process. In such cases, the issue is not elimination of the by-product but its minimization.

CHANGE IN THE RULE ECOLOGY

Changes in rule ecology occur when the social or physical context of a rule changes, thus mitigating the rule's usefulness. If there is any single factor that may account for the "red tape potential" in Title V it is the changes occurring in the *rule ecology* between the passage of Title V and its implementation. One obvious and sweeping change occurred when the Republican congressional majority emerged in 1994. Change in congressional partisan control does not *necessarily* change rules' ecologies, but in the case of Title V the Republican majority led to reduced support for environmental permitting. More generally, environmental policy directives began to have an "on-again-off-again" unpredictable quality. In such circumstances there is almost always high potential for red tape, even with the best intended rules. If the rules ecology changes dramatically and among those changes is a lack of clarity as to just what is required for compliance or implementation, then red tape is virtually inevitable.

To best explore how changes in Title V's rule ecology have affected its effectiveness, we begin with some background. The Title V provisions were devised in the midst of a political firestorm created by the acid rain controls and tailpipe standards of the 1990 CAAA, which pitted public health against economic growth. Title V's technical complexity also contributed to its lower profile. A former staff member for Congressman Henry Waxman (D-Cal.), chair of the Energy and Commerce's Environment and Public Works Subcommittee, made the following comment:

> Members cared about specific environmental issues, others were worried about particular industry interests and local utility allowances. Small businesses were concerned with permitting, but there were not a lot of people stirring up things on permitting.... Clearly permitting was not a pressing issue; it was just too complicated to explain. (Personal interview, April 16, 1996)

As a result of the legislation's technical complexity and low profile, Congress realized fairly late in the political process the potential cost to industry and states for Title V. This led to last-minute attempts by industry, environmentalists, and state officials to alter provisions of the proposed permit program. These efforts failed as the original version survived (nearly intact) intense conference committee negotiations and, finally, the House and Senate votes (Bryner, 1995: 180).

Ironically, the passage of the 1990 CAAA amendments marked the beginning of Title V negotiations. According to the Waxman staff member, the Bush administration enabled this negotiation by withdrawing support for the provision:

> By the time it passed, Bush was already apologizing for his own permitting title, got involved in negotiation and backed off immediately. This gave everyone the impression that (the administration and EPA) were really willing to rethink Title V, and that the EPA people were willing to hang in there. It would have been much better if the administration had just said: "This is the law." (Personal interview, April 16, 1996)

This nonsupportive stance carried over to regulatory development, as EPA submitted draft regulations to the Office of Management and Budget. The President's Council on Competitiveness, established as part of the regulatory review process during the Reagan administration to reduce regulatory burden on industry, reviewed this draft. The council proposed over one hundred changes to the draft regulations, including provisions to allow minor permit modifications with simple notification to the state and to exempt permit revisions from public review (Bryner, 1995: 196). Congressional staffers intimately familiar with the original legislation regarded the proposed rule changes as "substantially weaker than those mandated by Congress" (House Subcommittee on Health and the Environment, 1991: 2). The dispute between the council, EPA, and the original drafters of the Title V statute dragged on until 1992, when President Bush ordered EPA to make the changes sought by the council. As a result, EPA issued the final rules on July 21, 1992.

Support for Title V eroded further when Republicans won a majority of seats in the Senate and House and a majority of the nation's governorships in the November 1994 elections. It was the first Republican-dominated Congress in forty years and the first Republican majority of governorships since 1972. The Republican victors had campaigned on a platform of smaller government and fewer regulations. With strength in numbers, the new Republican majority engaged in a flurry of legislative activity aimed at reducing regulatory burden and federal discretion. The Unfunded Mandates Reform Act of 1995 required Congress to consider the costs of new mandates to states and localities and requires federal agencies to consider state and private sector costs in contemplating new regulations. The Paperwork Reduction Act of 1995 sets specific paperwork reduction goals for the entire government through 2001. The Regulatory Transition Act of 1995 imposes a moratorium on new rules and regulations. While various bills threatened to undermine the regulatory power of federal agencies, EPA authority specifically came under attack by federal budget cutters.

To summarize, Title V was conceived in political obscurity amidst a battle of economic and environmental forces over the high-stakes issues of acid rain control and automobile emissions standards. Its technical complexity compounded its already low-profile status, relegating serious discussion over its merits until after the amendment's passage. The resulting postamendment dialogue signaled to EPA, state air officials, and the regulated industries that there was room for negotiation, thus weakening chances for a Title V implemented as conceived.

Stakeholders reacting to their volatile political environment and continually changing the rules implementation have created Title V's red tape. Thus, rule ecology changes have been a driving force in—but not a direct cause of—Title V's red tape. The following is a comment made by one seasoned environmental consultant who has helped hundreds of companies with their Title V permitting:

> Conflicting advice from bureaucrats within the same state agency has produced needless cost for industries, where companies following one approach in filing permit applications find out later that the original direction provided by their agency representative was incorrect. (Personal interview, May 1996)

Implementation changes have led to overcompliance by risk-averse companies, inconsistent interpretations of Title V within state agencies, and wasted implementation efforts by regulated companies and state agencies.

TITLE V AS A RED TAPE REMEDY?

Title V, while clearly having already generated red tape and having potential for more, is both the disease and its cure. Let us consider an example of Title V's red tape-cutting potential. In each of the fifty states the printing industry is to some extent a contributor to pollution. Print shops are subject to two different air quality rules for a single pollutant: one as a general hydrocarbon and the other as a toxic agent. If the company is subject to two different control technologies, monitoring activities, or record-keeping requirements for the same pollutant, then there's a strong possibility that these activities are redundant or even conflicting, thus generating red tape. To address this red tape, EPA has issued Title V guidance that allows states to apply the most stringent of the two standards to the source's permit, thereby eliminating duplication of effort while accomplishing the goals of both rules. This simple example is repeated again and again in each of the states and the rule simplification effects of Title V must, ultimately, be weighed against the considerable costs of developing new and inevitably complex permitting systems. From a policymaking standpoint, the red tape, compliance costs, and inefficiencies generated must be considered in relation to the benefits derived from rules' implementation.

The question must not be limited to "How much red tape?" but "How much red tape for what benefit?" Some policies inherently involve more red tape than do others, even if well managed. For example, policies affected by unstable political environments cannot be excoriated for having more red tape than policies insulated from rapid political change. Changes in rules ecologies almost inevitably induce red tape. A complicated, but valid question, is "How much red tape is likely given the functional objectives, accountability requirements, and the ecology of a set of rules?" In some cases, red tape is unavoidable and perhaps best viewed as part of the overhead in program implementation. The issue, then, is the *acceptable* level of overhead. A first step in making such a determination is developing more useful theories and measures of red tape.

CONCLUSION

At the beginning of the chapter, three "utility tests" for red tape theory were identified. Theory (or, less grandly, ideas) can be useful as explanations, as organizing frameworks, and for generating hypotheses. The application of red tape concepts and theory to the case of Title V permitting fares poorly according to the strongest of utility tests, providing a valid explanation. In part this shows that the theory is underdeveloped; not really a theory in the scientific sense, only in the colloquial sense.

Red tape theory seems to fare better with respect to the second utility test. As even this relatively brief account makes clear, the politics and policymaking surrounding the Clean Air Act Amendments and Title V were complex, involving many different institutional actors, many of whom held perception at odds with the others. Title V is a story of multiple, often incompatible, "realities." Red tape theory does seem to help here by identifying "points of entry" to the multiple realities, key questions about the evaluation of rules and regulations. Similarly, red tape theory might well prove useful in developing hypotheses. The foregoing analysis was not a formal one. The aim was determining the applicability of concepts rather than developing hypotheses. Nevertheless, one could easily move to the next step and organize the red tape concepts and ideas into a series of hypotheses that could, with some imagination, bring some insight into complicated policies with multiple realities.

What about the "bottom line?" Has Title V generated enormous red tape or not? Unfortunately, even with a considerable investment in red tape concepts and measures, this question is not easily answered.

However, perhaps red tape theory allows us to better understand the question. For example, careful readers know where to look for differences in compliance burden, formalization, and red tape. These are not the same things, and judgments about red tape require us to analyze the differences among these and other related concepts. Similarly, careful readers know where to look for possible red tape threats. If the rules forecasts are inordinately complex, beware. If multiple, interdependent organizations promulgate rules that all must live by, beware. If the political or economic environment within which the rules are implemented changes rapidly, beware. None of these factors are necessary components of red tape pathology, but each is a marker.

In Chapter 9 we finally turn our attention to the "So what" question: "So what can we do about red tape?" In addition to providing a few cautious prescriptions, the concluding chapter once again underscores that efficiency and red tape reduction must be considered in light of other core values, including accountability and effectiveness.

CUTTING RED TAPE:
A BALANCE MODEL
OF BUREAUCRATIC REFORM

A concluding chapter of a book about bureaucracy is usually the place where the author says, in so many words, "Now we roll up our sleeves and do something about the problem." Then the author provides "ten steps for fighting red tape" or "a twelve-step program for recovering bureaucrats." In this day of reinvention, reengineering, privatization, and performance-based everything, we suffer no shortage of prescriptions for reforming bureaucracy. Unfortunately, the various prescriptions seem not to have cured all bureaucratic ills. Thus, in this chapter, we consider some additional ideas about bureaucratic reform, especially cutting red tape.

As discussed in Chapter 3, every set of bureaucratic reform prescriptions carries with it a set of assumptions—more or less innovative, more or less radical, more or less true. Taken together, these assumptions reveal the would-be reformers' philosophy of bureaucratic reform. In most cases the reader is left to surmise the reform philosophy. But in this chapter the underlying philosophy (whether or not innovative, radical, or true) is at least explicit.

The prescriptions presented here are within the framework of a *balance model* of bureaucratic reform. The theme of bureaucracy balancing core values has appeared throughout the book. When bureaucracy is Weberian "pure type" it focuses on control, performance, and efficiency. These remain important values. But these must be balanced with accountability and fairness.

There are two parts to this concluding chapter. First, the balance model is presented. Second, prescriptions consistent with the balance model are presented. In light of the large-scale and ambitious reform efforts now underway, it is important to emphasize the limits of pre-scriptions presented here. In the first place, our concern here is not bureaucratic reform writ large, but red tape. Many problems of bureau-cracy have little or nothing to do with red tape. Second, the prescriptions center on the manager's role in red tape fighting. Much red tape can be traced to legislators, judges, or controller agencies, less to line managers. But this is a book about bureaucracy and bureaucrats, so the focus is on steps managers can take in the absence of a grand mandate from a polit-ical superior. Moreover, even if managers generate only a minority of the world's red tape, they nonetheless bear the brunt of responsibility (and often blame) for it.

SOME PREMISES FOR RED TAPE REFORM: FROM ECONOMY AND EFFICIENCY TO A BALANCE MODEL

In the discussion of bureaucratic pathology in Chapter 3, we noted the interplay between theories of pathology and approaches to reform. For example, the reform instruments presented under the Government Performance and Results Act clearly imply that pathology results from lack of goal clarity and from imprecise measurement and evaluation of tasks. Other approaches to reform have different assumptions. Thus, most privatization initiatives assume government is inherently ineffi-cient, and when market prices can be established, goods and services should be provided by the private sector.

A balance model begins with core values of public management: efficiency, accountability, performance, and fairness. Since these terms are used many different ways, we begin with a simple definition of each. In the present context, *efficiency* is using the minimum level of resources to achieve a desired level of results. *Accountability* is achieved if policies and procedures are implemented in conformance with the purposes pre-scribed by higher authorities (whether the higher authority is a superi-or bureaucratic entity or even "the citizens)." *Performance* is the extent to which the values included in policy objectives are achieved. Finally, and most complicated, *fairness* means that people are dealt with in the prescribed manner. Fairness may imply impartial treatment and "neu-tral competence" in the bureaucracy or it may imply differential treat-ment, such as special preference for the underprivileged, for veterans, or for minorities. In short, fairness must be considered in the context of policy statements and assumptions. There may be some Platonic essence of fairness but, if so, it has not yet been a practical guide to policy or decision making.

What, then, is the relation of these core public management values

ANTIBUREAUCRATIC ENCOUNTER:
ONTARIO'S RED TAPE REVIEW COMMISSION

Let us consider an example of red tape fighting. One of the most extensive recent efforts at red tape fighting is the Red Tape Review Commission of the Province of Ontario in Canada. The commission engaged a consulting firm to "establish priorities for the elimination or amendment of inappropriate regulatory measures" (Carr-Gordon, Limited, and Erin Researchers, Inc., 1996: 1). Their report illustrates typical reform efforts in that it includes some measures that by almost any standard (including the one presented here) seem to attack red tape. But other proposals seem to substitute efficiency for other core policy and management values.

The methodology for the Ontario study included consulting with sixty business and government leaders in focused interviews and surveying, via a structured telephone-administered questionnaire, more than five hundred business and nonprofit organizations in Ontario. The survey asked respondents to assess a number of "problems with regulation." Some of these problems are straightforward red tape-related issues such as using plain language in regulations, but others seem simply to substitute one set of core values for another. One "red tape problem" is "approval processes defined in legislation or regulations cause undue delays in our operations." The majority (63 percent) of respondents agreed that this does occur. Similarly, 68 percent agreed that "reporting requirements are complicated and create unnecessary paperwork." Unnecessary for whom? No one likes paperwork. But it is at least possible that the respondents *really* mean "unnecessary for us." Moreover, it is not obvious that the respondents can even provide a valid assessment of "necessary," at least not unless the intent and use of the reporting requirements have been carefully explained. What is the lesson here? I am not suggesting that paperwork is good or that it does not result in burdens or even that it necessarily has any value. What I am suggesting is that assessing the value of paperwork is complicated and requires much more than simply asking those who suffer the burden. In all likelihood, some paperwork is totally superfluous, some is more of a burden than it really needs to be, and other paperwork, even if it presents a burden, is essential to the preservation of accountability and the assurance of performance or fairness variables. Asking industry officials to comment on paperwork—a common approach in assessments of red tape—provides no means of sorting out red tape from compliance burden.

Some of the changes considered by the commission similarly have potential to substitute values. Among the commission's proposed changes in labor regulations is "revising labor legislation to limit arbitration as a solution." Another is "continuing the minimum wage freeze." Neither of these has anything to do with red tape, bureaucratic reform or even, by most definitions, efficiency. These are, respectively, limitations of workers' rights and cost containment.

ANTIBUREAUCRATIC ENCOUNTER:
ONTARIO'S RED TAPE REVIEW COMMISSION (CONTINUED)

In setting priorities for reform, the Ontario study noted that organizations object to regulations when (1) the process has no clear benefit; (2) the process takes too long; and/or (3) regulation creates a high cost. Again, the red tape implications are not at all clear. If the process has no benefit, then we have identified a red tape problem. If it has no *clear* benefit, then we have identified a communication problem. If the process "takes too long" the implication is that there is a benchmark for "too long." Usually there is no such benchmark. Knowing that a regulation has "high cost" tells us nothing about its value. Low-cost regulations may be pure red tape (if no legitimate functional objective is served) and high-cost regulations may be purely beneficial if they achieve important social and policy goals.

What does this illustration tell us about red tape and bureaucratic reform? Again, there is no implication that the Ontario effort is a poor one or atypical. In many respects the approach taken is superior to many such studies. They begin by seeking some evidence and the study provides a wide range of proposals, many of which may turn out to be quite effective. But if we consider the Ontario study in light of the lessons presented in this book, it becomes clear that there is some potential here, as in most bureaucratic reform efforts, to confuse red tape fighting and bureaucratic reform with managerial and policy values. All too easily, red tape fighting evolves into cost cutting or abridgment of rights. Sometimes costs need to be cut and rights even need to be abridged, but these are not the same as red tape.

---

to red tape? If we take these as core values, no single one inherently more important than another, then red tape fighting becomes much more complicated. Even those reforms recognizing these values sometimes neglect the tension among them. Most reform efforts center on efficiency. Efficiency remains important but if efficiency is enhanced at the expense of other core values then, by the concepts included in this book, no red tape has been snipped.

By the concept of red tape used here, efficiency is not a sole criterion. Rules seek to achieve objectives efficiently, but often those objectives include accountability, fairness, or performance, not just efficiency. Thus, *reform efforts often result in elevation of efficiency at the expense of other equally important core values.* Red tape fighting often says, in effect, let us increase efficiency by paying less attention to accountability, fairness, or procedural guarantees (Gilmour and Jensen, 1998). This may be a bad trade.

Elements of a Balance Model

Now we turn to the question "Given what this book says about the nature of red tape, what can we conclude about approaches to bureaucratic reform?" While there are various lessons in this book serving various purposes, the following points made in previous chapters seem especially relevant to questions of bureaucratic reform:

1. Bureaucratic reform and red tape mediation should consider the balance of core values (accountability, performance, fairness), not just efficiency.
2. Bureaucracy is not popular even when functioning well. The very meaning of bureaucracy is standardization and control. People generally do not wish to be controlled and, typically, they want to be treated as unique individuals.
3. Red tape depends on one's perspective (e.g., client, manager, political superior) and assessing red tape requires judgment calls.
4. Red tape is not the same as formalization or the number of rules and procedures.
5. Red tape often evolves from rules and regulations once serviceable. Reasons for "good rules gone bad" include the presence of "organizational phantoms," rule drift, changes in the rules ecology, and changes in the objectives the rule serves.
6. All rules and regulations may be viewed as forecasts of behavior; when those forecasts are wrong, red tape often results.
7. Government organization and "more public" organizations tend to have more red tape. In large measure, this is due to the necessity of greater accountability. To some extent, this red tape propensity is an "overhead investment" in control and accountability. So long as there is a desire to keep tight reins on government, red tape will be an unfortunate byproduct.

Considering these points together, we can outline the premises of a balance model for bureaucratic reform.

1. A balance model seeks to remedy red tape and bureaucratic pathologies while, at the same time, doing minimal injury to the values bureaucracy serves.
2. A balance model recognizes that the sources of red tape lie in many places (the organization and its rules, managers, political superiors, controller organizations).
3. A balance model does not expect government organizations to be identical to private organizations and, thus, gives little credence to the curative powers of "making government more businesslike."

> ### FIGHTING RED TAPE: IF BUREAUCRACY IS THE PROBLEM, IS CONGRESS THE SOLUTION?
>
> Among the many roles played by members of Congress, one particularly popular with constituents is red tape warrior. As reported in the *Christian Science Monitor* (Dillin, 1994), a Virginia woman under siege by the IRS received several demands for payment of taxes until, finally, her bank account was frozen and then plundered. The problem—she owed no taxes. Like so many Americans, this harassed citizen turned to her friendly congressional representative, Frank Wolf (R-10th District) who immediately dispatched a staff member to solve the problem. The problem was solved, the IRS mistake admitted, and a letter of apology was sent.
>
> This tale is replicated again and again. Every legislator understands that constituent service—often taking the form of red tape fighting—ingratiates the champion to the beleaguered voter. As a result, Congress now employs thousands of staff who are, essentially, red tape caseworkers. As noted in the *Monitor* article, staff casework is especially prominent in such activities as replacing a lost Social Security check, working the maze of immigration bureaucracy, and dealing with the IRS. Sounds like a good deal for the taxpayer. But is it?
>
> During Congressman Wolf's more than twelve years in Congress, his staff has dealt with 80,000 cases. Is this boon or bane? One view: Without legislative staff working for constituents, citizens would have little ability to address the abuses of bureaucracy. Another view: Legislators complain constantly that they have insufficient staff to fully understand the many and diverse technical issues requiring legislative attention. Ironically, the red tape addressed by congressional staff sometimes is created by the passage of bad legislation that has suffered from too little scrutiny and insufficient expertise. What goes around comes around.

WHAT CAN MANAGERS DO ABOUT RED TAPE?

With so many agencies being reinvented and with the long arm of the National Performance Review reaching across the federal government, the market for bureaucratic reform seems nearly saturated. But this chapter adds to the suggestions provided by blue ribbon panels, agency task forces, and pundits. These suggestions differ a bit in intent and range. First, whereas most of the best-known (e.g., National Performance Review) approaches to bureaucratic reform have been broad and sweeping, the concern here is much narrower, limited to red tape. Second, these prescriptions are not system-wide but focus on factors that may be controllable by managers. Third, the concept of red tape addressed is different from most other studies in which red tape is a synonym for reduction of paperwork. The suggestions provided here do not elevate the value of efficiency above other core public management values, nor is there an interest in making government more business-like, or even cutting back the number of rules and regulations. Instead, a prescriptive approach taken within the framework of a balance model focuses on identifying those rules and regulations that have little value and dealing with them. None of this is a radical departure from various reform efforts, but it does provide a somewhat different emphasis.

In both bureaucratic reform and surgery, the best physician leaves the smallest scars. To put it another way, the objective in reforming red tape is to remedy the red tape, not simply to attack rules and regulations. The prescriptions presented in the following sections appear to do little damage to well functioning, needed rules, and regulations.

COMMUNICATE THE "FUNCTIONAL OBJECT" OF THE RULE

Red tape occurs when a rule entails a compliance burden but fails to contribute to the rule's functional object. As noted in the Ontario Red Tape Commission illustration, there is no difficulty agreeing on the need to eliminate rules, regulations, and procedures that provide no benefit. Unfortunately, determining whether there is a benefit and to whom is almost always challenging. Sometimes even communicating the rule's objective proves difficult.

Consider the Title V Clean Air Act Amendments case from the previous chapter. In this instance we have compliance costs in the millions, perhaps billions, of dollars, and the benefits are extremely difficult to measure. One alleged benefit of Title V is to bring more polluters into state permitting systems. Another is to provide greater information and information resources to states, EPA, and citizen groups. Yet another is to "level the playing field" for industry and make competition more equitable, with everyone incurring similar costs of pollution. Obviously these benefits are difficult to measure and, if they occur at all, will accrue over a long period of time. The point here is not the difficulty of measuring benefits, but the difficulty of even communicating the objectives of rules. Many of the industry officials we interviewed had very little idea of the benefits sought under Title V. While it is not necessarily the case that industry would be rabidly enthusiastic about Title V legislation if the objectives and benefits were better articulated, that is at least a start.

This guideline cuts two ways. First, managers must work hard to communicate the objectives and possible benefits associated with the rules they are either formulating or implementing. Whether these are high impact rules with huge compliance burdens, such as those pertaining to air pollution control, or low impact rules with small compliance burdens, such as requiring subordinates to file reimbursement claims within thirty days, communication reduces problems. Second, managers must seek information about rules and regulations to which they are subject.

QUESTION AUTHORITY! IDENTIFY THE RULE'S PURPOSES

Old 1960s bumper stickers are not always the best place to go for wisdom, but this is one stale admonition that bears repeating to red tape revolutionaries. In many instances, employees and clients bear the brunt of red tape in stoic silence or, if they do complain, it is to colleagues or friends who have no power to resolve the problem. In many cases, they overestimate the temerity of the authority responsible for what seems, from their perspective, damnable red tape. By questioning the authority, the disgruntled might find either that the "red tape" actually serves an important and legitimate function, or it might turn out that the person in authority was not aware of the compliance burden associated with the rule or red tape and will actually be gratified to learn about it. Remember the staying power of organizational phantoms. Questioning authority is sometimes the only way to exorcise organizational phantoms. If everyone blithely assumes "it's a rule, it must serve a purpose," then generations get to waste their time to no good end.

Questioning authority is like turning over rocks on the ground. Sometimes there is nothing there, sometimes disgusting creatures start scurrying, and sometimes one finds a pleasant surprise. But the experienced bureaucrat asks first, "What are the dangers of questioning authority?" Nor is this an unreasonable question. Some who have questioned authority, especially whistleblowers, have found themselves fired or reassigned to the bureaucratic equivalent of Siberia. First, the level of hazard in questioning apparently extraneous rules for procuring office supplies may be a bit less than one encounters questioning a $5 billion cost overrun on the latest X-for-the-unknown jet. Second, whatever the circumstance, questioning tends to bear minimal personal risk, hectoring quite a bit more. Simply asking, "Why do we have this rule?" often succeeds and at minimal risk.

DEVELOP CRITERIA FOR THE FORMAL AND THE INFORMAL

Rules are inherently formal. Indeed, one measure of organizational formalization is the extent to which there are rules to cover every situation. Many organizations simply have entirely too many rules and seek to substitute rules for good judgment or for informal socialization. Since Chester Barnard's time, organization analysts have been quite aware of the power and often the effectiveness of the informal aspects of organizations. But, whether from fear or a need to control, the promulgation of rules, the formalization of the organization, has proceeded unimpeded.

Organizations and their managers would do well to give systematic consideration to the question, "What should be formal and what should be left to the informal organization?" This question is particularly appropriate for managers because the high impact, externally imposed rules rarely deal with topics that might as easily be left to the informal organization. But the manger-imposed, intraorganizational rules often give leeway.

Simply stating that managers need to think carefully about requirements for rules and functions of informal organizations accomplishes little. What factors might the manager take into consideration in determining the formal versus the informal? In previous chapters we noted that many rules and much red tape comes from managers' attempts to exert control, often as a substitute for actual power. One issue in determining the need for a rule is whether the rule could reasonably be expected to contribute to any managerial value other than control. Will task performance be enhanced? Will the rule result in greater public accountability? Will the rule save money? If, upon reflection, the answer is simply "the rule will enhance my feelings of control," then the rule is probably a good candidate for extinction. Managerial control is often important but never as a cardinal value.

Here is a second issue: Does the contemplated rule solve a problem or a prospective problem? One of the chief reasons for overcontrol, a major culprit in red tape, is the wish to guard against problems that have never occurred and are unlikely to occur. One way to calculate the need for a rule is to expand the rules forecast to consider "what are the behaviors that will occur in the absence of a rule?" In previous chapters we examined the great difficulties in providing a correct rules forecast for complex behaviors and events. But forecasting behaviors for the *absence* of a rule is often much easier. If there is not an existing rule, one can monitor existing behavior, and absent any compelling reason to do otherwise, assume that behavior will continue in pretty much the same fashion as before. To put it another way, observing usually entails fewer perils than forecasting. Thus, if behaviors currently remain in the satisfactory range, new rules should require strong and effective rationales.

TEST THE RULE FORECAST

Chapter 4's section on the "anatomy of a rule" noted three dimensions common to all rules—behavior requirements, implementation mechanisms, and enforcement provisions. Typically, managers and policymakers give a good deal of thought to implementation and enforcement but too little to behavior requirements. Implementation and enforcement usually entail specific actions that must be planned before being executed. By contrast, behavior requirements can often simply be posited and one can just assume that the rule will effect the required behaviors. But glossing over behavior requirements, the rule's "logic," often leads to undesired outcomes, embarrassment, and red tape.

Managers promulgating and implementing new rules should first make explicit their rules forecast (as described in Chapter 5) and then move quickly to test the impacts of the rule. Simply explicating the rules forecast, including behavior requirements, can prevent red tape. Often rules that seem initially to make sense begin to look much less promising when held up to the light. By enforcing the discipline of examining the logic and assumptions behind a rule, the manager can prevent red tape and other embarrassing mistakes. After explicating the rules forecast, the manager may wish to show the rules logic and assumptions to someone else—perhaps a subordinate or a client affected by the rule. A fresh look by a knowledgeable person with a different perspective often serves the manager and the rule.

An excellent rules forecast improves the chances but fails to guarantee a rule's success. Usually, observation proves superior to projection. In many instances the manager can quickly test the rule by examining the actual behaviors it has engendered in the rule's early applications. In the more complicated cases and for more sweeping rules, the test of the rules' effects involve serious research. But for localized and simpler rules, a quick test is often possible. In Chapter 5, the simple example was a flextime rule aimed at reducing traffic congestion. This is the sort of rule for which a rough test can be easily undertaken and, if the results are not to one's liking, adjustments can be made.

DEVELOP SUNSET RULES

One of the more common guidelines proposed by bureaucratic reformers entails sunset provisions for rules and regulations. Some state governments have adopted sunset provisions for statues and these apply to externally imposed rules and regulations. That is, if the laws are not renewed by direct action they lapse after a specified period of time.

Usually sunset provisions entail sweeping legislation. But sunset provisions can also be employed on a organization-wide or even a division-wide basis. The appeal is obvious. In some cases, no one even remembers the original functions of rules but that does not always stop them from being enforced—often to the detriment of organizational members and clients. Sunsetting is one of the best defenses against "organization phantoms" and the entropy of rules (see Chapter 5). If rules go away without explicit review and reintroduction, then there is little chance for the continuance of rules no one understands or defends.

CONSIDER THE TECHNOLOGICAL FIX

The federal government spends more than $200 billion every year procuring goods and services, everything from tanks to toilet paper. By all accounts, red tape is rampant. But the technological fix is in. A presidential memorandum tells us that "moving to an electronic commerce system to simplify and streamline the purchasing process will promote customer service and cost-effectiveness" (President's Memorandum, 1993: 1). The federal government deals with more than thirty thousand vendors each year and the cost of even a little red tape is enormous. The new federal electronic commerce guidelines establish an architecture for a government-wide electronic commerce system, standardization in requests for quotes, purchase orders and notice of awards, capability for electronic payment and document interchange, all fully implemented during 1997. Does this technological fix actually fix? Or does it create new problems?

In many cases, the expected productivity gains from technology, especially computers and information management technologies, have proved disappointing. Technology is not a cure-all and, in the case of red tape, it has potential not only to reduce red tape but to add to it. For example, agencies with excess computing capacity have a tendency to keep more information than they need, sometimes increasing administrative burdens and red tape.

While one should be cautious about a technological fix for red tape, there are some good opportunities. For example, if paperwork and procedures are burdensome, automation can sometimes be the answer. With centralized data banks, the need for the tenth copy of the personnel form may be less evident. Indeed, many of the most glaring red tape problems are, *in principle*, subject to technological fix. Sometimes new technology produces great efficiencies and cuts red tape; sometimes technology produces new nightmares.

The history of technology in government provides some lessons useful in predicting success and debacle. First, technological solutions rarely work in agencies that have neither the technical skill to implement the solution or the technical expertise to ride herd on contractors charged with implementing the solution. Second, when a government agency is the first adopter of a new technology, the agency incurs the same high risk as any first (or early) adopter of untried technology. Third, if the personnel who must work with the technology are not convinced that it will help them or that it will work in their best interest (e.g., by *not* replacing them!) then the technological solution will almost certainly fail. Fourth, technology has limits. Agencies expecting technology to solve all their problems, quickly and efficiently, are usually disappointed. Clear goals must be in place before the technology is implemented and those goals must be relatively precise, measurable, and limited. "Improving management" is not a realistic goal for any technology; it is too nebulous and provides no benchmarks for determining that the technological fix fixes.

PROVIDE FOR PARTICIPATION
BY THE "OLIGARCHY OF THE INTERESTED"

In most organizations, especially government organizations, the cure for the problems of democracy is often more democracy. Under the purest of motivations, making sure others have a say, much red tape is created. In many cases, those who "have a say" certainly wish to. In some cases, however, an issue is perceived as sufficiently remote or tangential to one's interests that participation is neither needed nor desired. Simply determining whether the participants in a participative process really care to participate can eliminate much red tape.

The problem of "negative sum process" was introduced in Chapter 5. Several diagnostics were introduced to help identify a problem with negative sum process. These included the following: (1) a high percentage of potential participants passing up opportunities to participate; (2) declining attendance at meetings; (3) persons in the sign-off line (i.e., individuals needed to approve new rules or decisions) beginning to display limited knowledge or concern with decisions; and (4) a high percentage of organization's rules being *about* rules.

One managerial approach to negative sum process is establishing procedures or informal norms for participation by "the oligarchy of the interested." In some instances, managers appoint employees to committees or provide responsibilities for tasks erroneously assuming employee gratification. Likewise, some persons left off the committee or not given responsibility may, perhaps to the managers' surprise, feel left out. One simple yet powerful solution is to manage according to the method I refer to as the oligarchy of the interested. In the case of committee appointments, for example, this entails designating one person as chair or initial organizer (but only after determining that individual's interest in the appointment) and inviting others who are eligible (i.e., appropriate rank and duties) to "sign up." To be sure, this is not always a perfect solution. In some cases too many sign up and in some cases too few. But the sign-up rate is itself a good indicator. If everyone signs up, the issue is obviously important and salient. If few sign up, maybe the need for the committee should be examined. In most instances, though, appointment by the oligarchy of the interested method will yield a good result: having interested persons work on problems and saving the time and energies of persons who prefer to work on something else.

SEEK EXTERNAL STAKEHOLDERS' VIEWS

Chapter 4 distinguished between *organizational* red tape and *stakeholder* red tape, emphasizing that even when rules do serve a legitimate purpose, the rule may nonetheless be viewed as red tape by a stakeholder for whom the rule entails a compliance burden and for whom the rule's purpose has no value. Insular organizations or managers have a tendency to define red tape as "burdensome rules and regulations that affect *us*." However, many of the effects of red tape are born by external stakeholders: clients, customers, superior organizations, and vendors. Occasionally soliciting the views of stakeholders, either informally or formally (see section titled "The Red Tape Audit"), can provide a reality check.

Approaches to assessing external stakeholder views about red tape may be simple (such as asking during informal conversations whether there have been red tape encounters) or more elaborate. One example of a more elaborate and seemingly effective approach is a survey undertaken for the U.S. Patent and Trademark Office with the assistance of the U.S. Census Bureau (Commerce Department, 1993). The survey included such red tape-relevant issues as timeliness in decision-making, clarity of processes, time taken in communication of decisions, and other actions. The survey showed a relatively high level of satisfaction in some areas, including competence of staff and responsiveness, but both agencies ranked low in terms of customer assessments of red tape. Using the results of the survey, the Patent and Trademark Office addressed specific points raised by stakeholders. Some of the changes included redesigning its business processing to include performance measures, conducting customer focus groups each year, and installing more fax machines so customers could transmit documents with greater ease. The survey of stakeholders permits the agency to identify specific bottlenecks and sources of red tape and to develop remedies to address them.

THE RED TAPE AUDIT

Red tape often results from poor information. Since no one really wishes to create red tape (with the exception of those using red tape to achieve personal political goals), simply identifying red tape is often an excellent first line of defense. Many particularly virulent causes of red tape involve a lack of information. For example, changes in implementation usually occur with no knowledge of, or at least with no documentation of, those changes. Similarly, a change in the rule's ecology often implies an ignorance of key environmental factors having the potential to turn rules into red tape. Incorrect rules forecast often leads to red tape because information about behaviors is not collected. A red tape audit is a means of gathering the information needed to identify red tape, attack it, and improve management performance.

The purpose of a red tape audit is to determine which rules remain functional and which rules have evolved into red tape. This is a process that sounds simple in concept, but may be difficult in execution. While the red tape audit procedures may vary according to organizations' particular needs, the crux of the method is described in Table 9-1, which provides the six steps of the red tape audit method, each of which is discussed later in more detail, including a review of each of the required steps.

TABLE 9-1   RED TAPE AUDIT METHODOLOGY

STEP	PROCESS PHASE	ACTIVITIES	TECHNIQUES
1	Rules ID	Identify the universe of rules and regulations to which the organization is subject.	a. Employee interviews or focus groups b. Back-tracking rules through administrative process paper trail
2	Rules Source Sorting	Separate the rules and regulations under the control of the organization from those under the control of external authorities and focus on the former.	a. Informal consultation b. Legal interpretation
3	Stakeholder ID	Identify stakeholders to the rule, both internal (employees, managers) and external (clients, oversight agencies).	a. Focus groups b. Documentation through back-tracking rules c. Rule "tracer"
4	Stakeholder Process	Develop data from stakeholders for the purpose of (a) assessing the current impact of the rules and regulations; (b) measuring the impact against intended and preferred outcomes.	a. Surveys b. Panels and focus groups c. "Avoidee" assessment
5	Rules Assessment	Require a stakeholder delegate panel to categorize each rule and regulation as either (a) acceptable as is; (b) in need of modification; (c) a candidate for abolition. *Then, issue red tape audit and recommendations.*	a. Open panel b. Anonymous Delphi-like panel c. Measure convergence
6	Rules Reformation	Implement rules changes.	a. Managerial action or executive order b. Legislative request

RULES IDENTIFICATION

Some organizations are subject to an incredible number of rules. In many instances, a portion of the rules is not particularly salient to the organization. Thus, some rules are applied only rarely, some entail easy "automatic compliance," and some are routinely violated. One advantage of the rules identification stage of a red tape audit is systematically considering rules and, thereby, increasing the likelihood of organizational knowledge of violation.

An obvious pitfall of the red tape audit method is that it presents its own compliance burden. Here, and in subsequent steps, the focus is on achieving the information necessary for the audit and, at the same time, doing so with minimal compliance burden. The rules identification step has great potential to contribute compliance burden. A good rule of thumb for the rules identification stage is to use the "walk and talk" method of data gathering. Most employees have no difficulty identifying the rules they deal with day-to-day and can do so quickly and efficiently. The key, then, is knowing which employees to interview. Generally, interviews should proceed by organizational function rather than hierarchy. After identifying organizational functions and persons responsible for those functions, the auditor should interview two persons (unless only one fulfills the function) for each function. The rule of two provides convergent validity but, by interviewing no more than two, reduces compliance burden. At the end of the interview period the auditor will have a rough approximation of the rules to which the organization is subject. But is a rough approximation good enough? The red tape audit is not a scientific instrument. One must decide if the relatively low burden cost activity, rules identification, suffices. If not, a next step is a paper trail audit, following the administrative processes of the organization to backtrack the rules executed, interpreted, or obeyed. This may well be an order-of-magnitude increase in effort (at least for larger, more complex organizations) and a judgment will be needed as to whether the extra effort is compensated for in additional red tape revelations. In all likelihood, the higher effort paper trail rules identification process will be worth the effort if performed once every five to ten years, a good period for a thoroughgoing, all-out red tape cleansing.

RULES SOURCE SORTING

The source of red tape—internal or external—has many implications for approaches to red tape reform. In most instances, red tape audits focus on internally generated red tape on the assumption that most varieties of external red tape will be beyond the organization's control. In any event, the source of rules must be considered in developing an assessment. The source of the rule is usually easily identified and, if not self-evident, can be determined with informal consultation with employees who implement the rule. In rare cases it may be necessary to determine legally not only the source of the rule but also, when there are multiple sources, which has preeminence. Usually such legal interpretation will be straightforward. Source sorting should, in general, be a low burden part of the process but it is important not only for determining authority over the rule but as an early strategy-forcing process. The decision whether to examine only rules over which the organization has direct control or those in which it shares control or submits is a strategic choice. The factors to consider in the choice include the level of resources devoted to the red tape audit, expected returns from the audit, the nature of relationships with external controller organizations, and the focal organization's resources for influencing controller organizations.

STAKEHOLDER IDENTIFICATION

The stakeholder identification process, like rule sorting and much of the red tape audit, has strategy and planning benefits. Identification of stakeholders says much about an organization. There is no automatic stakeholder designation nor is there a natural order to stakeholder definition. If the organization identifies stakeholders as something less than the entire set of individuals, organizations, and groups with which the focal organization interacts (and, as a practical matter, almost all organization *do*), then stakeholder designation is a choice—a choice that says "These are the significant actors."

Any of a variety of processes can be used to identify stakeholders including informal discussions with employees and focus groups. Alternatively, stakeholders can be identified by backtracking rules through documentation, which is more complicated. Backtracking consists of reviewing the paperwork entailed in a rules implementation or enforcement. Another method, useful only when a particular rule or set of rules is deemed significant and its effects are unclear, is the use of a "rule tracer." This is similar to backtracking except that it involves real time observation of impacts of rules and the parties to rules. It may seem strange that organizations would not know the parties to their rules but in many cases rule implementation is not closely tied to the rule formulator. No better evidence exists than with environmental rules. The rules are promulgated and posted and it is assumed that target organizations will know about the rules and comply. Similarly, many occupational safety rules are published broadly but there is little knowledge of affected parties. In such cases, and especially for newly implemented rules, a "tracer" may uncover affected parties unknown to the focal organization.

STAKEHOLDER PROCESS

While the organization's employees can usually do a good job identifying rules, stakeholders (*and* employees) must be involved in rule evaluation. After the list of rules has been identified, sorted, and vetted, the assessment begins. Assessment includes two phases: stakeholder process—focusing on determining impacts—and rules assessment—focusing on developing an action plan from the process.

Determining impacts is a key to the entire audit process and, typically, more than one technique should be used to determine impacts. A useful beginning is to gather data from employees about impacts of rules. Not only will this yield some significant insights but it also gives data to compare to stakeholders' views about impacts. The difference between the two provides useful management decision-making data. Once the process of data acquisition begins, several techniques may be employed. First, a survey questionnaire is often useful, one identifying rules and asking specific questions about impacts. The survey may be administered by phone, by mail, or face-to-face. In any but the least complicated cases, face-to-face surveys are preferred. Interactive panels and focus groups are often useful and if questionnaires are employed the data from the questionnaires can be used as a point of departure for group analysis and feedback. One technique less common is "avoidee" assessment. If it is possible to identify a set of noncomplying individuals it may be useful to determine *why* they are not in compliance. Is it ignorance of the rules? A view that the compliance burden is too great? Are enforcement mechanisms viewed as toothless or erratic?

RULES ASSESSMENT

As a result of the stakeholder processes, a list of rules, objectives, and impacts should be available. These should be submitted to a stakeholder delegate panel (which also includes the focal organization's employees) and the panel should be charged with evaluating each rule as acceptable, in need of change, or in need of abolition. In order to avoid "groupthink" it is useful to first allow each member to make not-for-attribution evaluations. The lists derived from this panel should be compiled, with statistics of divergence-convergence, and submitted to the group as a beginning point of discussion. Actual recommendations can come only from an open process (rather than a vote without discussion) since any individual participant may have vital information pertaining to a rule's efficacy. Ultimately, the panel should develop a list of rules that need to be changed, including specific recommendations for change, and a list that needs to be abolished. These are the primary data for the red tape audit, which is now ready to be written, along with background information about methodology and an action plan.

ANTIBUREAUCRATIC ENCOUNTER: RED TAPE AUDITS IN MODESTO

Doubtless, red tape audits will never have the cachet or popularity of other major management reforms or innovations. Conducting a red tape audit implies the organization has red tape. Nevertheless, activities are underway that are much like red tape audits. In the city of Modesto (California) an elaborate procedure has been developed for permit streamlining, and the procedures closely resemble the red tape audit methodology described earlier in the chapter.

The motivation in the City of Modesto is to streamline building, zoning, and environmental permitting to enhance economic development. The process initially involved employees from the Departments of Planning, Environment and Health, Building and Economic Development, as well as appropriate "interest groups" (stakeholders). Data collection involved analysis of ordinances, regulations, and policies, the missions of each and the degree of consistency and coordination among them. Other data included annual reports (for historical analysis), benchmark information about average processing time, the number of permitting appeals and resultant decisions, and the number of agencies, groups, and individuals who must review an application. After review and analysis (an "inventory of existing permits"), the task force submitted recommendations about needs for permit consolidation, merging departments, or permitting functions and elimination of ineffective rules and regulations.

RULES REFORMATION

Rules reformation is less subject to standardization. Organizations and authoritative members of organizations will vary considerably with respect to their ability to act upon the action plan developed in a red tape audit. Obviously, if there is only limited capacity or commitment to implementing the action plan, then the red tape audit should not be pursued. Presumably, rules reformation will normally be within the authority of management. In some cases it may be useful to use the red tape audit process as data for requested legislation.

One should not underestimate the cost or "pain" associated with a red tape audit.. It is essentially a review of the organization's way of doing business. But even with high costs the red tape audit promises high yield. It also has several beneficial by-products, not the least of which is promoting communication among stakeholders and identifying different perceptions about the impacts and values served by rules and regulations.

Conclusion

As we cut red tape and seek bureaucratic reform, it is a good idea to remember that bureaucracy is not usually the enemy. Certainly bureaucrats are not the enemy. The enemy is bureaucratic pathologies and their harmful effects.

As bureaucrats see reformers reforming, it is a good idea for bureaucrats to give reformers the benefit of the doubt. Reformers' worst sin, usually, is naivete. There is a tendency among reformers to focus narrowly on cost and to equate rules with red tape. However, reforms and reform processes, so long as they are not punitive or mean-spirited, serve to revitalize bureaucracy.

Here is another suggestion for bureaucrats: Don't wait for the reformers. Organizational change has two faces. The first, the one receiving the most attention, is the massive, government-wide reform effort. The second, often invisible, is the small, intraorganizational adjustment or fine-tuning. The first gets the headlines, but in many cases the second gets the job done. Not that the two are unrelated. Broad social and political interest in reform signals bureaucrats that people care. Often large-scale reform spurs small-scale reassessment.

Sometimes the reformer's axe proves an unsatisfactory surgical instrument; other times a little enthusiastic hacking is just what's needed. However, the organization's fine-tuning may, in aggregate, contribute more to positive change than the more grandiose government-wide efforts. There are at least four reasons (discussed in the following sections) to expect that localized efforts will prove superior.

FEW GOVERNMENT-WIDE REFORMS ARE ORIGINAL OR INNOVATIVE

Consider a few examples. Many of the reinvention ideas at the core of the National Performance Review came from a popular book by Osborne and Gaebler (1992), *Reinventing Government*. The authors make no claim to originality. Their book simply catalogs reform activities observed in many government agencies. Presumably, some of those same government agencies that originated the reforms chronicled by Osborne and Gaebler are now being asked to reinvent themselves. Truly, it is a postmodern world.

The reform-as-imitation approach was not begun by the National Performance Review. To understand the structure and reasoning of the Government Performance and Results Act, one need go no further than the Johnson administration's planning-programming-budgeting innovations. The similarities are striking. The Carter administration's "next big thing," zero-based budgeting, was imported from Georgia State government, which had imported it from a popular book that, in turn, simply reported budget and accounting innovations pioneered by Texas Instruments (then owned by well-known prospective government reformer Ross Perot). Federal reforms are not the only ones that are ahistorical and, at the same time, derivative. Currently, forty-eight state governments have some sort of results-based or performance budgeting system. Performance budgeting is "hot," just as it was in the 1950s.

ONE SIZE DOES NOT FIT ALL

An obvious difficulty of government-wide reforms is developing standard solutions that can be applied to every agency, even the ones without the problem the reform is supposed to solve. This limitation sometimes is remedied by making flexible reforms and by decentralizing their implementation. Nevertheless, the problem does not occur with reforms originating locally.

MOST OF US PREFER TO BUY LOCALLY

In any bureaucratic reform one of the most important issues is "buy-in." If the people affected by the reform do not believe in it there is a strong likelihood it will fail. Public managers working in the Wyoming regional station of the Department of Agriculture may have a hard time getting excited about ideas that emerge from Washington, D.C. focus groups. The "not-invented-here" syndrome continues to thrive. In part, it is fear of the unknown. In part, it is a rational interpretation of events. Regardless of the source or the validity of "not-invented-here" syndrome, it is almost always an issue in commitment to reform. Reform alternatives developed locally rarely face this problem. Only in cases where local change is autocratically developed or applied is buy-in a problem. Sometimes it is possible to enhance buy-in of government-wide reforms by expanding participation and by providing test sites. The National Performance Review has successfully used these methods.

Whether reforms emanate from within the organization or from other institutions, one key to dealing with red tape and bureaucratic pathology is to be realistic in one's expectations. Bureaucracies are bulwarks of stability and change rarely comes quickly or easily. In some respects this stability is positive. Unpredictability is not often a virtue of bureaucratic organizations.

The most pervasive thread of unrealistic thinking is the notion that public bureaucracies will be better if only we can make them run like a business. So long as there are politicians who can capitalize on the public's antipathy for government bureaucracy this peculiar form of self-delusion will remain with us. Yes, business-like public bureaucracies may well be cheaper, perhaps even more efficient, but that does not always equate to better.

By remembering the term "balance model" it is perhaps easier to remember that bureaucracies usually serve multiple values, including efficiency, accountability, performance, and fairness. Sometimes the values conflict. If this book has reinforced that lesson, then perhaps it has instilled wariness about simple solutions. There is little that is simple about bureaucracy or its purposes.

GLOSSARY

change in the functional object   Rule-evolved red tape occurring because the functional object has changed in a way that renders the rule unnecessary or ineffective.

change in the rule's ecology   Rule-evolved red tape that results from an environmental change; the rule and its implementation may be unchanged, but some external change has undermined the rule's efficacy.

compliance burden   Total resources actually expended in complying with a rule.

compliance resource requirement   Total resources (time, people, and money) required to comply with a rule.

formalization   The extent to which rules, procedures, instructions, and communications are written.

functional object of a rule   The officially sanctioned objective of the rule.

illegitimate functions   Rule-inception red tape that occurs because rules are self-serving and do not promote a legitimate, official purpose.

implementation burden   Total resources actually expended in implementing a rule.

implementation change   Rule-evolved red tape resulting from a change in the way a rule is executed.

incorrect rule forecasts   Rule-inception red tape that occurs because rule-makers' assumptions about the relation of means to ends turn out wrong, resulting in ineffective rules.

negative sum compromise   Rule-inception red tape that occurs because rules are a compromise, serving more than one objective, none well.

organizational red tape   A rule that remains in force and entails a compliance burden for the organization but makes no contribution to achieving the rule's functional object.

over control   Rule-inception red tape that occurs when rules are established for no other reason than managerial control and accountability, and that objective is not obtained.

rule density   Total resources devoted by the organization to complying (i.e., compliance burden) with all its rules (i.e., its rule sum), as a percentage of total resources available to the organization.

rule drift   Rule-evolved red tape occurring because the rule changed incrementally (though not formally and not by intent).

rule ecology   That part of the social and physical environment that impinges upon compliance and upon the rule's effects.

rule efficacy   The extent to which a given rule addresses effectively the functional object for which it was designed.

rule incidence   The number and types of persons affected by a rule, regulation, or procedure.

rule incompatibility   Rule-evolved red tape that occurs as new rules are promulgated that may themselves be effective but at the same time undermine the effectiveness of old (but still active) rules.

rule strain   Rule-evolved red tape resulting from the sheer number of rules and corresponding increase in compliance burden; occurs when the marginal benefit from rules becomes less and less, then becomes negative.

rule sum   The total number of written rules, regulations, and procedures in force for an organization.

stakeholder red tape   A rule that remains in force and entails a compliance burden but serves no objective valued by a given stakeholder group.

subjects to a rule   Those people (individuals, groups, interests, organizations, or other social collectivities) whose behavior the rule seeks to remedy or reinforce.

REFERENCES

Aberbach, J. 1978. "Administrators' Beliefs about the Role of the Public: The Case of American Federal Executives." *Western Political Quarterly* 33, 4: 502–522.

Aiken, M., and J. Hage. 1966. "Organizational Alienation: A Comparative Analysis." *American Sociological Review* 31: 497–507.

Air Pollution Control Act of 1955, Chapter 360, 69 Statute 322.

Air Quality Act of 1967, Public Law 90-148.

Aldrich, H. 1979. *Organizations and Environments*. Englewood Cliffs, NJ: Prentice Hall.

Allison, G. 1979. "Public and Private Management: Are They Fundamentally Alike in All Unimportant Respects?" Paper presented at the Public Management Research Conference, The Brookings Institution, Washington, D.C., November 19–20, 1979.

Anderson, P. 1992. "Emergency Agency Is under Fire." *Miami Herald* (September 6): 4.

Anechiarico, F., and J. Jacobs. 1996. *The Pursuit of Absolute Integrity: How Corruption Control Makes Government Ineffective*. Chicago, IL: University of Chicago Press.

Angle, H., and J. Perry. 1981. "An Empirical Assessment of Organizational Commitment and Organizational Effectiveness." *Administrative Science Quarterly* 26, 1: 1–15.

Antonsen, M., and T. Beck Jorgensen. 1997. "The 'Publicness' of Public Organizations." *Public Administration* 75, 2: 337–357.

Apgar, W., and H. J. Brown. 1987. *Microeconomics and Public Policy*. Glenview, IL: Scott-Foresman Publishing.

Argyris, C. 1957. "The Individual and Organization: Some Problems of Mutual Adjustment." *Administrative Science Quarterly* 2: 1–24.

Baker, S. M., A. Etzioni, R. A. Hansen, and M. Soutag. 1973. "Tolerance for Bureaucratic Structure." *Human Relations* 26: 775–786.

Baldwin, J. 1987. "Public versus Private: Not That Different, Not That Consequential." *Public Personnel Management* 6, 2: 181–193.

Baldwin, J. 1990. "Perceptions of Public versus Private Sector Personnel and Informal Red Tape: Their Impact on Motivation." *American Review of Public Administration* 20: 7–28.

Barton, A. 1980. "A Diagnosis of Bureaucratic Maladies." In *Making Bureaucracies Work*, ed. Carol H. Weiss and Allen H. Barton. Beverly Hills, CA: Sage.

Barzelay, M. 1992. *Breaking through Bureaucracy*. Berkeley, CA: University of California Press.

Bayer, C. W. 1990. "Maintaining Optimum Indoor Air Quality." *Journal of Property Management* (March–April): 37–39.

Beck Jorgensen, T. 1993. "Rescuing Public Services: On the Tasks of Public Organizations." In *Quality, Innovation, and Measurement in Public Sector Organizations*, ed. H. Hill, H. Klages, and E. Loffer. Frankfurt: Peter Lang, pp. 161–182.

Bendor, J., S. Taylor, and R. Van Gaalen. 1987. "Politicians, Bureaucrats, and Asymmetric Information." *American Journal of Political Science* 31: 796–828.

Bennett, J. R., and M. H. Johnson. 1979. "Paperwork and Bureaucracy." *Economic Inquiry* 17: 435–451.

Benveniste, G. 1983. *Bureaucracy*. San Francisco, CA: Jossey-Bass.

Benveniste, G. 1987. *Professionalizing the Organization: Reducing Bureaucracy to Enhance Effectiveness*. San Francisco, CA: Jossey-Bass.

Berle, A., and Gardiner C. Means. 1932. *The Modern Corporation and Private Property*. New York: MacMillan.

Blau, P. M., and R. Schoenherr. 1971. *The Structure of Organizations*. New York: Basic Books.

Blau, P. M., and R. Scott. 1962. *Formal Organizations*. San Francisco, CA: Chandler.

Blumenthal, W. 1983. "Candid Reflections of a Businessman in Washington." In *Public Management: Public and Private Perspectives*, ed. J. Perry and K. Kraemer. Palo Alto, CA: Mayfield.

Bozeman, B. 1977. "Epistemology and Futures Studies." *Public Administration Review* 37, 5: 544–549.

Bozeman, B. 1979. *Public Management and Policy Analysis*. New York: St. Martin's Press.

Bozeman, B. 1987. *All Organizations Are Public*. San Francisco, CA: Jossey-Bass.

Bozeman, B. 1993. "A Theory of Government Red Tape." *Journal of Public Administration Research and Theory* 3, 3: 273–304.

Bozeman, B., and S. Bretschneider. 1994. "The 'Publicness Puzzle' in Organization Theory: A Test of Two Alternative Explanations of Differences between Public and Private Organizations." *Journal of Public Administration Research and Theory* 4: 197–223.

Bozeman, B., and M. Crow. 1991. "Red Tape and Technology Transfer in U.S. Government Laboratories." *Journal of Technology Transfer* 16, 2: 29–37.

Bozeman, B., and L. DeHart-Davis (in press). "Red Tape and Clean Air." *Journal of Public Administration Research and Theory*.

Bozeman, B., L. DeHart-Davis, and G. Kingsley. 1999. *Compliance Costs, Red Tape, and Title V Air Permitting: Final Report to the USEPA*. Atlanta, GA: School of Public Policy, State Data and Research Center.

Bozeman, B., R. Deyle, and R. O'Leary. 1987. *A Survey of New Jersey Small Quantity Hazardous Waste Generators*. Report prepared for the New Jersey Hazardous Waste Siting Commission.

Bozeman, B., and G. Kingsley. 1998. "Risk Culture in Public and Private Organizations." *Public Administration Review* 58, 2: 109–118.

Bozeman, B., and S. Loveless. 1987. "Sector Context and Performance: A Comparison of Industrial and Government Research Units." *Administration and Society* 19: 197–235.

Bozeman, B., and W. E. McAlpine. 1977. "Goals and Bureaucratic Decision-Making: An Experiment." *Human Relations* 30: 417–430.

Bozeman, B., and H. Rainey. 1998. "Organizational Rules and the Bureaucratic Personality." *American Journal of Political Science* 42, 1: 163–189.

Bozeman, B., P. Reed, and P. Scott. 1992. "Red Tape and Task Delays in Public and Private Organizations." *Administration and Society* 24, 3: 290–222.

Bozeman, B., and P. Scott. 1996. "Bureaucratic Red Tape and Formalization: Untangling Conceptual Knots." *American Review of Public Administration* 26, 1: 1–17.

Bozeman, B., and J. Straussman. 1990. *Public Management Strategies*. San Francisco, CA: Jossey-Bass.

Bretschneider, S. 1990. "Management Information Systems in Public and Private Organizations: An Empirical Test." *Public Administration Review* 50: 536–545.

Bretschneider, S., and B. Bozeman. 1995. "Measuring Red Tape: An Approach Based on a Theory of Administrative Delays." In *Public Management Challenges*, ed. A. Halachmi. San Francisco, CA: Jossey-Bass, pp. 81–116.

Brower, R., and M. Abolafia. 1997. "Bureaucratic Politics: The View from Below." *Journal of Public Administration Research and Theory* 7, 2: 305–331.

Bryner, Gary C. 1995. *Blue Skies, Green Politics: The Clean Air Act of 1990 and Its Implementation*, 2nd ed. Washington, D.C.: CQ Press.

Bryson, J. 1988. *Strategic Planning for Public and Nonprofit Organizations: A Guide to Strengthening and Sustaining Organizational Achievements*. San Francisco, CA: Jossey-Bass.

Buchanan, B. 1975. "Red-Tape and the Service Ethic: Some Unexpected Differences between Public and Private Managers." *Administration and Society* 6: 423–444.

Burns, Tom, and G. M. Stalker. 1961. *The Management of Innovation*. London: Tavistock.

Caiden, G. 1991. "What Really Is Public Maladministration?" *Public Administration Review* 51, 6: 486–493.

Calista, Donald J., ed. 1986. *Bureaucratic and Governmental Reform*. Greenwich, CT: JAI Press.

Carr-Gordon Limited, and Erin Research, Inc. 1996. *Responsible and Responsive Regulation for Ontario: A Report to the Red Tape Review Commission*. Shelburne, Ontario.

Castenda, R. 1993. "It's Paperwork That Gets a Social Worker Down." *Washington Post* (March 29): B1, B6.

Cherniss, Cary, and Jeffrey S. Kane. 1987. "Public Sector Professionals: Job Characteristics, Satisfaction, and Aspirations for Intrinsic Fulfillment through Work." *Human Relations* 40, 3: 125–136.

Chernow, Ron. 1998. *Titan: The Life of John D. Rockefeller*. New York: Random House.

Child, J. 1972. "Organizational Structure and Strategies of Control: A Replication of the Aston Study." *Administrative Science Quarterly* 17: 163–177.

Christenson, J., and C. Sachs. 1980. "The Impact of Government Size and Number of Administrative Units on the Quality of Public Service." *Administrative Science Quarterly* 25: 89–101.

Editorial. 1991. "University Charges for Research." *Christian Science Monitor* (April 18): 20.

Chubb, J., and T. Moe. 1990. *Politics, Markets, and America's Schools*. Washington, D.C.: The Brookings Institution.

Church, T. W., and R. Nakamura. 1993. *Cleaning up the Mess: Implementation of Strategies in Superfund*. Washington, D.C.: The Brookings Institution.

Clarkson, K. W. 1972. "Some Implications of Property Rights in Hospital Management." *Journal of Law and Economics* 15: 363–384.

Clean Air Act of 1963, 42 USC Ch. 85, 1857–18571, 1964.

Clean Air Act of 1970, 42 U.S.C. 7401a, 1970.

Clean Air Act of 1977, 42 U.S.C. 7401b, 1977.

Clean Air Act of 1990, 42 U.S.C. Ch. 85, 1990.

Clegg, S. 1981. "Organization and Control." *Administrative Science Quarterly* 26: 545–562.

Clinton, B., and A. Gore. 1995. *Putting Customers First '95: Standards for Serving the American People*. National Performance Review. Washington, D.C.: USGPO.

Congressional Record, S. 3163, March 26, 1990.

Cope, G. 1997. "Bureaucratic Reform and Issues of Political Responsiveness." *Journal of Public Administration Research and Theory* 7, 3: 461–471.

Coursey, David, and Barry Bozeman. 1990. "Decision Making in Public and Private Organizations: A Test of Alternative Concepts of 'Publicness.'" *Public Administration Review* 50: 525–535.

Coursey, D., and H. Rainey. 1990. "Perceptions of Personnel System Constraints in Public, Private, and Hybrid Organizations." *Review of Public Personnel Administration* 10, 2: 54–71.

Cowen, R. 1994. "Snipping the Red Tape That Keeps Private Enterprise Earthbound." *Washington Post* (September 14): A4.

Crewson, P. 1995. "A Comparative Analysis of Public and Private Sector Entrant Quality." *American Journal of Political Science* 39: 628–639.

Crow, M., and B. Bozeman. 1998. *Limited by Design: R&D Laboratories in the U.S. National Innovation System*. New York: Columbia University Press.

Crozier, M. 1964. *The Bureaucratic Phenomenon*. Chicago, IL: University of Chicago Press.

Cyert, R., and J. March. 1963. *A Behavioral Theory of the Firm*. Englewood Cliffs, NJ: Prentice Hall.

Darby, M. R., and E. Karni. 1973. "Free Competition and the Optimal Amount of Fraud." *Journal of Law and Economics* 16.

Davies, D. 1971. "The Efficiency of Public vs. Private Firms." *Journal of Law and Economics* 14: 149–165.

Davies, D. 1977. "Property Rights and Economic Efficiency." *Journal of Law and Economics* 20: 223–226.

Davis, P. 1992. "$20 Billion Bill for Andrew at Government's Door." *Congressional Record* (September 5): 2633.

De Alessi, Louis. 1969. "Implications of Property Rights for Government Investment Choices." *American Economic Review* 59: 13–24.

Demsetz, Harold. 1967. "Toward a Theory of Property Rights." *American Economic Review* (papers and proceedings) 57: 347–359.

Demsetz, Harold. 1969. "Information and Efficiency: Another Viewpoint." *Journal of Law and Economics* 1: 1–22.

Dillin, John. 1994. "Caught in Red Tape? Who Ya Gonna Call? Congress!" *Christian Science Monitor* (June).

Di Lorenzo, T., and R. Robinson. 1982. "Managerial Objectives Subject to Political and Market Constraints." *Quarterly Review of Economics and Business* 22: 113–125.

Donahue, J. 1989. *The Privatization Decision: Public Ends, Private Means*. New York: Basic Books.

Downs, A. 1967. *Inside Bureaucracy*. Boston, MA: Little Brown.

Downs, G., and P. Larkey. 1986. *The Search for Government Efficiency: From Hubris to Helplessness*. New York: Random House.

Druyan, A. 1977. "Earth's Greatest Hits." *New York Times Magazine* (September 4): 24–26.

Dubin, Robert. 1951. *Human Relations in Administration: The Sociology of Organization, with Readings and Cases*. New York: Prentice Hall.

Duggar, W. 1985. "Centralization, Diversification, and Administrative Burden in U.S. Enterprises." *Journal of Economic Issues* 19: 687–701.

Duignan-Cabrera, A. 1993. "As Some Reopen, Other Stores Caught in Red Tape." *Los Angeles Times* (June 25): B1.

Edwards, R. 1984. "Work Incentives and Worker Responses in Bureaucratic Enterprises: An Empirical Study." *Research in Social Stratification and Mobility* 3: 3–26.

Federal Register, Vol. 57, no. 140, July 21, 1992: 32251.

Federal Register, Vol. 57, no. 215, November 5, 1992: 52951.

Federal Register, Vol. 40, August 19, 1994: 44460.

Foster, J. L. 1990. "Bureaucratic Rigidity Revisited." *Social Science Quarterly* 71: 223–238.

Foster, J. L., and J. H. Jones. 1978. "Rule Orientation and Bureaucratic Reform." *American Journal of Political Science* 22: 348–363.

Frant, H. 1993. "Rules and Governance in the Public Service: The Case of Civil Service." *American Journal of Political Science* 37, 4: 990–1007.

Fredrickson, G. 1996. *The Spirit of Public Administration*. San Francisco, CA: Jossey-Bass.

Friedman, Milton. 1953. "The Methodology of Positive Economics." In *Essays in Positive Economics*, ed. M. Friedman. Chicago, IL: University of Chicago Press.

Friedrich, C. 1952. "Some Observations on Weber's Analysis of Bureaucracy." In *Reader in Bureaucracy*, ed. R. Merton. Glencoe, IL: The Free Press.

Furlong, S. 1997. "Interest Group Influence on Rule-Making." *Administration & Society* 29, 3: 325–347.

Gawthrop, L. 1969. *Bureaucratic Behavior in the Executive Branch*. New York: The Free Press.

Gilmour, R., and L. Jensen. 1998. "Reinventing Government Accountability." *Public Administration Review* 58, 3: 247–258.

Glisson, C. A., and P. Martin. 1980. "Productivity and Efficiency in Human Service Organizations as Related to Structure, Size, and Age." *Academy of Management Journal* 23: 21–37.

Golden, M. 1998. "Interest Groups in the Rule-Making Process: Who Participates? Whose Voices Get Heard?" *Journal of Public Administration Research and Theory* 8, 2: 245–270.

Golembiewski, R. 1985. *Humanizing Public Organizations.* Mount Airy, MD: Lomond.

Goodnow, F. 1900. *Politics and Administration.* New York: Macmillan.

Goodsell, C. 1981. "Looking Once Again at Human Service Bureaucracy." *Journal of Politics* 43: 763–768.

Goodsell, C. 1984. "The Grace Commission: Seeking Efficiency for the Whole People?" *Public Administration Review* 44: 196–204.

Goodsell, C. 1994. *The Case for Bureaucracy: A Public Administration Polemic*, 3rd ed. Chatham, NJ: Chatham House.

Gore, A. 1996. *The Best-Kept Secrets in Government.* Washington, D.C.: USGPO.

Gore, A. 1993a. *From Red Tape to Results: Creating a Government That Works Better and Costs Less.* Report of the National Performance Review. Washington, D.C.: USGPO.

Gore, A. 1993b. *Creating a Government That Works Better and Costs Less: Reengineering through Information Technology.* Washington, D.C.: USGPO.

Gormley, W. T. 1989. *Taming the Bureaucracy.* Princeton, NJ: Princeton University Press.

Gouldner, Alvin W. 1950. "The Problem of Succession in Bureaucracy." In *Studies in Leadership*, ed. A. Gouldner. New York: Harper, pp. 644–659.

Gouldner, Alvin W. 1952. "Red Tape as a Social Problem." In *Reader in Bureaucracy*, ed. Robert K. Merton. New York: The Free Press, pp. 410–418.

Gouldner, Alvin W. 1954. *Patterns of Industrial Bureaucracy.* Glencoe, IL: The Free Press.

Gruber, J. 1987. *Controlling Bureaucracies: Dilemmas in Democratic Governance.* Berkeley, CA: University of California Press.

Hage, J., and M. Aiken. 1969. "Routine Technology, Social Structure, and Organizational Goals." *Administrative Science Quarterly* 14: 366–376.

Hall, R. H. 1963. "The Concept of Bureaucracy: Its Empirical Assessment." *American Journal of Sociology* 69: 32–40.

Hall, R. H. 1968. "Professionalism and Bureaucratization." *American Sociological Review* 33: 92–104.

Hall, R. H. 1991. *Organizations: Structures, Processes, and Outcomes*, 5th ed. Englewood Cliffs, NJ: Prentice Hall.

Hammond, T. H., and G. J. Miller. 1985. "A Social Choice Perspective on Expertise and Authority in Bureaucracy." *American Journal of Political Science* 29, 1: 1–28.

Heimann, C. F. L. 1993. "Understanding the Challenger Disaster: Organizational Structure and the Design of Reliable Systems." *American Political Science Review* 87, 2: 421–435.

Heimann, C. F. L. 1995. "Different Paths to Success: A Theory of Organizational Decision-Making and Administrative Reliability." *Journal of Public Administration Research and Theory* 5, 1: 45–71.

Helmer, O., and N. Rescher. 1959. "On the Epistemology of the Inexact Sciences." *Management Science* 6, 1: 25–52.

Hempel, C. 1966. *Philosophy of Natural Science*. Englewood Cliffs, NJ: Prentice Hall.

Hempel, C. 1968. "Explanation in Science and in History." In *The Philosophy of Science*, ed. P. Nidditch. London: Oxford University Press, pp. 54–79.

Hickson, David J., Richard J. Butler, David Cray, Geoffrey R. Mallory, and David C. Wilson. 1986. *Top Decisions—Strategic Decision-Making in Organizations*. Oxford, UK: Basil Blackwell and San Francisco, CA: Jossey-Bass.

Holdaway, E., J. F. Newberry, D. J. Hickson, and R. P. Heron. 1975. "Dimensions of Organizations in Complex Societies: The Educational Sector." *Administrative Science Quarterly* 20: 37–58.

Hood, Christopher, and Andrew Dunsire. 1981. *Bureaumetrics*. University, AL: University of Alabama Press.

House Subcommittee on Health and the Environment. 1991. *The Vice President's Initiative to Undermine the Clean Air Act*. 102nd Congress, 1st session (May 1).

Huck, S., and H. Sandler. 1979. *Rival Hypotheses*. New York: Harper and Row.

Hummel, R. 1992. *The Bureaucratic Experience*, 2nd ed. New York: St. Martin's Press.

Hunt, G., ed. 1995. *Whistleblowing in the Health Service: Accountability, Law, and Professional*. London: E. Arnold Publishing.

Ingraham, P., J. Thompson, and R. Sanders, eds. 1998. *Transforming Government: Lessons from the Reinvention Laboratories*. San Francisco, CA: Jossey-Bass.

Ivancevich, J. M., and J. H. Donnelly. 1975. "Relations of Organizational Structure to Job Satisfaction, Anxiety-Stress, and Performance." *Administrative Science Quarterly* 20: 272–280.

Jacoby, H. 1973. *The Bureaucratization of the World*. Berkeley, CA: University of California Press.

Jurkiewicz, C., T. Massey, and R. Brown. 1998. "Motivation in Public and Private Organizations: A Comparative Study." *Public Productivity and Management Review* 21, 3: 230–250.

Kaufman, Herbert. 1976. *Are Government Organizations Immortal?* Washington, D.C.: The Brookings Institution.

Kaufman, H. 1977. *Red Tape: Its Origins, Uses, and Abuses.* Washington, D.C.: The Brookings Institution.

Kaufman, Herbert. 1986. *Time, Chance, and Organization: Natural Selection in a Perilous Environment.* Chatham, NJ: Chatham House.

Kaufman, Herbert. 1993. Personal communication (February).

Kelly, M. 1994. "Theories of Justice and Street-Level Discretion." *Journal of Public Administration Research and Theory* 4: 119–140.

Kelman, S. 1990. *Procurement and Public Management: The Fear of Discretion and the Quality of Government Practice.* Lanham, MD: AEI Press.

Kendall, P., and Art Barnum. "Traffic Red Tape Takes Toll in Lives." *Chicago Tribune* (July 21) Southwest section: 1.

Kerwin, C. 1994. *Rulemaking: How Government Agencies Write Law and Make Policy.* Washington, D.C.: CQ Press.

Kerwin, C., and S. Furlong. 1992. "Time and Rule-Making: An Empirical Test of Theory." *Journal of Public Administration Research and Theory* 2, 2: 113–138.

Kettl, D. 1994. *Reinventing Government? Appraising the National Performance Review.* Washington, D.C.: The Brookings Institution.

Kilborn, P. 1992. "Snarl of Red Tape Keeps U.S. Checks from Storm Areas." *New York Times* (September 5): A1.

Kingsley, G. 1998. Personal communication.

Kingsley, G. (in press). "Decision Participation in Public and Private Organizations." *Knowledge and Policy.*

Kirlin, J. 1996. "What Government Must Do Well: Creating Value for Society." *Journal of Public Administration Research and Theory* 6, 1: 161–185.

Kohut, J. 1995. *Stupid Government Tricks: Outrageous (but True!) Stories of Bureaucratic Bungling and Washington Waste.* New York: Plume Publishing.

Kriess, K. 1993. "The Sick Building Syndrome in Office Buildings: A Breath of Fresh Air." *New England Journal of Medicine* (March 25): 877–878.

Kuttner, R. 1997. *Everything for Sale: The Virtues and Limits of Markets.* New York: Knopf.

Lan, Z., and H. Rainey. 1992. "Goals, Rules, and Effectiveness in Public,

Private, and Hybrid Organizations: More Evidence on Frequent Assertions about Differences." *Journal of Public Administration Research and Theory* 2: 5–24.

Lancaster, K., and R. Lipsey. 1956. "The General Theory of the Second Best." *Review of Economics and Statistics* 24, 1: 11–32.

Landau, M. 1969. "Redundancy, Rationality, and the Problem of Duplication and Overlap." *Public Administration Review* 29: 346–358.

Landau, M. 1991. "On Multiorganizational Systems in Public Administration." *Journal of Public Administration Research and Theory* 1: 5–18.

Landau, M., and R. Stout. 1979. "To Manage Is Not to Control: Or the Folly of Type II Errors." *Public Administration Review* 39: 148–156.

Landy, Mark K., M. J. Roberts, and S. R. Thomas. 1994. *The Environmental Protection Agency: Asking All the Wrong Questions, from Nixon to Clinton.* New York: Oxford University Press.

Langton, J. 1984. "The Ecological Theory of Bureaucracy: The Case of Josiah Wedgwood and the British Pottery Industry." *Administrative Science Quarterly* 29: 330–354.

LaPorte, T., and P. Consolini. 1991. "Working in Practice but Not in Theory: Theoretical Challenges of High-Reliability Organizations." *Journal of Public Administration Research and Theory* 1, 1: 19–47.

LaPorte, T., and C. Thomas. 1990. "Regulatory Compliance and the Ethos of Quality Enhancement: Surprises in Nuclear Power Plant Operations." Paper presented at the American Political Science Association, San Francisco, CA.

Lau, A. W., and C. M. Pavett. 1980. "The Nature of Managerial Work: A Comparison of Public-Private-Sector Managers." *Group and Organization Studies* 5, 4: 453–466.

Leazes, F. 1997. "Public Accountability: Is It a Private Responsibility?" *Administration & Society* 29, 4: 395–411.

Ledeen, Michael. 1988. *Perilous Statecraft: An Insider's Account of the Iran-Contra Affair.* New York: Scribner.

Leen, J., and S. Freedberg. 1992. "What Took So Long?" *Miami Herald* (September 6): 1A.

Lewis, Greg. 1991. "Turnover and the Quit Crisis in the Federal Service." *Public Administration Review* 51, 2: 145–155.

Lewyn, M. 1993. "How Not to Buy 300,000 Personal Computers." *Business Week* (March 8): 47–51.

Lieberson, S., and J. O'Connor. 1972. "Leadership and Organizational Performance: A Study of Large Corporations." *American Sociological Review* 37: 117–130.

Light, P. 1995. *Thickening Government.* Washington, D.C.: The Brookings Institution.

Light, P. 1997. *The Tides of Reform: Making Government Work, 1945–1995.* New Haven, CT: Yale University Press.

Lindblom, C. E. 1959. "The Science of Muddling Through." *Public Administration Review* 19, 1: 79–99.

Lindblom, C. E. 1977. *Politics and Markets.* New York: Basic Books.

Lindsay, C. 1976. "A Theory of Government Enterprise." *Journal of Political Economy* 84: 1061–1078.

Lippman, Walter. 1955. *The Public Philosophy.* London: Hamish Hamilton.

Lynn, L. 1981. *Managing the Public's Business.* New York: Basic Books.

McAllister, B. 1993. "Ruling Out Postal Rate Overseers: New Regulations Limit Commissioners' Visits." *Washington Post* (July 27): A15.

McGarrity, T. 1991. "The Internal Structure of EPA Rulemaking." *Law and Contemporary Problems* 54: 57–65.

Magat, W., A. Krupnick, and W. Harrington. 1986. *Rules in the Making.* Washington, D.C.: Resources for the Future.

Mansfield, E. 1991. "Academic Research and Industrial Innovation." *Research Policy* 20, 1: 1–19.

March, J., and H. Simon. 1958. *Organizations.* New York: Wiley.

Marcuse, H. 1968. "Industrialism and Capitalism in the Work of Max Weber." In *Negations: Essays in Critical Theory.* Boston, MA: Beacon Press, pp. 201–226.

Martin, Shan. 1983. *Managing without Managers: Alternative Work Arrangements in Public Organizations.* Beverly Hills, CA: Sage Publications.

Maser, S. M. 1986. "Transactions Costs in Public Administration." In *Bureaucratic and Governmental Reform,* ed. Donald J. Calista. Greenwich, CT: JAI Press, pp. 55–71.

Merton, R. 1940. "Bureaucratic Structure and Personality." *Social Forces* 18: 560–568.

Merton, R., A. Gray, B. Hocky, and H. Selvin. 1952. *Reader in Bureaucracy.* Glencoe, IL: The Free Press.

Meyer, M. 1979a. *Change in Public Bureaucracies.* London: Cambridge University Press.

Meyer, M. 1979b. "Debureaucratization?" *Social Science Quarterly* 60: 25–33.

Meyer, J., and B. Rowan. 1977. "Institutionalized Organizations: Formal Structure as Myth and Ceremony." *American Journal of Sociology* 83: 340–363.

Meyer, J., W. R. Scott, and D. Strang. 1987. "Centralization, Fragmentation, and School District Complexity." *Administrative Science Quarterly* 32: 186–201.

Milward, B., and Hal G. Rainey. 1983. "Don't Blame the Bureaucracy." *Journal of Public Policy* 3: 149–168.

198   REFERENCES

Mitnick, B. 1980. *The Political Economy of Regulation.* New York: Columbia University Press.
Mladenka K. 1981. "Citizen Demands and Urban Services: The Distribution of Bureaucratic Response in Chicago and Houston. *American Journal of Political Science* 25: 693–714.
Moe, T. 1984. "The New Economics of Organization." *American Journal of Political Science* 28, 4: 739–777.
Moloney, S. 1996. "The Lady in Red Tape." *Policy Review* 79: 147–154.
National Performance Review. 1996. *Reaching Public Goals: Managing Government for Results.* Washington, D.C.: USGPO.
Neuberg, L. 1977. "Two Issues in the Municipal Ownership of Electric Power Distribution Systems." *Bell Journal of Economics* 18: 303–323.
Nickel, N. 1991. "The Race to Regulate." *1991 Environmental Forum* 18–22 (January–February).
Novello, David, G. F. Hoffnagle, G. D. McCutchen, and K. N. Weiss. 1995. *Clean Air Operating Permits: A Practical Guide.* Pittsburgh, PA: Air & Waste Management Association.
Nutt, P. 1984. "Types of Organizational Decision Processes." *Administrative Science Quarterly* 29: 414–450.
Nutt, P., and R. Backoff. 1992. *Strategic Management of Public and Third Sector Organizations.* San Francisco, CA: Jossey-Bass.
Nystrom, P., and W. Starbuck, eds. 1981. *Handbook of Organizational Design.* New York: Oxford University Press.
Occupational Health and Safety Administration. 1995. *Reinventing Worker Safety and Health.* Washington, D.C.: USGPO.
Osborne, D., and P. Plastrik. 1997. *Banishing Bureaucracy: The Five Strategies for Reinventing Government.* Reading, MA: Addison-Wesley.
Osborne, D., and T. Gaebler. 1992. *Reinventing Government.* Reading, MA: Addison-Wesley.
Pandey, S. 1995. *Managerial Perceptions of Red Tape.* Unpublished Ph.D. dissertation. Syracuse, NY: Syracuse University.
Pandey, S., and S. Bretschneider. 1997. "The Impact of Red Tape's Administrative Delay on Public Organizations' Interest in New Information Technologies." *Journal of Public Administration Research and Theory* 7, 1: 113–130.
Pandey, S., and G. Kingsley. 1995. "Perceptions of Red Tape in Public and Private Organizations." Paper presented at the Third National Public Management Research Conference, Lawrence, Kansas, October, 1995.
Paperwork Reduction Act of 1995. Public Law 104-13, 44 USC 101, Ch. 35.
Parade Magazine. December 29, 1991: 16.

Percival, Robert, A. S. Miller, C. H. Schroeder, and J. P. Leape. 1992. *Environmental Regulation: Law, Science, and Policy.* Toronto, Canada: Little, Brown & Company.

Perrow, Charles. 1972. *Complex Organizations: A Critical Survey.* Glenview, IL: Scott Foresman.

Peters, G. 1994. *The Politics of Bureaucracy*, 3rd ed. New York: Longman.

Pffefer, J., and G. Salancik. 1977. "Organizational Context and the Characteristics and Tenure of Hospital Administrators." *Academy of Management Journal* 20: 74–88.

Phillips, D. C. 1987. *Philosophy, Science, and Social Inquiry.* New York: Pergamon Press.

President's Memorandum. 1993. *Streamlining Procurement through Electronic Commerce.* Washington, D.C.: Memorandum for Heads of Executive Departments and Agencies (October 26).

President's Private Sector Survey on Cost Control. 1982. Washington, D.C.: USGPO.

Pugh, D. S., D. J. Hickson, C. R. Hinings, and C. Turner. 1968. "Dimensions of Organizational Structure." *Administrative Science Quarterly* 13: 65–91.

Pugh, D. S., D. J. Hickson, C. R. Hinings, and C. Turner. 1969. "The Context of Organization Structures." *Administrative Science Quarterly* 14: 91–114.

Pyhrr, P. 1973. *Zero-Base Budgeting.* New York: John Wiley and Sons.

Radin, B. 1998. "The Government Performance and Results Act (GPRA): Hydra-Headed Monster or Flexible Management Tool?" *Public Administration Review* 58, 4: 307–315.

Rai, G. S. 1983. "Reducing Bureaucratic Inflexibility." *Social Service Review* 57: 44–58.

Rainey, H. 1979. "Perceptions of Incentives in Business and Government: Implications for Civil Service Reform." *Public Administration Review* 39: 440–448.

Rainey, H. 1983. "Public Agencies and Private Firms: Incentive Structures, Goals, and Individual Roles." *Administration and Society* 15: 229–250.

Rainey, H. G. 1989. "Public Management: Recent Research on the Political Context and Managerial Roles, Structures, and Behaviors." *Journal of Management* 15: 229–250.

Rainey, H. G. 1997. *Understanding and Managing Public Organizations*, 2nd ed. San Francisco, CA: Jossey-Bass.

Rainey, H., and B. Bozeman. 1996. "Comparing Public and Private Organizations: Empirical Research and the Power of the *A Priori*." Paper presented at the Annual Meeting of the American Political Science Association, San Francisco, California (September).

Rainey, H., S. Pandey, and B. Bozeman. 1995. "Public and Private Managers' Perceptions of Red Tape." *Public Administration Review* 15, 2: 207–242.

Ranson, S., B. Hinings, and R. Greenwood. 1980. "The Structuring of Organizational Structures." *Administrative Science Quarterly* 25, 2: 1–17.

Reason, J. 1990. *Human Error.* New York: Cambridge University Press.

Regulatory Transition Act of 1995, S219, introduced January 21, 1995, by Senator Nickles (R-Okla.), 104th Congress.

Richardson, Elliot. 1996. *Reflections of a Radical Moderate.* New York: Pantheon.

Risk Assessment and Cost-Benefit Act of 1995, HR690, introduced January 25, 1995, by Representative Zimmer (R-N.J.), 104th Congress.

Roethlisberger, F. J., and W. J. Dickson. 1939. *Management and the Worker.* Cambridge, MA: Harvard University Press.

Rose, R. 1984. *Understanding Big Government: The Programme Approach.* London: Sage Publishing.

Rosenblatt, R. 1994. "Electronic Fraud Eludes IRS." *Los Angeles Times* (February 11): 1.

Rosenfeld, R. A. 1984. "An Expansion and Application of Kaufman's Model of Red Tape: The Case of Community Development Block Grants." *The Western Political Quarterly* 37: 603–620.

Ross, S. 1973. "The Economic Theory of Agency: The Principal's Problem." *American Economic Review* 62, 1: 134–139.

Rourke, F. 1984. *Bureaucracy, Politics, and Public Policy.* Boston, MA: Little, Brown.

Sanders, D. L. 1997. "Mistrust of Doctors Lingers after Tuskegee." *Washington Post* (April 15) Health News Section: 8–9.

Savas, E. 1982. *Privatizing the Public Sector.* Chatham, NJ: Chatham House Publishing.

Savas, E. S. 1987. *Privatization: The Key to Better Government.* Chatham, NJ: Chatham House Publishing.

Schein, E. 1985. *Organizational Culture and Leadership: A Dynamic View.* San Francisco, CA: Jossey-Bass.

Scott, P. 1994. *Assessing Determinants of Bureaucratic Discretion: An Experiment.* Unpublished Ph.D. dissertation. Syracuse, NY: Syracuse University.

Scott, P. 1997. "Assessing Determinants of Bureaucratic Discretion." *Journal of Public Administration Research and Theory* 7, 1: 35–57.

Scott, W. Richard. 1987. *Organizations: Rational, Natural, and Open Systems,* 2nd ed. Englewood Cliffs, NJ: Prentice Hall.

Seidman, H. 1970. *Politics, Position, and Power: The Dynamics of Federal Organization.* New York: Oxford University Press.

Simon, H. 1957. *Administrative Behavior*, 2nd ed. New York: Macmillan Publishing.

Slevin, P., and D. Filkins. 1992. "More Destruction Than Any Disaster." *Miami Herald* (August 28): 1A.

Snizek, W., and J. Bullard. 1983. "Perception of Bureaucracy and Changing Job Satisfaction: A Longitudinal Analysis." *Organizational Behavior and Human Performance* 32: 275–287.

Solow, R. 1957. "Technical Change and the Aggregate Production Function." *Review of Economics and Statistics* 39: 312–320.

Sorenson, J. E., and T. L. Sorenson. 1974. "The Conflict of Professionals in Bureaucratic Organizations." *Administrative Science Quarterly* 19: 98–106.

Starr, P. 1989. "The Meaning of Privatization." In *Privatization and the Welfare State*, ed. S. B. Kamerman and A. J. Kahn. Princeton, NJ: Princeton University Press.

Stavins, Robert. 1989. "Harnessing Market Forces to Protect the Environment." *Environment* 31, 1 (January/February): 4–7, 28–35.

Stevenson, W. 1986. "Change in the Structure of Bureaucracy: A Longitudinal Analysis." *Sociological Perspectives* 29: 307–336.

Thayer, F. 1981. *An End to Hierarchy and Competition: Administration in the Post-Affluent World*, 2nd ed. New York: Franklin Watts.

Thelen, D. P. 1996. *Becoming Citizens in the Age of Television: How Americans Challenged the Media and Seized Political Initiative during the Iran-Contra Debate*. Chicago, IL: University of Chicago Press.

Thompson, Fred D. 1975. *At That Point in Time: The Inside Story of the Senate Watergate Committee*. New York: Quadrangle Books.

Thompson, V. 1961. *Modern Organization*. New York: Alfred A. Knopf.

Thompson, V. 1975. *Without Sympathy or Enthusiasm: The Problem of Administrative Compassion*. University, AL: University of Alabama Press.

Tietenburg, Tom. 1996. *Environmental and Natural Resource Economics*, 4th ed. New York: HarperCollins.

Tullock, G. 1965. *The Politics of Bureaucracy*. Washington, D.C.: Public Affairs Press.

Tyson, J. 1993. "Midwesterners Face a Flood of Red Tape." *Christian Science Monitor*: 1222.

Unfunded Mandates Reform Act of 1995. Public Law 104-4, 2 U.S.C 1501.

U.S. Bureau of Census. 1987. *U.S. Census of Governments*.

U.S. Commission on Wartime Relocation. 1983. *Personal Justice Denied*.

U.S. Congress. 1992. Committee on Governmental Affairs of the U.S. Senate, *Report on the Government Performance and Results Act*, Report 102–429, 102nd Congress, 2nd session.

U.S. Congress. 1993. PL 103-62. *Government Performance and Results Act of 1993.*

U.S. Congress, Subcommittee on Energy Conservation and Power of the Committee on Energy and Commerce U.S. House of Representatives. 1996. *American Nuclear Guinea Pigs: Three Decades of Radiation Experiments on U.S. Citizens.* Report by the Subcommittee, 99th Congress, 2nd session.

U.S. Environmental Protection Agency. 1991. "The New Clean Air Act: What It Means to You." *EPA Journal* 17, 1 (January/February).

U.S. Environmental Protection Agency. 1995. "White Paper for Streamlined Development of Part 70 Permit Applications." Lydia Wegman Memorandum (June 10).

U.S. Environmental Protection Agency. 1995. "White Paper #2 for Improved Implementation of Part (September 5).

U.S. Environmental Protection Agency. 1995. "Regulatory Impact Analysis and Regulatory 70 Operating Permits Program." Lydia Wegman Memorandum (March 5).

U.S. General Accounting Office. 1993. *Whistleblower Protection: Agencies' Implementation of the Whistleblower Statutes Has Been Mixed.* Washington, D.C.: USGPO.

U.S. General Accounting Office. 1995. *University Research: Effect of Indirect Cost Revisions and Options for Future Changes.* Washington, D.C.: USGPO.

U.S. General Accounting Office. 1997. *The Government Performance and Results Act: 1997 Government-Wide Implementation Will Be Uneven.* Washington, D.C.: USGPO.

U.S. Office of Management and Budget. 1979. *Paperwork and Red Tape: New Perspectives, New Directions. A Report to the President and Congress.* Washington, D.C.: USGPO.

U.S. Treasury, Bureau of the Public Debt. 1997. Web site report of national debt (http://www.publicdebt.treas.gov/opd/opd.htm).

Van De Ven, Andrew H. 1986. "Central Problems in the Management of Innovation." *Management Science* 32, 5: 590–609.

Vickers, J., and G. Yarrow. 1991. "Economic Perspectives on Privatization." *Journal of Economic Perspectives* (Spring).

Vogel, D. 1996. *Kindred Strangers: The Uneasy Relationship between Politics and Business in America.* Princeton, NJ: Princeton University Press.

Waldo, D. 1946. "Government by Procedure." In *Elements of Public Administration*, ed. Fritz Morstein-Marx. Englewood Cliffs, NJ: Prentice Hall.

Walker, J., and H. Vatter. 1997. *The Rise of Big Government in the U.S.* New York: M. E. Sharpe.

Wamsley, G., and J. Wolf. 1996. *Refounding Democratic Public Administration*. Thousand Oaks, CA: Sage Publishing.

Warwick, D. 1975. *A Theory of Public Bureaucracy*. Cambridge, MA: Harvard University Press.

Waterman, R. W., and K. Meier. 1998. "Principal-Agent Models: An Expansion?" *Journal of Public Administration Research and Theory* 8, 2: 173–202.

Waterman, R. W., A. Rouse, and R. Wright. 1998. "The Venues of Influence: A New Theory of Political Control of the Bureaucracy." *Journal of Public Administration Research and Theory* 8, 1: 13–38.

Weber, Max. 1946. *From Max Weber: Essays in Sociology*, ed. H. H. Gerth and C. W. Mills. New York: Oxford University Press.

Westman, D. 1991. *Whistleblowing: The Law of Retaliatory Discharge*. New York: Bureau of National Affairs.

Wildavsky, A. 1969. "Rescuing Policy Analysis from PPBS." *Public Administration Review* 29, 2: 160–165.

Williamson, Oliver E. 1975. *Market and Hierarchies*. New York: The Free Press.

Wilson, W. 1887. "The Study of Administration." *Political Science Quarterly* 2: 197–222.

Wittmer, D. 1991. "Serving the People or Serving for Pay." *Public Productivity and Management Review* XIV, 4: 369–383.

Wittmer, D. 1992. "Ethical Sensitivity and Managerial Decision-Making." *Journal of Public Administration Research and Theory* 2, 4: 443–462.

Wittmer, D., and D. Coursey. 1996. "Ethical Work Climates: Comparing Top Managers in Public and Private Organizations." *Journal of Public Administration Research and Theory* 6, 4: 559–572.

Wolf, P. 1997. "Why Must We Reinvent the Federal Government? Putting Historical Development Claims to the Test." *Journal of Public Administration Theory and Research* 7, 3: 353–388.

Wood, B. D., and R. Waterman. 1991. "The Dynamics of Political Control of the Bureaucracy." *American Political Science Review* 85: 801–828.

Woodward, J. 1965. *Industrial Organization*. London: Oxford University Press.

Woodward, B., and C. Bernstein. 1994. *All the President's Men*, 2nd ed. New York: Simon & Schuster.

Yarwood, D. 1996. "Stop Bashing the Bureaucracy." *Public Administration Review* 56: 611–613.

York, R., and H. Henley. 1986. "Perceptions of Bureaucracy." *Administration in Social Work* 10, 1: 3–13.

Zhou, X. 1993. "The Dynamics of Organizational Rules." *American Journal of Sociology* 98, 5: 1134–1166.

INDEX